Lions, Liars  IS

The Killing of Alison

Tom Bell

All I have is a voice to undo the folded lie, the romantic lie in the brains of the sensual man-in-the-street and the lie of authority whose buildings grope the sky.

W. H. Auden

Lions, Liars, Donkeys and Penguins – The Killing of Alison

Author – Tom Bell

Able and patient editorial assistance – Sarah Daniel

Version 1.1 – May 05th 2020

Published by HIPSS Ltd (Honesty and Integrity in Public Sector Services) 12589044

Foreword

For Alison. Now we are casting each other's shadows.

If you hadn't been abandoned by the thoughtless, surrounded by the misguided and preyed on by the selfish, you would have been so much more, to so many more, for so much longer. You were harmed by people trusted to protect you and by a health system that too often protects its own ahead of those it is supposed to care for. You have since been utterly failed by our justice system. You would laugh at how incompetent the police have been. I still see your smile and hear you laughing.

It's said all we have is a voice and the time it takes to learn how to use it. Though it's taken me a while I think I might be getting there. This book is my way of telling your story, it may be the closest we get to any form of justice. Your big sister Sarah, who always looked out for you in life has helped me. Her attention to detail has been incredibly useful. I talk a bit about myself in this book, but you wouldn't expect anything else from your annoying little brother.

To Debbie my rock. Sarah, my family, friends, work colleagues, fellow members of a sadly growing social media tribe and anyone else who has put up with me, encouraged me, listened, held my hand on the rollercoaster, lived with my anger and despair, and kept me afloat with kind words, your support means more than you could know. Keith, you deserve a medal. And to the many, many others who didn't know me yet were still generous with their time, knowledge and money, asking nothing in return, I will be forever grateful, thank you.

Music, you have been a refuge. You refuelled my righteous anger when I needed energy and held me and gave me light when I was in dark places. Glastonbury, you are the sanest place in a crazy world, and Homer Simpson, you keep me laughing.

Thank you to Inquest and every other voluntary organisation doing incredible work across the UK, especially the Samaritans who soaked up the pressure when it all became too much. You are the Florence Nightingales walking the wards of our fractured society. You hold our fragmented dysfunctional healthcare services together as they struggle with their own ineptitude and the impossible demands an increasingly complex world is placing on them.

To the NHS, I have been clapping, loudly each Thursday evening in support of the leaderless heroes putting their lives at risk treating the victims of a global pandemic. I want to protect the best of you, but I have no wish to preserve you as an organisation in your current state. For the sake of us all, you need to change, to become what you set out to be, what we need you to be and always hoped you would be.

To my many nieces, nephews and godchildren; question everything.

I swear...I will follow that system of regimen which, according to my ability and judgement, I consider for the benefit of my patients, and abstain from whatever is deleterious and mischievous. Into whatever houses I enter, I will go into them for the benefit of the sick and will abstain from every voluntary act of mischief and corruption; and further, from the seduction of females or males, of freemen and slaves.

From the Oath of Hippocrates.

While grooming is most associated with child sexual abuse, it is also possible for adults, especially vulnerable adults to be groomed – or prepared – for abuse. As with children, this is more common in situations where there is a power differential – for example by someone older or physically stronger, or by a professional who has a measure of control. One of the key results of grooming is that the survivor is left carrying the shame of the events, often represented in a sense of complicity – that they let it happen. This self-blame once again makes the abuse difficult to talk about. Grooming makes it more difficult to identify when abuse is happening, and more difficult to identify and talk about in retrospect. The law is clear; when consent to sex is coerced, including emotionally coerced sex, it is not consent.

Adult grooming and its effects; Survivors UK website.

This section considers a number of offences, including offences against those who have the capacity to consent but have a mental disorder which makes them vulnerable to inducement, threat or deception...the guideline for offences where there is a mental disorder impeding choice should adopt a similar structure to the guidelines for rape, assault by penetration and sexual assault...the victim may appear to have acquiesced to sexual activity, but that has occurred due to exploitation or manipulation by the offender... Maximum sentence if penetration, 14years' custody.

Extract from UK Sentencing Council Sexual Offences Guideline Consultation 2012.

It became apparent after a very short time that he was spending more time with Alison May Bell than any other patient. He had to be spoken with on more than one occasion regarding the time spent with Alison May Bell. A colleague particularly remembers an incident he witnessed where the two were too close together in the Games Room despite the warnings given. Concerns were raised. Sometime after early 1988 Alison May Bell was witnessed entering Beech Lodge (male nurse's residence) where he was living at the time.

Another colleague who had overall responsibility for Ward 26 remembers Alison May Bell being on the ward and that concerns were raised about his over familiarisation with her and noticed that he was spending a lot of time with this patient. Concerns were raised about the unethical behaviour. The situation did not improve and there were further meetings. One meeting resulted in him being clearly told that his behaviour was inappropriate and that the matter would be formally reported.

It was brought to attention that he had developed a relationship (sic) with Alison May Bell, a young female patient who was extremely ill and disturbed at that time. This was addressed with him; however, he continued.

Notes from witness statements taken by Cumbria police, December 2001 & January 2002.

On the 12th August 1988, records show Alison May Bell had a pregnancy termination at Carlisle General Hospital. The abortion was a result of sex acts committed illegally on hospital premises by an NHS employee called Robert Scott-Buccleuch, a 35yr old trainee mental health nurse at Garlands NHS Mental Health Hospital where Alison was a patient.

I was unaware I was doing anything wrong.

Robert Scott-Buccleuch's rationale for the acts he committed.

Contents

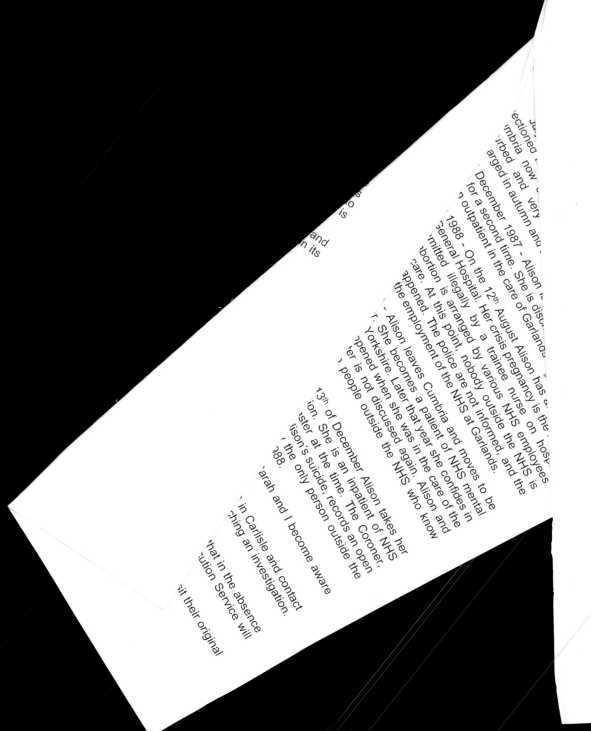

Feb 2017 – The former trainee mental health nurse, Robert Scott-Buccleuch, finally admits his actions under caution. He goes on to tell Cumbria police that Alison's psychiatrist, along with numerous others, was fully aware of what was going on.

May 2017 – Cumbria police inform us that even though they are now in possession of supporting documents and a confession, the CPS will not be prosecuting the individual in question. We appeal their decision.

December 2017 – Our appeal to the CPS is thrown out. We are "very disappointed" and arrange to meet them.

May 2018 – The CPS tell us they will block any attempt to pursue a private prosecution.

Spring 2019 – A national charity called Inquest who provide support for the bereaved in relation to deaths that occur in the care of the state, help us launch a crowd-funding campaign. Th... is to raise the money needed to pay legal fees in an attempt... obtain a fresh inquest into Alison's death. The amount required... raised.

Spring 2020 – The appeal to quash the original inquest ... secure a new one is currently underway; correspondence is ... way to the Attorney General's Office.

The future remains unwritten...

Introduction

What is the price of experience? Do men buy it for a song? Or wisdom for a dance in the street? No, it is bought with the price of all that a man hath.

William Blake

My name is Tom Bell, Alison was my sister. In the Spring of 2019, I found myself between jobs. As it turned out, the time and space I was given were a welcome well-timed present, an extended punctuation mark in life's journey that gave me the opportunity to write this book. The need to tell this story has been burning a hole in my consciousness for some time.

I want to bring to life the human side of what all too many texts written by so called experts do not, cannot. The world seems full of counsellors without knowledge who offer views and solutions without experience and pontificate about issues they have no understanding of.

They say what doesn't kill you makes you stronger, I'm unconvinced. 2017 was a strange year for me. I was embroiled in a highly emotive energy sapping battle for justice. I had been bullied out my job in the NHS and mental illness was tearing the stuffing out of me. I was ripped off by a rogue builder who left our home without a roof in a wild and windy November. I was admitted to hospital with chest pains. My father died, and then to top it off, I was knocked off my bike by a driver who was over the drink drive limit. If I had placed odds at the bookies on all these things happening, I would be lying on a bed made of fifty-pound notes under a Caribbean Sun right now. I didn't. My only prizes were anxiety, depression and thoughts of suicide running riot in my head. My mind got so tired of going to hell and back it just hovered somewhere in between as serotonin dictated.

Events and emotions led me to a place where happiness became an imposter and Sertraline the solution. A passage in time in which I feel life has been so unjust there were moment's I questioned if it was worth living. I used to love life, I believed it was a gift. I tried to rise each morning with enthusiasm. I thought the days were precious and the future held great promise. I was the former brewery salesman, outwardly confident with a good sense of humour and a large and when appropriate, crude repertoire of jokes. I was the mildly annoying guy arranging party games at the barbecue. Cajoling and encouraging anyone and everyone to take part and have fun. Take a big slug of your drink, run down the garden, place your hand on the ground, spin round ten times and run back in a straight line, if you can. I was the bloke who whisked out the guitar to get people singing round the campfire at festivals. My voice is so bad I think onlookers felt obliged to sing over me, but the good intent was there. I liked to have a good time and help others have one too.

Perhaps sometime during the last few years I had inadvertently, maybe after a heavy drinking session or smoking something stronger than cigars, agreed to join a secret club that offers its members all the downsides of life. A sort of opposite to the Freemasons. In this gang there are no benefits, in fact you are proactively excluded and denied favour or privilege. Justice is beyond reach, a career with progression is out the question and as your mind careers out of control, the universe waves its shitty stick of fate at your forehead with increasing intensity while asking itself, just how much can Tom Bell take before he cracks?

This book is part of my answer. It is the cathartic if lengthy email of the sort we are encouraged to write and never send when we feel aggrieved. But I have been pushed beyond the point a person should be, so I am pressing the send button and copying-in the world. It may seem an unkind uncouth at times irreverent email, but it is honest. I have prioritised other's feelings to my own detriment for too long. Writing has become part of putting me back together. It is me exercising my right to tell a story that needs telling. A right denied by my upbringing, a right each of us has. This is a firm fuck you to the notion of karma, who in the absence of hell has become the lazy thinker's modern solution to natural justice. If she has shown herself to be a bitch it is only because she cannot be relied upon.

I don't believe in fate, but as I wrote this book, I had the feeling I was doing exactly what I should be. It has felt so empowering, right, logical, necessary even. Thinking about what happened to Alison has also allowed me to examine my own life.

And writing seems to be giving me the therapy the NHS cannot give me, but that it owes me; more than you can imagine at this point. It cannot give me it in part because there is no therapy service entitled, support for people and their families we have fucked up, and in part because it cannot cope with the general levels of everyday demand being placed on it. A fact Covid-19 has graphically reinforced.

I couldn't easily find a publisher for this work. Some made encouraging noises but when faced with contentious content, shied away. This book contains much that was hidden that needs placing in the light. It will make uncomfortable reading for those who continued to enjoy their lives as ours fell apart in the wake of their choices. We have been without Alison nearly three decades, it is time for names and deeds to come out from the shadows.

I've been battling depression while I have been writing. My mental health has become the fight of my life. It was also the fight of Alison's life, a fight she ultimately lost. A fight she could not win. A fight I defy anyone to win when their hands are tied as tightly behind their back as Alison's were. I told myself the purpose of this foreword would be to convey the intensity of my feelings and emotions along with a sense of how they came about. Jarring unsettling emotions, I am becoming uneasy bedfellows with. Anger, rage, fury, frustration, sadness, despair, isolation, more anger, a sense of complete hopelessness, of feeling utterly insignificant. And a touch more anger for good measure. I now realise you will only get a real sense of how and why I feel this way, when you have read this book.

For anyone struggling with their mind who feels they are losing hope, whatever the trigger, if you recognize it is happening to you, then that is the first step to getting help and finding a way forward. Even if the next step is just to stand still and breathe for as long as it takes. Ask for help and don't let anyone make you feel bad about your mental health. Mental illness and depression are not a slight to the people you have in your life, or the things you have around you. They just are, like a broken bone, a torn muscle, or a fever. Nobody has a bag of hope they can give you, believe me I have looked. But thankfully there are people who will listen, and as crass as it may sound, I have found the benefit of being listened to when I have felt on the edge, is immense.

Thank you for making time for this book, to hear this story.

Chapter 1 - Happy Christmas

Have yourself a merry little Christmas, let your heart be light. From now on our troubles will be out of sight.

Have Yourself a Merry Little Christmas; R Blane, H Martin

Christmas Eve 1991. And I am stood shaking, numb with cold and disbelief by the side of my sister Alison's freshly dug grave, watching as the grim, sombre, and almost always awkward funeral formalities unfold. Blacks, greys, some dark browns, the whites of clean shirts and the obvious inability or unwillingness to make eye contact with each other. This is a funeral without colour, not a modern affair where a life lived is celebrated and funeral goers are encouraged to wear clothes that remind them of the person, they are saying goodbye to. The atmosphere today is strange, stranger than most funerals. The awkwardness everyone feels is amplified under a long dark shadow of suicide that hangs over the proceedings.

There are many of the born-again Christian brigade present. The congregation and the topic for this occasion are like oil and water. Happy clappy shiny religious types, men and women who exist in a faith-fuelled state of ignorant certainty are not comfortable in the grey areas of life days like this showcase. The pastor of the local evangelical church mum attends is particularly conflicted, and it shows. He says little, jumbling and confusing the few words he utters, Alison was, we will never know, we are all God's children, blah, blah. He has only agreed to bury Alison because it is mums wish.

He does not comprehend it is guilt that has paved the way to the place we find ourselves on this day. The irrational guilt of original sin and the gnawing crushing biblical torment of killing the unborn, needless guilt and torment he and his kind fuel and absolve. As far as he is concerned the act of Alison's suicide would be a selfish squandering of the blessing of life she was given. A deliberate choice to insult God and hurt the people who loved her. He has no idea her death, this grim unforgettable day, is the twisted gift he and his vengeful psychotic god, the role model for coercive control, gave to Alison, to my family.

For these faithful, poor mental health is a spiritual issue, the result of a flawed relationship with the Almighty. Nothing to do with genetics, chemical imbalances, circumstance or the scars of the past. True born-again believers have shed their past so to acknowledge its role in the present is a slight to God. There are no references to Serotonin, Melatonin, manic-depression, schizophrenia, bipolar, bulimia, abandonment issues, adverse childhood experiences or post-abortion trauma in the well-thumbed pages of the pastors King James Bible. Cosy and warm wrapped in the manmade fibres of an oversize synthetic jacket, this is a man more inclined to believe Alison was possessed by demons than acknowledge the presence of a chemical malfunction in her brain. The atheist in me now shudders when I think of such self-inflicted ignorance and people like the pastor who continue to peddle it so enthusiastically.

But the faith I have at this point in my life, a belief in the unprovable and intangible that was thrust upon me and that I misguidedly acquired following a nervous breakdown when I was eighteen is being stretched beyond its limit. Before I found the truth, I myself was an enthusiastic evangelical Christian until God played god with Alison. Her death and the horrific nature of it was the slap round the face I needed to stop me believing in fairy tales. I have embraced science and discovered Dawkins and Harris since then.

It was in my mid-twenties I finally summoned up the courage to tell God to fuck off, in a fit of honest anger in a layby off the A6 near Carlisle. It felt good, liberating, courageous and dangerous. I meant it, and though I laugh at myself now I was genuinely afraid because I truly believed God existed; I just couldn't go along with what I was told were his ways any longer. As I pulled back onto the road, I was sure I would be wiped out by the next lorry.

Such was the strength of my beliefs the feeling I would be maimed or killed stayed with me for years. Perhaps he is still serving his revenge. The great thing about telling God to fuck off is that you realise no one is above criticism, and the bad thing is that no one becomes above criticism.

Early the following year when a coroner in Doncaster records an open verdict at the inquest into Alison's death, the pastor of the church will be there to welcome the news Alison did not officially take her own life. His relief expressed in the words, "thank goodness for that I couldn't have buried a suicide". He then assures mum that because her daughter did not die by her own hand, she is now safe in heaven, essentially because a man in a wooden panelled room in South Yorkshire deems it so. Whether mum believes this or not I don't know, she needs to hear it and he knows she needs to hear it.

Alison had taken off her new blue coat, doubtless with mum's words about it still being in good condition and useful to someone less fortunate ringing in her ears. She placed it with her handbag on the nearest seat on the platform of Rotherham Railway Station, before slowly and deliberately making her way down the stairs onto the line and into the path of an oncoming train. I have wondered for many years why a coroner would record a verdict other than suicide when it was clear to anyone Alison's intent was to kill herself.

Our father left us when I was three years old and even though I was the youngest of three children I have occupied a place as the male of the family for many years. Digging the garden, mowing the small square lawn on the front of our boxlike council house in Penrith and carrying the shopping home from town. These were my childhood chores and they were expected, not rewarded with generous amounts of pocket money, which in any case mum did not possess to be able to give me. I am supposed to be the strong one, the tall upright male figure to lean on. But I don't know how to feel, and I am wondering how a brother should feel at his sister's funeral, a sister who has left to enter the collective world of myth and memories at the age of just 25. My head is spinning, jumbled thoughts tumbling and spilling over the brim of my brain, perhaps a hat would have held them in place, it would certainly have kept my head warm. So many thoughts. What the fuck has just happened, has she gone to a better place, is this part of God's plan for her, for us, for mum?

My experience of later years would suggest that if there is a god then Alison was not supposed to die and there has been an unholy cock-up in the order of things. But Heavens public relations advisors will already be over it, mapping out the stakeholders and advising the Holy Trinity against any unsanctioned outburst of honesty and openness. After they have falsified the paperwork, shredded the emails and created a new audit trail, they will issue a bland yet sincere sounding statement to the press and an expectant needy public.

Unlike the spin-stories we are told by the public sector after someone has been found to have dropped the ball, that everyone is deeply sorry, lessons have been learned etc., etc. Heavens press release will not acknowledge the need for learning or better staff training. It will include phrases along the lines of, God working in mysterious ways, and it's not for the likes of us mere mortals to question events, just to deal with them. Safe in the knowledge everything is part of a greater plan and the Lord will be there for us in our hour of need. The same hour of need he has just created. It's the ultimate business model, define the problem then offer the solution. Steve Jobs eat your heart out, you might have been good, but the church wrote the book when it comes to building a brand based on intangible services.

My father is at the funeral. He is wearing a warm well-made coat. A Geordie with time for beer, the Freemasons, former schoolmates and everyone except his children. Though he is undoubtedly a very intelligent man he remains to this day one of the most emotionally blind people I have ever known. Andy Capp with a chemistry degree. And on this funeral day he is of little use to his two remaining children. He has been little use on any day. If it seems harsh to air such thoughts while recounting a father attending his daughter's funeral, forgive me, but I feel entitled. He has not been there for us since he left for a younger model in 1971.

I can still remember Alison clinging to the back of his car. Screaming for him not to leave as he drove off after the occasional conscience salving dutiful visit to see his children and explain to his former wife why he did not have any money for his jettisoned family. As Alison clung to his car begging him to take her with him, mum would tell us to get back in the house as she prized my sister's fingers from the rigid sharp silver metal bumper.

Mum was left to hold her sobbing broken daughter in the middle of the road. We lived near the bus stop; our neighbours watched what went on. Manna from heaven for any self-respecting curtain-twitcher in a small market town in Northern England. Mum would pick up the pieces, calm the waters and hold the remains of a shattered fragile family together.

Despite his obvious shortcomings I do not recall mum ever saying anything negative about my father. By his absence and indifference, he played a significant part, perhaps an unwitting unknowing part, yet an important part nonetheless in the implosion of Alison's mental health. And ultimately in her reaching a point where she decided taking her own life was the only option left. It will strike me in later life he is part of the reason for this most miserable of days. But I will also discover his role in bringing us to this moment turns out to be more of a supporting actor than the leading protagonist.

At this point in the story of Alison's death, the main villain, his accomplices and the parts they have played are unknown to us. Amongst the messy spaghetti of thoughts in my head on this cold

December day, allocating blame to outsiders does not feature. I blame myself, for not being there for her when she needed me.

In my profound ignorance, I blame her for taking her own life. It is not just the pastor who does not understand mental health. The toxic shameful lingering aftertaste of the acrid confused thoughts flooding my mind will stay with me for a decade. I hold back my tears. Why has Alison done this to us, what right have I, to indulge in self-pity. I will look back from the future and feel deep regret that religion and ignorance robbed me of my right to grieve.

But it turns out there are people to blame. Each with varying degrees of responsibility for the scene unfolding on this bitter Christmas Eve. And unknown to us on this wretched day we are not just laying Alison to rest, we are burying a casket of untold truths, lies and secrets. Traces of other's sins will eventually leach upward from Alison's coffin, finding their way to the earth's surface. Revelations which mean she has never truly been laid to rest. Today, the 24th December 1991, everyone except mum is blissfully unaware of the insidious forces that have led Alison and us to this point.

As for my dad's indifference towards his children, this is something I will broach with him in a few years when the last vestiges of tolerance I have for his families need to maintain a shop window at all cost eventually evaporates. Dads side of the family are interesting, use of that word is so much more polite than the alternatives. Their desire for acceptance and disempowering need for approval would appreciate my diplomacy in the sensitive area of family dysfunctionality. One of my grans favourite phrases was that it was better to be dead than out of fashion. A mantra guaranteed to get advertisers of apparel in trouble nowadays, one probably even Benetton would shun.

I'm told the origins of the phrase came from the wearing of corsets which caused great discomfort to women who wore them. But in an age when netting a husband was the key to securing a future and some ladies waists were measured at fifteen inches, women were forced to put up with such discomfort in anticipation of the better life it would bring. The insensitivity of my gran repeating this phrase to three children who lived in hand-me-down clothes because her son would not pay their mother enough maintenance, should not be wasted on anyone. Anyway, fashion be fucked. I'd have settled for the underpants and jumper from the school's lost property that didn't have holes in.

But we are the way we are for a reason. Perhaps dad didn't stand a chance of being anything other than emotionally illiterate growing up in the shadow of such shallow mantras. If my gran had been the marketing executive for Loreal, her strapline would have been, prove you're worth it by buying this, even if it gets you in debt. I think the sentiment is very similar to their thinly veiled appeal to low self-esteem. Granny Bells message would have been much more direct.

Winter has enveloped the large municipal cemetery in a tight icy grip. The thin cheap and slightly oversized suit I am wearing is no match for it. The cold seems to mask the numbness I feel. We are pressed further into misery by a dark iron grey sky that hangs over Doncaster. It is suitably inscrutable and seems to mirror the mood of the nation and the monotone character of its post-Thatcher Prime Minister, John Major. The overwhelming greyness and the biting cold seem to hold our heavy moods in an unforgiving vice. The passing of the hours will be our only means of escape.

The sun does not shine on days like this, it seems to have the wisdom to show restraint. Its presence today would only intensify the emotional conflict that already exists between where we find ourselves, what we find ourselves doing and the festivities coming to a climax all around us. The contrast is stark and strange enough without the sun making an appearance.

Despite our pleas, Christmas Eve was the first available slot at the local cemetery. We were told this time of year is a busy time for arranging funerals due to the number of older people dying of cold related ailments. The aged progress unceremoniously from bed-blockers of the NHS to bottlenecks of burial demand at the cemetery. What a legacy for the elderly. How did that plan to create a country fit for heroes come along?

Roger Daltrey's words now seem prescient and logical, not the outrageous rebellious statement we took them to be. Perhaps we should all hope to die before we get old. But Alison is not old, she was not supposed to be here at this point in the story of our lives, this was not what was planned. I don't know what was planned, but it was surely not this. It was not saying goodbye to the vibrant, beautiful, intelligent, scarred and mentally unstable girl that was Alison. She was a mocker of pomp. She would have laughed at the sombre atmosphere and our obvious awkwardness.

The pastor, the leader of the local evangelical church mum attends is accompanied by a posse of the faithful. Debbie my wife is standing next to me, fidgeting uncomfortably, not knowing what to say. We have been married for five years but are still very young. We met at school and were teenagers of eighteen and nineteen when we married. We are part of the awkward shuffling shivering group of people who have come to show their support and say last goodbyes to the gentle tortured soul of Alison.

The elephant in the graveyard, the word that cannot be spoken, is suicide. Just ignore it, it will go away eventually. Perhaps she had dropped something off the platform and was looking for it when she was killed. Maybe she simply hadn't noticed the oncoming train. There must be a logical reason she was on the railway line. The gentle redheaded girl that was Alison would never have done something like this deliberately. After watching the coffin being carefully placed into the cold insatiable ground, we gaze for a moment into the hole, scattering a handful of earth onto the coffin before we move slowly, not too obviously towards the waiting cars. I don't want to leave my sister and her unspent life in the hard-frosted earth of a cemetery in South Yorkshire.

The drive back to Cumbria after the funeral is long, strange, too quiet. After what seems an eternity of silence, I turn the radio on to a low setting. Freddy Mercury sings wistfully into the car that those were the days of our lives, we can't turn back time or the tide. If only he knew. I turn it off, I don't have the headspace to cope with the added emotion hearing another soulful lyric might bring. Music can be as cruel as it can be kind. Driving a car in a straight line is the extent of my abilities at this point.

The Christmas eve traffic is quietening down, and darkness is falling as we cross the county boundary taking mum and my sister Sarah to stay with friends for the festive season. In later years I will chastise myself for not staying close to them during this painful period. I just couldn't face it. Mum has become a shadow of herself in the back seat of the car. She seemed brave at the funeral, now she has shrunk, tiny and fragile in my rear-view mirror. She has changed, we have all changed, but the difference in mum is immediately visible, pronounced. The God she loves, the omnipotent loving selfish psychopathic amalgam of contradictions who asked Abraham to kill his own son, has taken her daughter and pushed her beyond the point any mother should be pushed. She is confused, in utter turmoil. Does she thank him for selecting her as worthy of trial and tribulation, or is it ok to mourn?

She tries to talk about the need for us to remember it is still Christs birthday tomorrow, a cause for celebration and reverence. She keeps saying, partly to herself and partly to us it seems, that at least Alison has gone to a better place, it must have been part of the Lords plan. Her voice is shaky, low, more a mumble than a recognisable string of words.

I don't know what to say, no one knows what to say. It doesn't feel like Alison has gone to a better place, it feels as if we have left her alone for Christmas in the cold crowded graveyard of a spent mining town, a place she had no ties to or natural affinity with. Alison has been abandoned again. If this is all part of a plan, it's the worst plan I have ever come across. The Almighty was on the golf course when this one was hatched. I don't think any of us really understand what has just happened. We haven't yet realised things will never be the same, a bomb has gone off and we cannot put the pieces back together.

At this point in time only mum knows the secrets of Alison's time at the mental health hospital in Carlisle. And we don't know it now, but we may never outrun the sadness sitting on our shoulders, however hard we try.

Chapter 2 - Born under a bright sun

Take me to this land of sweet sugar cane and Mount Gay Rum, I want to taste its sweetness and feel its tropical sun, take me to Barbados.

Charmaine J Forde

There is a low barely perceptible humming from the daylight lamp hanging on the wall above the corner of my desk. Mum gave me the money for the lightbox a few years ago. Having lost a daughter to suicide she is living the ultimate impact of poor mental health and I know she worries about mine. She also worries about my spiritual wellbeing, my red wine intake and propensity for cigars, which ironically escalated during five-years working in the NHS. My liking of festivals and desire to listen to music other than Cliff Richard is just the bitter icing on the unevangelical devoutly atheist flavoured cake that is her son.

The lamp is blindingly bright. Its brilliant clean white light floods my home-office, a loft we converted in the little terraced house in Penrith Debbie and I have lived in for almost thirty years. To any nosey neighbour it looks like we spend a lot of time on a sunbed. We don't, my legs are like hairy milk-bottles and my face is nearly always pale. I can't look at the lamp directly for long. The two high wattage tubes sitting vertically next to each other are just visible beneath the thin transparent plastic cover that harnesses and diffuses the substitute sunlight I have come to depend on each year. I dread winter.

It's not that I dislike the season or the weather it brings, but the lack of sunlight affects my mental health to the point where there are times I can barely function. My mood can sink to a point where I have thoughts I couldn't share with any life-insurance company, thoughts I don't share with those around me because I wouldn't want them to carry the burden of knowing. My memory suffers terribly. I forget people's names, everyone gets labelled bud, mate or fella, and if you're female I struggle, I'm not a darling kind of person. I call Debbie Chicken, not because I have forgotten her name it's just a term of affection.

My capacity to carry out the simplest of tasks is massively reduced. I can't think straight, and I need periods of quiet and repeated reference to lists if I am reading, cooking or need to concentrate at all. There are days, dark days where it feels as if someone has taken my batteries out while I was asleep, and I don't want to get out of bed. I mean I really don't want to get out of bed. I force my body to rise and keep reminding myself the way I feel will not last forever. I talk to myself and I tell me to just deal with each moment and not think about what comes next. I get up, wash my face, brush my teeth then shave, one step at a time. Slow and steady is the way I have learnt to live through winter these last few years.

Seasonal Affective Disorder is very real to me. I am one of a small proportion of the population for whom the winter blues as it's sometimes called, can be debilitating. My lightbox, exercise when I can motivate myself, a patient wife, understanding friends, occasional periods of mindful reflection, online forums, and latterly conversations with Alexa and Google help me weather the mental winter storm that takes me in its grip each year. I took St John's Wort for many years, an old widely used form of natural medication used to help people suffering with low mood, but it no longer does the job. I rely on prescription anti-depressants now.

Finding someone who knows much about SAD in the UK is a real challenge, in fact finding a doctor who demonstrates empathy or understanding can be quite a challenge. I don't blame them for not seeing it as important. Many GPs by their own admission haven't been trained adequately in the complex field of mental health. When someone comes to the surgery saying they feel anxious about the onset of winter it probably doesn't feel like much of a priority compared with a global pandemic, Elsie's Dementia, Jim's terminal struggle with pancreatic cancer, climate change, the seemingly imminent demise of the NHS, the upcoming inspection from the Care Quality Commission or their own anxieties about paying this year's university fees for the children; I get it. But the lack of awareness and knowledge of SAD amongst mental health professionals themselves puzzles me. I've met a lot and I've never met one with an interest in understanding it.

I've hidden feelings of inadequacy behind a mask of confidence for much of my life. I wouldn't have openly acknowledged my SAD or depression ten years ago without feeling weak, deficient, flawed. No one likes winter Tom, we all feel a bit low when the dark nights come, you know there is really no such thing as Seasonal Affective Disorder, don't you, it said so in the Daily Mail. Pull yourself together, whistle a happy tune. Read some Deepak Chopra, a wealthy advocate of quantum healing hocus pocus, a trendy softly spoken swarthy skinned stylish glasses wearing pseudo-intellectual and self-appointed self-help alternative medicine espousing guru whose Twitter account spews such bullshit laden phrases as, mysticism heals the wounds inflicted by reason, to an eager audience of over three million followers. And if all that fails, as it will, then just play some M People and go search for the hero inside yourself.

I was born under a bright sun in the newly built Queen Elizabeth Hospital in Bridgetown Barbados on February 26th, 1968. The youngest of three and the only boy. My two older sisters Saran and Alison were also born on the island. My father was a senior brewer in the employment of Banks, the best known of the brewers on what many refer to as the jewel of the West Indies and most beautiful island in the Caribbean. A place of eternal summer.

William, Bill to those he knew, was a failed if fun loving medical student turned brewer who worked in many countries spreading the pleasures and ills of alcohol all over the world. Over the course of his life my father worked in the West Indies, Ceylon, now Sri Lanka, Scandinavia, Europe and Nigeria. And he practiced what he preached. He was by any modern standard of the definition an alcoholic. It may have been hot near the equator but not everyone drinks lager for breakfast, Glastonbury excluded. They were different times. British expatriate workers, expats as they are more commonly known were gainfully employed and tempted abroad to posts in developing nations with good terms and conditions. A house, a live-in servant, a nanny and sometimes a driver, were all part of the gig. The expats were there to share their knowledge and expertise in the drive to bring the delights of western consumerism, modern manufacturing and all its associated prosperity to aspiring economies across the globe.

Dad died a couple of years ago. He spent the last years of his life living on the island of Sri Lanka with his second and much younger Sinhalese wife. My greatest regret is that I never really knew him enough to mourn his passing. As a teenager I visited him when he was working in Nigeria, the company he worked for paid for the flights. In a rare and misguided moment of candour, he told me that sooner or later I would see that life must be about the pursuit of pleasure. I prefer to think he was being insensitive rather than cruel in saying this to a son he abandoned in pursuit of his own.

The only thing worse than missing your dead dad is not missing your dead dad. I can't remember him ever telling me he loved me. When he died, I found myself grieving for what might have been, not what was.

I don't know where to start describing mum. She is still very much alive, in mind if not entirely in body. In her late eighties now, she has been waiting for God to return to Earth to take her and her fellow born-again Christians for many years. The post-war life that promised so much has been utterly unfaithful to her, delivering a relentless string of barely tolerable disappointments and unbearable heartbreak. I'm not sure she wants to be here anymore. She seems impatient God hasn't come for her yet. I think she curses the failure of the millennium bug to spew forth the chaos and hell-like disruption we were all promised. For her and her religious kin it was supposed to be the starting gun that unleashed the four horsemen of the apocalypse, a trigger point signalling the beginning of the end of days, the imminent destruction of the world as we know it and the commencement of the rapture. She has changed from the beautiful beaming young woman who smoked cheroots, loved chocolate, enjoyed dancing, watching rugby, who laughed, smiled and sang along to the Beatles.

The rapture is a peculiar Evangelical Christian notion. It is a single and as yet unknown point in time in which all the born-again brothers and sisters will be transported to heaven to live in eternal bliss with their saviour. Around half of all Americans who are Christians say they believe in the rapture; bless them. My mum believes when the truly faithful are taken from the earth the rest of us will be left at the mercy of the devil and his demons. The remaining sinners will then be left to battle it out in what can only be described as the largest cage fight of all time, just without the cage.

There will doubtless be a demonic organisation chart somewhere at Satanic HQ outlining the responsibilities and project milestones for each malevolent being. Good chaos requires directing and even a piss-up in a brewery needs organising; I have a t-shirt to prove it. In the unfolding chaos, humanity will disappear up its own orifice in an insatiable evil and ugly orgy of selfish self-interest where we pursue our own pleasures and satisfy our basest needs and darker vices at the expense of those around us. Clearly the rapture has already happened; I just can't bring myself to break the news to mum. If she has missed her turn in the lift to the executive floor due to administrative error, God will never hear the end of it.

Mum would like nothing more than to be taken to heaven. Even more so than many of the people living in deprived parts of Doncaster. Her zealous religious beliefs have distanced her from what is left of a small family, her health is letting her down, and she is increasingly dependent on the work and goodwill of others for her wellbeing. Sometimes non-believers, and on occasion even those of other faiths. It's strange to think the indignities of old age are forcing the great religious ideologies of our time to come together in one of the afterlife's waiting rooms owned by the Railway Housing Association of South Yorkshire. Born-again Christians being dressed and cared for by Muslim's and atheists working for a charity on minimal wages. Infirmities are blind to religious preference and the universe has a wicked sense of humour when it comes to putting our petty prejudices in their place. If mum is resentful her life has worked out this way, she has a right to be. Her god has treated her abysmally.

I remember when the millennium was approaching. Talk of a mysterious bug, a computer glitch known as Y2K that was going to wreak havoc on our increasingly computerised world, was rife. The media were feasting on it. Planes were going to fall out the sky, traffic lights would fail, trains crash, power stations malfunction, nuclear reactors explode, prison security systems crash, the internet would shut-down and your desktop computer would start talking to you in a voice like the exorcist, come to life and possess your soul just before you were raped or murdered by a violent escaped prisoner or pierced through the head by debris falling from the sky. Y2K was going to make the Day After Tomorrow look like The Wizard of Oz shown on an outdoor screen as a matinee on a sunny Saturday.

But this carnage was manna from heaven, literally, for any self-respecting born-again Christian. This was it, the beginning of the end, the final act they knew was coming, the end of ridicule by those who lacked the faith or wisdom to understand the will of god that had only been made known to them. This was a glorious and righteous performance they had a starring role to play in and it opened the door to the start of their eternity in heaven. Nuts to Songs of Praise, mum and her gang were getting ready to sing in the presence of the holy trinity, the saints and the angel Gabriel. For the record mums singing is as bad as mine, but she tells me in heaven her voice will be transformed to that of an angel; X-Factor take note. And yes, people are really encouraged to believe these things.

So, as Y2K approached, as far as mum and her fellow churchgoers were concerned, they had served their apprenticeships, applied for the parts and the director of the play would soon be on the phone begging them to accept. They were utterly convinced the end was nigh. In what can only be described as some majorly screwed-up thinking, they were jubilant the end-times were imminent. Seemingly righteous pillars of the community, ecstatic about its imminent destruction and the end of all within it who didn't share their views. With some power and a nicely starched uniform, I think the elders of her church would give Hitler a run for his money in the sanity stakes.

Mum sincerely and earnestly told me not to worry. She explained that though the millennium bug was going to be the start of the end, the actual rapture might not occur for a little while afterwards. Apparently, their god wanted to test his true believers by leaving them in the chaos for a wee bit and leave a window of opportunity open for any late conversions. Only after the faithful had proved themselves within the fire of a world of disorder and temptation would he deliver on his promise to give them a lift to heaven. Jim, one of the other believers from their little church had shared these insights through prophesy with the group at a recent prayer meeting and so they were duly preparing for a short period of life amidst the chaos that was about to be unleashed.

Preparation involved the purchase of fishing rods, tents and tinned food, but surprisingly few toilet rolls. The plan was to go and camp by a Loch in Scotland. The precise destination was not yet known but the group were waiting for guidance, perhaps another prophesy from Jim to give precise map coordinates. We are talking pre-Google Maps and smartphones, pre-Blackberry even, dark times indeed. Mum was serious about the Scottish Loch; she had the tins in her pantry to prove it. She hadn't ordered a fishing rod as she felt fishing would be the men's job, but she had seen a nice one in a magazine and cut out the advert for a friend. Jim's prophesy turned out to be inaccurate or premature. The inevitable non-occurrence of the apocalypse was explained away as simply a further test of their faith; one they all passed with flying colours.

Though I smile as I think about these things, my laughter hides a deep sadness and anger that my mum became so absorbed in a crazy and worrying set of beliefs that her convictions about the future meant she was genuinely if needlessly worried for my safety. This was the same woman who relied on herself to bring us up and worked all her life. She laughed and made me laugh, she introduced me to the joy of reading; Asterix, Tales of Narnia and Spike Milligan. We watched the Two Ronnie's together, howling hysterically at the Phantom Raspberry Blower of Old London Town.

My earliest memories of mum are of a woman who never stopped. Always on the go, working, looking after us, cooking, washing, cleaning, digging potatoes in her tatty old coat and gardening shoes, a pair of worn out brown brogues. Dragging us to church on Sundays, taking us to see friends or relatives on the train or knocking on doors collecting money for Save the Children. Irony becomes clearer with hindsight. We had no money and no car, we walked everywhere to get anywhere. But mum could be funny, she had a spark in her eye and a good sense of humour. There are still glimpses, but I haven't recognised her for many years now. Perhaps the reasons will become clearer as this book unfolds.

Sarah, Alison and I, were never permitted our own story. We were not allowed to think much about ourselves, to complain or highlight the things that mattered to us as children. Dad's decision to run off with his young secretary was never discussed and the resulting financial constraints we lived in were explained away and brushed aside. If we moaned, as we did, about being the last children we knew without a telly, we were simply told by mum, that there was always someone worse off. Reminded we should be grateful for what we had and where we were, no matter what the situation. Like the scene from Monty Python, were each person outdoes the others story of how hard their lives were, in a bid to claim the ultimate childhood hardship. No-one's experiences are acknowledged or discussed, just countered with worse alternatives. But being brought up to be constantly grateful life has not spat on you is only a short step from expecting nothing of it.

If I muttered dissent that it wasn't normal for ten-year olds to wear cord jackets with patches on the elbows, or the second-hand clothes from the schools lost property were embarrassing or didn't fit. The sizing service of the lost property department was very imprecise. I was countered with the argument there were countless children in the world running round in dirty loin cloths and less, who would be grateful to own a pair of baggy shorts and an oversized brown and orange jumper with a patch on the arm and just a small white paint stain on it. If I dared to suggest the mixing of platform shoes, these were always left over and cheapest in the winter sale, with shorts was not new fashion in the making, but unbearably embarrassing, I was reminded of all the people walking miles in bare feet for water who would gladly sell their soul for a pair of Clarks leather shoes from McVities footwear shop. The sheer luxury, what was I talking about. I clearly didn't know I was born. The radical look I was sporting sometimes made me wish I hadn't been!

Had we still been living in Bridgetown Barbados or Colombo in Sri Lanka, the argument about loin cloths might have carried the day. But we were living on a newly built council estate in a small market town in northern England. I just wanted a pair of blue jeans, non-branded would be fine, and a non-scratchy jumper with a star on it. Yes, equally cringeworthy with hindsight, but all the rage at the time. I was conscious I was different, that I wasn't from around here, a rootless young boy, an offcomer who spoke with a confused mix of dialects whose mum was a bit weird and whose family had no money. The last thing I wanted was to stand out any further because of mum's sartorial choices. More than most children I wanted to fit in. I don't anymore.

The older I get the more empathy I have with those who subscribe to the view that our parents fuck us up. I thought for a great many years, foolishly I now realise, that upbringing didn't really matter, it was what we made of ourselves that ultimately determined who we are and what we might become. Who cares if my mum had abandonment issues, low self-esteem, potentially undiagnosed mental health needs and arcane radical religious beliefs, or if Dad walked out on when I was three, everything will be just fine and I will turn out hunky dory. If these things are true, then good parenting can be written off as surplus to requirements.

Of course, I now know that's bullshit. Childhood experiences and upbringing matter. It's like saying to a car, if you should choose to speak to one, that its immaterial how well it was designed, developed and put-together, it is still capable of performing however it wants to. No, it's not. If you came off the Lada Production line in the eighties when the night shift were hungover there's a good chance you may have problems with gear changes, your doors might fall off and you will struggle to keep up with a Ferrari. Sure, it's not a perfect analogy, and one of the greatest gifts of being human, we are not cars, is that your parents and your upbringing do give you gifts, if you are prepared to see them that way.

Mine are naivety, unrealistic expectations, assumptions of others character attributes, an over propensity to trust and depression. And though these can feel like a prison at times, honesty is a barred window through which you get to see others reap the rewards of more flexible approaches to truth, I try to see them as gifts. They give me a view of the world that is unique, slightly different to many of my peers, and in a world of increasing conformity, they give me views and perceptions differing from the norm. I think it's a good thing, not always a feel-good thing, but a good thing. Our childhoods matter on the journey to who we become. I realise that now.

This Be The Verse

They fuck you up, your mum and dad.
They may not mean to, but they do.
They fill you with the faults they had,
And add some extra just for you.

But they were fucked up in their turn,
By fools in old-style hats and coats.
Who half the time were soppy-stern,
And half at one another's throats.

Man hands on misery to man.
It deepens like a coastal shelf.
Get out as early as you can,
And don't have any kids yourself.

Philip Larkin

Chapter 3 - And so to Penrith

A small town has as many eyes as a fly.

Sonya Hartnett

Penrith can be the very best of places. It can also be the worst. There is a story, I like to think of Greek origin, of two young men who visit a neighbouring town to find out if it is a suitable place to live. They travel separately and as they arrive each asks a question of the wise old man who sits at its entrance. It seems an unlikely, slightly Hollywood influenced scenario in which every Greek town has a wise old man, a Gandalf style white bearded philosopher who sits at its gate, but indulge me, let's run with it.

The young men each ask the wise old man what the town is like as a place to live. He replies by asking them to tell him about the place they have come from. The first young man replies that the town he comes from is full of dishonest ungenerous people, it is an unkind place he has grown to despise, hence his desire to move somewhere else. Upon hearing this the wise old man says to him he will find this town to be much the same. The second young man says the town he lives in is a kind place where people are honest and generous, to which the philosopher replies he will also find this town to be much the same

The message is clear if somewhat kitsch; life is what you make it and you will find people to be much the way you expect them to be. Be mean and selfish and you will see this reflected back to you, be kind and generous and you will likewise notice these qualities in those around you. It's a nice sentiment. The truth I think is that if you feel people are kind and generous you are simply less likely to notice the harm they are doing, to you and those around you; deliberately or unintentionally. Though I know I am imperfect to my core, I like to think I am kind, considerate and generous. I was brought up to believe the best in those around me, unfortunately, it has proved a crippling disability in a world which increasingly rewards their opposites.

I have lived in Penrith for nearly fifty years, almost all my life and certainly all my adult life. There is lots about it and the people who live here to love. But looking back I see the Penrith of the Seventies and early Eighties as a horrible bigoted little place, small and introverted in so many respects. Selfish, self-righteous, insecure and insular. It has changed, but even though our worlds are no longer the streets we live in, the minds of many have still not travelled far. But perhaps that could be said about anywhere.

I am told any residual wariness to welcoming outsiders to this part of the world is a hangover from the times of the Reivers. These fearsome lawless raiders drawn from both sides of the nearby Scottish border ran amok across the remote contested parts of Britain for four centuries. Penrith is still overlooked by a signalling beacon, part of a large network that kept a watchful eye for trouble and from where a fire would have been lit to notify the towns people the outlaws were on their way, giving them time to prepare or flee. If the Scots invaded now, I think most of us would stay and apply for citizenship.

Like me, my older sister Sarah was born in Barbados and though she is as white as snow with parents as traditionally English as Tea and Scones, a Geordie and a girl from Salisbury, she was called a Wog at school when we first arrived in the Eden Valley. Children can be as stupid as they are cruel. Eden and Cumbria still have some of the lowest levels of ethnic diversity in the UK. The taunting only got worse when it became known we were the children of a divorced single parent. In a time when the Second World War was not yet a distant memory to be the children of a widow was excusable. But to be the offspring of a single parent whose husband had divorced her on the grounds of unreasonable behaviour was a badge of shame.

Sarah, like me when I reached her age, discovered the necessity of pugilism to survive; sometimes a punch in the face is the only language that works. Try explaining divorce, fatherly infidelity, dual-nationality and the subtleties of being born abroad yet still being white to children who have never travelled more than twenty miles. Alison, whose red hair and large plastic framed national health glasses courted even more taunts from the school bullies, avoided conflict whenever she could. Sarah did her best to protect her, but Alison was the archetypal bullies dream, the victim who won't hit back. Though I love where I live, I can understand why Sarah left Penrith at the earliest opportunity and has no desire to come back. It is over fifty years since the first stretch of motorway reached Penrith in 1968, but things take time to change round here.

A neglected Wikipedia page clearly in need of updating, describes Penrith as a market town and civil parish in the county of Cumbria. The Wikipedia page omits all references to the infamous Penrith Pong that plagued the town for decades. Pong is a polite euphemism for the strong pungent wretch-inducing odour that emanated from the local rendering plant. The aroma would waft across the town like, well, you know, entering open windows and doors and lingering in homes like an unwelcome uninvited constantly farting tramp.

The Guardian ran an article in 2013 called Let's move to Penrith, in which a journalist described the town as a place of gruff, stony beauty. In the article the notorious pong was cited by residents as the worst thing about living in Penrith. Following a lengthy and highly fractious court action, the pong was officially dealt with in 2014 but rumours of its return are rife, and a group of residents have started a fresh petition to once again highlight the issue. A local punk band released an anthemic if unsubtle ditty called, This Town Stinks.

The tourist information website offers a slightly more aspirational take on things, pointing out that Penrith was formerly known as the Old Red Town due to all its sandstone buildings. Then in the finest of waffling traditions public sector copywriters are best known for, the site goes on to claim Penrith is a market town rich in history which combines the advantages of being located in a beautiful inspiring area with the amenities of a vibrant local community. Many of the town's young people leave to pursue education and work opportunities elsewhere, a great number never come back.

If you have travelled through Penrith on the West Coast mainline you may recall it as the town with the old castle ruins opposite the rail station. The castle ruins themselves sit at one edge of the towns public park. From behind an unkempt moat the ruins stand guard over the obligatory tennis courts, crazy golf, bandstand, and of course empty paddling pool now filled with sand by the faceless fun police to avoid the risk of drowning. You can of course still climb what is left of the castle ruins and achieve death or serious injury by gravity, but the twelve inches of treacherous tepid water that posed such an unacceptable hazard to life are gone.

A modern looking newly built tea shop and changing rooms overlook the pristine bowling green. They replaced the old wooden pavilion burned down by vandals a few years ago. I remember watching it blaze brightly from our back garden. We used to buy single cigarettes from the old wooden hut, sharing one between two, three, sometimes four of us. On a good day we would chip in and buy a whole pack of ten.

As well as playing host to King Richard the Third, Penrith's castle ruins have seen countless games of football, hide and seek, tag, a great deal of adolescent fondling and many an after-school fight. I and my teenage friends spent much of our formative years drinking, smoking, picking and eating magic mushrooms and sniffing glue around the damp smelling sandstone remains. I'm sure it wasn't what the castle builders had in mind or quite the photo opportunity the party of Japanese tourists expected but it didn't stop them whipping off their lens caps to capture the impromptu moment. Perhaps hanging on walls somewhere in Tokyo there are photos of two wild-eyed spaced-out schoolboys, shirts untucked, ties pulled tightly down into thin knots, breathing heavily into bags of Evo-Stik? It was dangerous and looking back seems incredibly foolish, and not all who entered made it through. But this was Britain in the early eighties, it was what bored frustrated skint angry teenagers did before smartphones, Xboxes and cheap cocaine.

Cumbria, home of the Lake District and the county Penrith sits at the heart of, would be the undisputed first choice for a British remake of the Dukes of Hazard. Apart from being overly cold for the frequent wearing of hot pants, we have most of the ingredients required. Some rough and ready drinking holes, I should know, wide expanses of lawless rurality, a hapless police force, a jolly if decidedly dim police commissioner, no shortage of incompetent public servants, and the obligatory gaggle of entitled landowners and favour pulling businessmen.

Macauley's history of England refers to the Wild men who live in West Cumbria, calling it a place only accessible by treacherous mountain passes. Anyone who has driven across the A66 will recognise this description. Cumbria is big geographically, but amongst the great and the good, those who move and shake at the level where decisions are made, it is a small place where everyone knows everyone. I recall the head of one local agency who sat on the boards of twenty-two other local and regional agencies; surely enough to secure a place in any self-respecting hall of fame for rural nepotism?

Penrith is at the quieter less touristy northern end of Cumbria's Lake District. The town has a population of around Seventeen thousand and sits at the epicentre of a local authority district called the Eden Valley. Eden's claim to fame is being the most sparsely populated rural district in England. Its population of just over fifty thousand is spread across more than two thousand square kilometres. An area of land one third larger than Greater

London with its population of nearly nine million. I and my next-door neighbour often go out cycling for a couple of hours on a Sunday morning and if we steer clear of the main roads and the tourist traps round lake Ullswater, we can travel a good few miles and still count the number of cars we see on one or two hands at most.

In 2019 the Eden Valley was hailed as the fifth best place in the UK to live in the Halifax's annual quality of life survey, ahead of St Albans, South Oxfordshire and the Cotswolds; praise indeed and now only a matter of time before we get our very own detective drama or perhaps scripted reality television show filmed on the patch. The Only Way is Eden would be less Midsomer Murders and more Joey Essex meets the Keystone Cops.

When it comes to the running of our public services, we have a bad habit of celebrating ineptitude and welcoming the detritus discarded from elsewhere that is unable to find refuge in any other place. Behind Cumbria's picture postcard scenery is a patchwork quilt of poorly performing public services who owe our continued tolerance of them on a mix of stoic rural self-reliance, community spirit and an army of committed volunteers.

Cumbria has never been and is unlikely to become a beacon of brilliance attracting the brightest and best of the public sector. Then again, do the words brightest, best, and public sector, even belong in the same sentence? On the rare occasions leading-edge thinkers might seek employment in public services, it's an unfortunate reality that isolated rural areas like Cumbria lack the critical mass needed to attract them. Unable to tempt the good and providing sanctuary for the inept, places like Cumbria deliver a double whammy to rural populations who need their public services to be innovative if they are to be effective.

The current Chief Constable of Cumbria's police force, Michelle Skeer, achieved her role in-spite of being closely linked to the infamously and tragically botched investigation into the death of Poppi Worthington. This horrific tragedy and the subsequent policing fiasco surrounding it rightly garnered UK wide press attention. One of her predecessors Craig Mackey, also earned recent national infamy in his role as acting commissioner of the Metropolitan police. He was labelled Commander Coward and condemned by colleagues following a decision to remain safely locked in his car as a fellow officer was being stabbed during the Westminster terror attack of 2017. As well as regularly losing crucial evidence from high profile cases, driving dangerously, blowing up the wrong cars in controlled explosions, unlawfully accessing the police database, committing fraud, child neglect and inciting children to engage in sexual activity, media coverage of officers being disciplined for watching porn on their smartphones and having sex on duty has cemented Cumbria's role as the undisputed clown prince of British policing.

If Cumbria's police force are a laughingstock, our NHS hospitals are an undisputed basket case. The NHS in Cumbria has been in crisis for as long as anyone cares to remember. The county's healthcare system is regularly highlighted by NHS England itself as one of the most challenged and dysfunctional in Britain. North Cumbria NHS has had fourteen different chief executives in the last twenty years, a national record. As inept management, consistent failings and a culture of collusion and wilful blindness have inevitably led to serious harm and even death, the NHS in Cumbria has been forced to pay out tens and tens of millions of pounds in compensation to patients and their families. The cost to UK taxpayers of continually baling Cumbria NHS out of the crap it appears unable to climb out of, is only exceeded by the tragic personal cost and often irreversible damage done to those it has failed and their loved ones.

As for the county's council services, I've yet to meet anyone who expresses delight in them, then again is anyone ever delighted with their local authority. Cumbria's six small district authorities and its countywide council are widely regarded by citizens as unfit for purpose, particularly children's services which are regularly lambasted in the local and national press. We will leave the state of Cumbria's education for another day. Suffice to say neither competence nor courage are obvious qualities in the upper echelons of Cumbria's public services.

We make such a wonderful hiding place for dross that recently an unqualified psychiatrist, which I guess means she wasn't really a psychiatrist, was discovered in the employment of Cumbria's NHS providing counselling to some of the county's most vulnerable people. Even pre-Corona, Cumbria's NHS was so stretched it would have welcomed Harold Shipman if he could be resurrected with a pulse. Mind you, this could help reduce our ageing population and if his services were publicised adequately, deter further retirees from coming here to see out their days in rural tranquillity.

If proof were needed of Penrith's distance from many urban ills, it is the content of our local paper. One prominent article told how the local police pursued a man on a mobility scooter on suspicion of shoplifting from a supermarket. For the local cops, this chase was probably the highpoint of their year, the adrenalin fuelled equivalent of young men getting to play with machine guns. Resources were deployed and the suspect was duly apprehended after a highly coordinated pursuit through the town centre. I can only imagine the congratulatory call from the police commissioner, the fist-pumping and belly-bumping that occurred upon the suspects apprehension. Such evil has no place in Penrith. And as for the absolute news scoop of the millennium, nothing has yet topped the time when three of the actors who played Hobbits in Lord of the Rings visited Penrith in 2003. Ah, the safety of the shire.

For me, the most telling indicator of the place Penrith is, is a view from the front door of the Royal, one of the towns oldest and arguably best watering holes. If you stand outside the pub and look directly across the road you will see the Town Hall looking proudly back at you. This is the mildly ostentatious headquarters of Eden District Council, one of the smallest local council administrations in England. Its reputation amongst locals as a hidey hole for detritus was cemented when a former Chairman and long-standing councillor was jailed a few years ago for multiple child-sex offences. If you then cast your gaze a little to the left across the street from the Town Hall, looking less overtly proud but no less substantially back at you, is a sturdy functional looking building of dark sandstone. This is home to the local Freemason lodges. The large window of the councils main meeting chamber where the great and good gather to discuss the important business local authorities deal in, planning applications, parking, dog fouling, councillors expenses, how much to pay themselves and the like, faces directly into the darkened windows of the Masonic Lodge. Is there any other place in England where the workings of a small market town and the links between the elected and the entitled are implied more obviously?

The brotherhood, yes, the Freemasons has officially existed for over three hundred years and they are still an actual thing. Some observers suggest they have been around in one form or another for over twice that length of time. No mean feat. Outwardly munificent, misguided, mischievous, at times malevolent, these masked clandestine Morris Dancers of the modern day are a fascinating anachronism. Superficially philanthropic but hungry for positions of influence at every level, and still secretive. The measure of each depending on who you talk to. Many masons do a great job of playing the philanthropy and fellowship card as the reason for their getting together. But now Freemasonry just feels a bit weird, a concept whose time has passed. My dad was a long-standing mason, so we should add irresponsibility, heavy drinking, emotional blindness and the inability to remember birthdays or Christmas's to any list of budding mason's qualities.

In my mid-thirties when I worked for Carlsberg, I was told by a local businessman I had been put forward to join the lodge. He put me on the spot. I had no desire to join or to offend by refusing. I was simply told a prominent member had recommended me for consideration. He explained I might be expected to run some errands, occasionally help some people and told it would be good for my career. I decided I needed to find a diplomatic way of refusing his offer so I constructed a polite and unnecessarily lengthy letter citing the amount of time I was investing in studying for a degree as the reason I could not join their esteemed society. I explained that while I greatly appreciated the opportunity, I was not prepared to commit myself to something I could not give my full attention to.

I should have been more honest. There are at least two good reasons I would not consider joining. The first is my father. As far as I was concerned, he had never been a role model for anything obvious; quite the contrary. There have been many times in my life when my decision-making compass has been guided by a deliberate choice not to act like him, I don't imagine I am alone in this. Like writhing snakes shedding their skin, many of us spend our lives trying to wrestle free of any vestiges of parental influence, often with good reason. I am told one of the greetings used when a member enters the Freemason lodge, presumably once aprons and other garb are adorned, is to state, good and worthy Mason am I. I have often found myself wondering how goodness and worthiness in this context is defined?

Though he fits many definitions of it, I would never say my father was a bad person, just utterly bloody thoughtless and blissfully, perhaps wilfully, blind to the consequences of his actions. Shortly after they separated and his estranged wife and three children landed back in England with no money or anywhere to live, Dad headed to Australia with his new love, a young Asian secretary. This venture entailed spending the family savings on a luxury cruise to get them there. These were the same savings he had told mum would be used to pay the deposit on a house for us to live in upon our ignominious arrival back in the UK. Having reneged on his promise he managed to balls-up his own escape plan in quite spectacular fashion. In the haste to start a new life and escape the chaos and growing mushroom cloud of shame he had left behind he did not realise his new Sri-Lankan partner would need different documentation if she was going to be allowed to stay in Australia. Upon arrival her application for residency was turned down and so after a period touring the country, they slinked back to the UK.

The savings had gone and instead of a place to live we each got cuddly toys covered in kangaroo skin. Mine was a koala. Nothing quite says I love my children like running off and spending the money to house and maintain them on a luxury cruise with your young lover. Good and worthy; hmmm. I was just three years old; I did not even know my father had run off with someone else. But at least I had a new teddy bear. It would be several years before mum sat me down and explained the reason we only saw Dad occasionally was nothing to do with him working away, this being the story I had been telling ever since coming to Penrith, and which was by now causing some embarrassment, but that he had left us.

I wish mum had spoken more openly and honestly about my dad when we were growing up. Sometimes I think it is to her great credit she didn't, but also our great loss. She said she wanted us to make our own minds up about him. On reflection I think this is a kop out. I can't help thinking it would have been helpful in the forming of our judgements if we had known what he had done. Young boys desire nothing more than the love and approval of their fathers, I would have settled for acknowledgement I existed. His leaving had a huge and lasting impact on all of us. If I had known he had left us through choice, I like to think I could have saved myself a lot of heartache in later life. I wouldn't have wasted the time and effort I did, on trying to impress and build bridges to a man who clearly did not care for me.

I think of the few occasions we did spend time with him and the lengthy lectures we were subjected to about what was right and wrong. How we should behave, how we should address people, what we should aspire to be. What a hypocrite. To add salt to our wounds my father had lost his own dad when he was eleven, killed in a car crash near the village of St Bee's in West Cumbria. The keys to a new family home were in his trouser pocket when he died. I was named after my grandfather.

My dad's mum was devastated by the death of her husband. She felt the loss of Bill's father explained, in some way excused the choices he made in later life. To me it makes them less understandable, less excusable. To know the pain of losing your own dad when you were young yet decide to inflict this on your own children through choice seems selfish beyond belief. My perceptions of my father's behaviour are one reason I could not join a club of any kind that grants favour to a man who behaved in such a way. Good and worthy my arse.

The second reason I could not justify being a Freemason, is I hate the idea of old boys' clubs. Undermining democracy, exercising influence behind closed doors, choosing who should be favoured and rewarded, even in the small things. Clubs by definition do not welcome everyone. Where there are people winning because they are on the right side of the club door, there will always be those outside who lose, left out in the cold, whose expense they are winning at. I have dealt with vested interests and petty small mindedness most of my life. I am the person outside the club door, I know what a difficult lonely place it can be. Dress Freemasonry in whatever wrapping you like, people who want to grant favours beyond friendship behind closed doors are doing no less than spitting on democracy and defiling the memory of those who fought to defend it. I lacked the courage to say this in the polite refusal letter I sent, I'm past caring now.

Perhaps stupidly, rather than developing a raging appetite to gain access, my experience of being on the outside has given me an empathy for the dispossessed and the underdog. I both blame and thank my upbringing and my mother's relentlessly naive view of the world and the good she tried to tell me existed in it for the optimism that tells me to stick to my principles in the hope things can change for the better.

In Spring 2017, my father died following a lengthy period of illness. He spent the last years of his life in Sri Lanka with his second wife, the same loyal secretary he ran off with all those years ago. She sent me some videos of the funeral, a slightly surreal, morbid if fascinating viewing experience. Mind you, I should be grateful of the time difference between Sri Lanka and the UK which meant an invitation to attend live via Skype or Facetime wasn't possible. Filming the dead hasn't caught on at funerals in northern England, yet.

A shadow of his former self, a frail bony old man lying in a casket, he was surrounded by a dozen evangelical happy clappy

Catholics, one of whom crooned wistfully while playing an acoustic guitar. There was lots of crying. I think it must have been sadness as the guitarist wasn't that bad. Along with anger and a bone-marrow-deep sense of low self-esteem, he left me an old cygnet ring and a battered pocket watch.

As I've grown older and started to think I understand what matters in life, I find myself increasingly resenting him. I have begun to understand the significance of the choices he made, and watching his funeral in grainy shaking pixelated images, I found myself getting angry at him dying without ever trying to make amends for the damage he caused. For being so blind he couldn't even see it. Here was a man who had the chance to build relationships with three intelligent young people who needed a father, more than he knew it, and he blew it.

When I was younger, I recall him being abroad at every opportunity, making little time for us. I blame him for the impact his leaving had on Alison's mental health. With the benefit of hindsight, I see his actions as the start of my sisters slippery, now strangely inevitable slide toward suicide. I find it difficult, infuriating even when I think of how differently things should have been. I tried so many times to reach out to him, phoning him, writing to him, visiting him when he was in the UK seeing his friends, friends who always seemed to come ahead of his own flesh and blood. His fourth change of Skype address should have been all the indication I needed. But I've never been the sharpest knife in the drawer, and I kept trying to build bridges.

In my twenties I was so desperate to gain his acknowledgement I ignored the evidence of his indifference. Like a beaten dog returning to its abuser seeking affection, I just created more and more opportunities to hurt myself. It broke my wife's heart watching my efforts to try and ingratiate myself, to become visible to him. She could see my adoration and respect, as ill-judged and misplaced as it was, was completely unrequited. I always had a sense my father was disappointed in me. At the time I couldn't see how misplaced my thinking was. Not only was he the architect of any disappointment he may have felt, he forfeited the right to an opinion of me. It's not so long ago you needed a licence to have a dog.

Just before the turn of the millennium, after I found out what happened to Alison when she was a patient of the NHS in 1988, I met with my father to tell him what we had discovered. I was burning with anger. I told him of the illegal sex that occurred, of a crisis pregnancy that arose and the discreet hastily arranged abortion that followed. I explained how knowledge of these events had been hidden within the walls of Garlands hospital in Carlisle, brushed under the executive carpet for over ten years. I expected something, I wanted something, a reaction from him. He was our father, Alison's father, my father, the person in a family who is supposed to stand tall in moments like these. But he said nothing, he did nothing. There was no offer of support to help me uncover the truth. No disgust expressed at what he had just been told. No anger visible in a man who had just been told his daughter had been used as the sexual plaything for an ill-disciplined under-supervised trainee nurse. My father just stared at the carpet as I spoke, his obvious discomfort making me feel awkward, uncouth for telling him such things. For daring to bring such a sensitive subject to his doorstep when he spent so much of his life avoiding any of the responsibilities he might have to his children.

I am in no doubt I would be a hellishly over-protective dad. I get agitated if another cat strays into our garden and upsets one of mine. I would knock seven shades of shit out of anyone who bullied or abused my own. I understand that I feel this way because I grew up without a father's interest or protection. You have to stand in the cold without a coat to really know what being cold feels like.

This encounter was one of those flashpoints in a person's life where they reveal what they are made of. I don't mean their levels of courage or bravery, or skill or mastery of specific tasks, just the presence and depth of intent. The expressing of desire to be present, to do something, anything. I knew he had never been there for us in the past, but surely this was different, an occasion, perhaps the occasion, for stepping up. This was his chance to show he loved us, that he cared for his children. Why didn't he want to hurt the man who had broken Alison beyond repair? Maybe one of the thoughts ultimately leading Alison to suicide was a realisation she was not the precious daughter of any father. Love is deeds.

Following his death in 2017, I was told my dad left instruction with his wife and close friends to set-up a charity with the purpose of gathering donations to help poor children in Sri Lanka. This last thoughtless, clumsy and entirely typical act summed up the utter emotional blindness of the man and highlights his hypocrisy and indifference in a most painful ironic way. Here was someone who had ignored his own children in life, trying to create a legacy that would paint an entirely different picture of his time on earth. This was the man who ignored attempts to arrange for him to meet his only granddaughter. This was the man who denied his children a modicum of financial security by spending the family silver cruising the Indian Ocean with his mistress while his wife and three young children were being hounded from a flat in Penrith for non-payment of the rent.

This was the same man who paid little if any maintenance for the upkeep of his children, yet here he was in death, wanting to be remembered for charitable acts toward the less fortunate. We were his less fortunate, I was his less fortunate, and he had made me so.

The contradiction in this final act is so thick you can feel it. Like a criminal setting up a trust fund to support the victims of other's crimes. When I heard what had been planned the disbelief was like being hit with a brick. Twisted to my core, what I felt was beyond description. Listening to people talk about what a fine fellow my father had been and how the setting up of a charity for poor children was a fitting tribute to him was unbearable. And they did it without any sense of irony? My dad never worked in public relations but managed to pull off a spectacular feat of rebranding. If I had ever doubted how invisible and insignificant I was to him, I don't anymore. But I will never understand why.

As I have aged, I have also developed a great sense of pity and sadness for my mum. She is the unsung hero and unwitting villain of my life. A woman who has been to hell and back and never come to terms with the demons following her since childhood. I can't imagine how she felt being cast adrift from the life of an expat's wife, with a housemaid, a nanny for her children and a driver, to bringing up three young children on her own. Her future turned from dreams of Downton Abbey, dips and dhal with Ceylon's first lady to the challenges of being a single mum on a council estate in Northern England.

Mum carries a mountain of baggage she has never allowed herself to acknowledge. Her own mum walked out on her when she was just three, leaving her and her father for another man. Her father was relatively young when he then died. It was only a few years ago we discovered mum had a half-sister and brother. Her estranged mother and new partner went to such lengths to leave their old lives behind that they never spoke of their previous relationships and faked their wedding anniversaries to give children and friends the impression they were married for longer than they had been.

The expectations of that generation and the gifts of shame so readily given to those who slipped between the cracks into real life have shaped and destroyed many lives. The presence and avoidance of shame has been a huge factor in my family over the years. If asked, mum would tell you Jesus is the only person she needs the approval of now. But in the moments of truth which truly reveal us, her upbringing bursts through the fragile devout shell she has built to protect herself. Her need to smooth over life's jagged edges has caused her to conceal truths she should have spoken but was too ashamed to share.

Chapter 4 - Growing up in the Shire

In the great cities we see so little of the world, we drift into our minority. In the little towns and villages there are no minorities; people are not numerous enough.

W B Yeats

In Spring 1971, following our parent's separation we arrived in the UK from Ceylon. Sarah my oldest sister was approaching seven, Alison was five and I was three. Mum now had three children to look after, less than seven pounds to her name and nowhere to live.

In Ceylon we'd recently had tea with the world's first female prime-minister, Mrs Bandaranaike, on the eve of her second election victory. Dad had a good job at the brewery, which was owned by an influential Sinhalese family supportive to her cause. Back in the UK we had nothing. We stayed for a short while in a small flat with an aunt in Leicester and then came to live with my granny in Appleby-in-Westmorland. Beggars couldn't be choosers and mum had to tolerate months of living with a disapproving mother-in-law until she could find a job and a place to live. I have no idea the yarns and tall tales my dad must have spun to his mother that she could feel justified being hostile to my mum, rather than angry toward the son who deserted his wife and three young children.

Being incredibly status conscious and in what seems like a desperate effort to save what remained of her families face after her son's affair, Granny Bell insisted the reasons for the upcoming divorce between my parents should not reflect badly on her son and her side of the family. So, despite the fact Dad had run off with his secretary, one of the oldest of clichés, mum was persuaded it would be in everyone's best interests if she shouldered the blame. This meant agreeing to be legally cited as the cause of the marriages' irretrievable breakdown. The rationale used would be her unreasonable behaviour.

This was in the days when divorce petitions were placed in the district paper and so the lie was duly laid out in the pages of the local press for all to see. Again, the irony is beyond words. Mum tolerated it at the time because she was too busy trying to hold us together. The more hindsight she has acquired the more bitterly she resents the way she was treated.

That my mother was held up and labelled as unreasonable and hence responsible for a marriage breakdown would be laughable were it not so tragic. Perhaps she would not give in to my father's requests for a polygamous relationship on foreign soil; unreasonable indeed. The result of being labelled as the cause of the breakdown meant her, and we her children, were frowned on by many who should have known better. People doubtless felt the subtle pressure of their peers to treat such nefarious off-coming urchins with disdain.

The vicar of St Andrews, the local Church of England where the faithful came to participate in the best hat competition every week, made a point of never shaking my mother's hand as we left his service each Sunday morning. I remember being dragged to that place for years, an uninspiring unimaginative blockish sandstone building. I hated it. Little of the kindness we received in Penrith came from the middle-class faithful of St Andrews.

My mum, for reasons unknown to me at the time, but which have since become clearer, still wanted to think we were an aspiring middle-class family. Though we lived as one of only a handful of single parent families on a newly built council estate. She had fallen a long way from having tea with dignitaries, a secure future and a relatively affluent lifestyle in the tropics. And though she must have taken it hard, my mother kept on telling us what she wanted to believe we still were, despite all the evidence to the contrary. I think she thought if she kept on repeating her mantras, that eventually, somehow, we would believe her. She practiced a very English version of fake it to make it. Mum would have made another good public relations practitioner.

I never bought into it. My young years meant any bonds tying me to the glossy future we had lost were the thinnest of threads. I think I found it far easier to accept the status quo of the situation we were in than my sisters, especially Alison. As eagerly as I unwrapped the expensively printed magazine addressed to me from the British Airways young flyers club that came twice each year, it didn't change the fact I wore second-hand underpants until the age of eleven. I struggled with the idea we were in the same social strata as the dear old ladies with big hats who seemed to have little trouble getting their hands shaken by the vicar on a

Sunday morning. If only they could see the frayed state of my underwear, they might insist we stop attending their nice church?

My mum's stepmother, a former housekeeper who stepped in after mum's real mother left her and her father, like Granny Bell, had also been incredibly status conscious. As well as controlling my mum when she was growing up using the incredibly cruel hoax of telling her she could read her mind, she also told her never to admit in class when she didn't know the answer to a question. She told my mum it would only show her ignorance. Maybe she was the forerunner for all modern politicians, spin-doctors and public sector managers; don't admit what you don't know has been one of the destructive mantras of recent times.

Unfortunately for me, one of the side effects of having lived in the tropics amongst the aspiring middle class, sending your offspring to a school for the children of privileged expats, is that you think all young boys should wear shorts; nearly all the time. Mum insisted I wore short pants until I went to secondary school. I remember longing for the day. I was the tallest boy in my class in primary and junior school and the only one wearing shorts in nearly all weathers. Her insistence on my dress code felt like part of her delusion. A denial of the fact we were no longer one of the prosperous itinerants of Ceylon, but were in fact living in a small, often wet cold market town situated on a more northerly latitude than most of Newfoundland.

There is an upside. I was forced to learn to look after myself. A bit like being the boy called Sue I stood out like a sore thumb. I got so hacked off with the jibes and taunting that I grew a thick skin and learnt how to throw a decent punch. I was too young to consider any lasting mental scars that may have been developing. In later years it would be suggested mum had deliberately made my life difficult because I looked so much like my dad, reminding her constantly of him. I like to think her lack of concern for my appearance was just that we were poor, and she was preoccupied with putting food on the table, rather than managing my wardrobe. As a single parent family, we lived beneath the official breadline my entire childhood. Dad did not make regular payments to support us and mum was constantly juggling, negotiating terms with the local bank manager and robbing Peter to pay Paul.

Mum could have had more money by claiming from the state, but she preferred to work. She was a qualified nurse and held a job as the school-matron at the local comprehensive school. A rough and ready educational melting pot in which children of all abilities and attitudes from a collection of disparate rural villages and backgrounds were thrown into a melee of bullying and fighting. Her nickname at school was the aspirin queen. She quickly realised most of the kids coming to see her, other than those with bloody noses, just wanted to get out of lessons. Giving them a soluble aspirin caused no harm and made them think they were being taken seriously.

We had next-door neighbours whose dad couldn't work due to a medical condition. In those days if you were out of work you could go to the DHSS office in town and they would give you cash or vouchers to buy the things you needed. A far cry from the ritual dehumanising the less fortunate experience today. They had a decent colour TV; we didn't have a telly and I liked watching it at their house.

I remember Neil our neighbour as a tall gentle man. He placed me on his shoulders once after I came home distraught. I had lost a shoe in the mud when I was out playing and walked home across the estate in one scruffy shoe and a sock. Money for footwear didn't grow on trees and I knew mum would be upset. He picked me up and carried me around the estate looking for it. I felt like a million dollars sitting high on his shoulders. I can still remember how good it felt. I wondered what it might have been like to have grown up with a dad who would do that for me anytime.

The state failed to step up to the plate when we first arrived back in the UK. Mum found a small first floor two bedroomed flat for rent in the heart of Penrith and it was only thanks to the commercial altruism of the Midland Bank and the good graces of its local branch manager we obtained the funds to pay the rent. I think he had a soft spot for mum, as did the local butcher. She was a good-looking woman. And it was thanks to the sympathetic, pay me when you can old school approach of Mr Bowerbank, the local ironmonger, we were able to get a gas stove to heat the flat and enjoy hot food during the power strikes of 1974. There was already a small stove in the flat, but the landlady took it back when the electricity shortages started. She didn't feel the need to keep three children warm and well-fed in winter was greater than her own. She lived alone.

We moved from Granny Bells house near Appleby into the flat on Brunswick Square around Christmas time. I dimly recall a man from Social Services who would come and see mum to assess our situation and make sure we were coping. In what seems to be the ethos of many of our publicly funded support services, Council Social Services were spectacularly unable to offer any practical help but were keen to monitor our wellbeing. He would sit in the small flat, puffing on a pipe and telling mum he admired her tenacity, that he did not understand how she seemed to be dealing with everything life was throwing at her and generally offer sympathy and understanding. Public services are still obsessed with assessment fifty years later. Assessing, ticking a box before signposting to the next agency who will then assess again before referring to another organisation is so much easier than real work.

He would then suggest hare-brained schemes mum could pursue to remove the pressure of being constantly threatened with eviction by the landlady. She should buy a caravan and move onto the gypsy site on the edge of town or buy a car that enabled her to find better paid work elsewhere. These schemes involved money we didn't have and which if we did would have meant we could easily have found somewhere else to rent.

No-one said you had to be good to succeed in public services, my experience suggests the opposite is true. He would drink tea, eat her homemade shortbread, which admittedly was brave, and then leave. We got nothing from him, he was less use than a chocolate fireguard. His inability to add value to our situation, to understand and make a difference to us in our world was of course no barrier to progress inside the warm insulated bubble of the public sector. When the county of Cumbria was officially created in 1974 and council services restructured, he was duly promoted to a senior post.

Shortly after the role mum didn't play in the irretrievable breakdown of her marriage became public, the landlady, a righteous bitter old battle-axe who owned the block of three small flats we were living in, formed a decidedly different view of us. She made no secret of wanting mum out at the earliest opportunity and pulled every trick in the book to evict us. She said she was trying to sell the building and therefore needed to remove the tenants. I don't think she ever tried to evict the residents of the other two flats. Mum protected us from knowing what was happening. She would pretend she was going elsewhere, when in reality she was appearing in court to appeal the case and delay our eviction.

We were exactly one week from being thrown out when we were given the keys to a new council house on a freshly built estate called Pategill. Mum cried with relief and elation. She had been working fulltime, and bringing up three small, boisterous and fast-growing young children in a confined space was becoming an increasingly thankless task. Our new council house at 47 Pategill Road was a simple three bedroomed box with paper thin walls. It was a huge leap forward from where we had been. We had a downstairs toilet, a spacious kitchen and living room and I was no longer sleeping on the sofa. I had a room of my own. We had a garden. It felt like home to me.

The estate was built round an old white farmhouse on fields at the edge of town. There was a selection of safe green spaces outside where we could play, including a pitch with goalposts and swings. It may be hard for readers to believe now but single mums were the exception back then. As the child of a single parent I was often viewed with suspicion and generally frowned upon. Penrith in the early 1970s was a small parochial place where the influence of the church going middle classes and the sway of Freemasonry was as strong as the smell from the auction mart. Times have changed. But back then being a single parent because your husband had left you was an oddity, it was most definitely not the norm in this small market town. The absence of a father figure gave little minds a licence to exercise petty vindictiveness. None more blatantly than the dinner ladies of the local junior school.

Picture the scene if you will. I am nine years old. There are two hundred other young boys in my school. I'm the only one wearing shorts, and one of only three from a single parent family. Cumbria Council, who run the school I attend, are in the throes of introducing a new lunch scheme. It means parents of pupils must pay for school meals or provide their children with a packed lunch. We can't afford school meals and so I am duly sent off with a packed lunch. Corned beef sandwiches and mum's infamous shortbread.

I am the only pupil bringing a packed lunch to school. Unsurprisingly but unbeknown to me the formerly pleasant and normally decent women who are employed as dinner ladies, are not in favour of anyone bringing their own lunch. They, like most people are fearful of change and unsure about the future of their jobs if the idea of packed lunches catches on. The solution they arrive at is to discourage others from bringing their own lunches by making an example of me. They inform the head who in turn instructs me that because I am not eating a school meal, I will not be allowed to eat with my friends in the canteen. Their reasoning to justify this decision is they are afraid I may be offered and tempted to eat food I have not paid for and this would not be fair on people paying for their meals.

In a cruel social experiment Dr Zimbardo would be proud of, the dinner ladies sit me alone outside the canteen, positioning my table cynically and deliberately right outside its entrance. I am to be sat at a small table on my own with my packed lunch in front of me. This means I must eat my sandwiches sat in my shorts looking directly into the queue of boys waiting in line down the long corridor to enter the canteen for their lunch. Being placed under the clock in the corridor at school is the favoured form of punishment and my peers are looking at me with a mix of curiosity and pity. As thick skinned as I am becoming, I am ashamed and embarrassed. I am on show and I feel like I am on show. The message to everyone is clear and stark. We are singling out this boy, and if anyone else chooses to bring their own packed lunch to school they will be similarly humiliated. My poverty was held aloft for all to see.

Their behaviour, which most reasonable people would condemn as bullying on a greater scale than the bullying dished out by my peers, was carried out in view of and with the full knowledge of the head and my teachers. To their great shame, these people sat back and let it happen. Their silence was all it took to facilitate my humiliation. It was an emotionally painful encounter with the unreasonable behaviour of otherwise reasonable people, who with the support of their peers excused their actions because the end justified the means. Their collective effort ensured no one individual needed to feel responsible or accountable. Each of them could say I just went along with the group; this would be the salving retort from their consciences. Like the chimps we are and with who we share 95% of our DNA, the individual members of the troop were simply doing all they could to ingratiate themselves to each other and cement their place within the group. Stick together or stick out and be lambasted. It's always easier to follow the gang than be the one who speaks out.

If it wasn't the adults making life difficult it was one pre-adolescent arsehole or another who wanted to have a go at the shorts wearing boy from the single parent family who didn't speak with the same twang as them. I never backed down in the school yard and I never hesitated to go to the aid of friends who were being bullied. I think if you have been picked-on and isolated it gives you some empathy, you see what a lonely place it can be. I became the person to stand behind if you felt threatened. I could have done with a me to stand behind these past few years. I tried to tell mum how I felt when I was forced to eat my packed lunch in the school corridor in front of everyone, she didn't understand. There are people worse off than you was her standard well-rehearsed response.

It was at moments like these I really missed not having a dad, a father figure in my life who could come to school and stick up for me. What I wouldn't have given to stand behind an angry passionate man as he tore strips off the dinner ladies, perhaps threatening the spineless cowering head of school with his fists. Just thinking about the possibility of it makes me feel good.

I am sure most people hold a fantasy list somewhere in their heads of the people they would like to meet down a dark alley with vigour in their muscles and baseball bat in hand. As time goes on, I also hold a growing list of graves I would merrily piss on. The dinner ladies from County Boys School would get a proper soaking.

As a child, each night I would shake my head forcefully from side to side for prolonged periods before going to sleep. I stopped at a friend's house once, in the morning his mum noticed impressions in the plasterboard wall that hadn't been there the night before. I couldn't explain it. I remember doing this until I was in my teens. I'm told it is a form of self-soothing, quite natural in young children. I think there were things going on in my head I didn't understand, and I couldn't process. I now realise if these things were happening in me even subconsciously, their impact would have been far greater in Alison. But our stories didn't matter, mum's response and coping mechanism was always that there was someone worse off. She didn't want to listen to any of us telling her we missed having a dad, that we just wanted to fit in. There was little room for emotional awareness in our lives.

I made it almost unscathed, or so I thought, to my teenage years. I was about to turn sixteen when mum, who in modern parlance had become increasingly radicalised, albeit by the local born-again branch of the Pentecostal church as opposed to a rural offshoot of Al-Qaeda, gave me an ultimatum. She had been talking with the pastor and elders from her church, who in their wisdom had concluded I was old enough to decide my spiritual future. I was given a choice, I should either accept Jesus into my heart as Lord and saviour or leave home.

As ultimatums go, to ask this of a Mohican sporting, make-up wearing, studded leather jacket wearing, bondage trouser clad, pot smoking, magic mushroom eating, soap avoiding, Clash listening teenage tearaway, its ambitious. I think the phrase is shit or bust. It's also an ultimatum to which there is only ever going to be one answer from the hormone fuelled teenager in question, up yours. There's no denying I had become difficult, obnoxious even, and I was too tall and volatile to be clipped round the ear anymore. I packed a case and out the door I went.

Don't forget Jesus loves you Thomas; yea, I'm really feeling it. The church and the idea of a god who really loves you but is reluctantly forced to exile you if you don't play the game his way, is surely the greatest example of a controlling bully whose affection is entirely conditional. I think mum thought I would come back before the day was out, I didn't. I walked my battered old case with its peeling British Airways stickers across town to a squat and rejoiced in my new-found freedom. I could smoke indoors. All I needed was coffee, cider, cigarettes and hair-gel, how hard could this be? I was terrified at first and didn't sleep a wink the first night I was away. But I put on a good front.

Dressing how I did in my teenage years was a way of countering how I had been dressed when I was younger. Shorts and cheap platform shoes made me stand out for the wrong reasons. But studs, tartan, leopard print, make-up and red, pink, blue or bleached hair could make me stand out for the right reasons. Again, when you stand out for whatever reason there is always someone who will have a go, especially in a conservative town like Penrith. I was beaten up more than once, but some instances were more memorable than others. On one occasion I ended up in hospital urinating blood and with a broken nose, one of three if memory serves. I recall no-one really wanted to know, who had done this to me; but I do recall being told in no uncertain terms it was my fault for dressing outlandishly.

It is no surprise I wanted to identify with and found solace in the remains of the Punk scene. Here were the people of difference, odds and sods who didn't fit anywhere else. I knew how that felt. All the establishment offered was mixed messages and hypocrisy. Rules for some and not others. I kept hearing I should give respect, but it was never made clear what I would get out of this, and my respect was seldom earned by those who deemed themselves worthy of receiving it.

By the time I was sixteen I was sticking two very angry fingers up at the establishment. I had been kicked out of school as well as home and when I wasn't freezing my nuts off; sleeping rough in an unforgiving February was not the teenage adventure I envisaged, I was sofa surfing, sleeping on a floor or squatting. I don't blame school for wanting shot of me, I was disruptive. There was only one teacher who made time for me, encouraged me and could see any promise beneath the surface. The rest were all cartoon caricatures from a Pink Floyd video.

The teachers and tabloids at the time said punk and its influence would be the undoing of our traditions and the end of our moral compasses. It's been fascinating to see how the icons society held aloft at the time, Saville and his ilk, turned out be a far greater threat than the young rebels the press decried. There was something honest if not perfect about punk. The angry music found a welcome home in my head. What was said was what was felt and for better or worse, the messages were not subtle or hidden.

Then I found myself slipping rapidly between the cracks of the system. I was homeless and though I had been expelled from school I wasn't able to claim any assistance because I was officially still registered as a pupil. There was no accommodation available, even temporarily, for someone in my situation. My appearance and living arrangements meant I wasn't the preferred candidate for any of the menial jobs I applied for. I resorted to theft.

I stole thousands of cigarettes, easily tradable currency I could sell on quickly to pay for the essentials; food, clothing, generally ill-fitting, cider, records, hair-gel and dye. I regret stealing and the hurt and hassle I caused, and I quickly acquired a lengthy juvenile criminal record. However, there is a strange almost funny irony to it all. I stole because I was falling through the cracks, I couldn't get support from the institutions there to supposedly help people, because I didn't tick their boxes. The system spent more money prosecuting me and putting me through the courts than it would ever have spent setting me up in a bedsit and helping me find a job.

I appeared in court as a juvenile charged for three crimes with a further half dozen minor offences taken into consideration. I thought I would be sent to a juvenile detention facility and I was more scared than I ever let on. But this was my first appearance in court, and thankfully leniency was applied. After having my name sombrely announced in court as Thomas Bell of no fixed abode, surely a high point in anyone's life, I pleaded guilty. My punishment was a fine and two-year's probation.

I had progressed from my mother's view I was mixing with the wrong crowd to firmly establishing my role as a wrong crowd in the eyes of my friend's parents. My probation officer did not have the first idea how to relate to a troubled disaffected young man who wanted to talk religion and politics, though he was always generous with his cigarettes. He sent me to the careers service who told me because I was pretty good at maths, I might have a future in carpet fitting or the merchant navy.

Not one of the publicly funded agencies seemed to care about my needs, my living arrangements, physical wellbeing or state of mind. They offered no real help. Each just wanted to tick a box and pass me on to the next one. It was the kindness of strangers who I still remember, a beautiful fellow young misfit with a stunning smile who later became my wife, the power of enterprise and less obviously, a mental breakdown and religious delusion, that ultimately arrested my journey into chaos.

I can't help wondering if I initially, albeit unconsciously and unwittingly, inherited my healthy if career terminal disrespect for authority and the figures and institutions of authority from my father. From his actions if not his example.

But while I was busy rebelling, Alison was slowly, almost unnoticeably drifting further and further into the treacherous and still largely unchartered waters of mental illness that would ultimately claim her. The smiling enthusiastic peddlers of the radical unregulated side of acceptable religion were pervasively, steadily and irresistibly burrowing their way deeper and deeper into the fabric of our small family.

Alison, an increasingly conflicted young woman in need of professional help, was now firmly under the influence of the Pentecostal witch doctors in suits. Ill-informed ignorant people of certainty who thought the reasons for her low self-esteem, erratic behaviour and emerging eating disorder, were a flawed relationship with God. The solutions for which lay in the pages of the bible or could be answered by prayer.

If mum thought I had gone off the rails, she had no idea of the powerful destructive influences coming over the horizon. Or of the irreparable damage the unwitting agents of carnage she welcomed into our lives would cause. She still has no idea, or perhaps is unable to admit, that the havoc and unhappiness the wolves in sheep's clothing wreaked on us all, is in part down to her. Dad had gone, mum was the last line of parental defence. She had brought us so far. I wish she could have seen through the misguided religious alchemists who zealously promised they could turn the strewn rubble of a broken life into gold.

Chapter 5 - Reach out and touch faith

Feeling unknown and you're all alone, flesh and blood on the telephone, lift-up the receiver, I'll make you a believer.

Personal Jesus; Depeche Mode

Like primitive predators scenting traces of weakness in their prey from miles away, hustling pedlars of religious hope seem able to sniff out the needy and vulnerable. Once located, they are drawn to the zealot's lair, isolated and fed on voraciously. Time, money, attention and adulation are then sucked from them for as long as they have it to give. Ultimately victims are robbed of the most precious things they possess, their freewill and mind. As the potential for free thought is stolen from them, thinking is discouraged and the true natural magic and miracle of life itself is replaced with a cocktail of fairy-tails and dogma.

Radical religious beliefs of all persuasions thrive amongst the disaffected masses others cannot reach. The outlandish unevidenced claims they make appeal to people who need to make sense of the seemingly senseless and constantly shifting evolutionary chaos we live in. Jesus saves; saves what? Where is the advertising standards authority when you need them?

Mum had always been religious in the polite traditional English sense of the word. Church bells, songs of praise, vicars, cups of tea served in Indian Tea crockery, choirs, cucumber sandwiches, confirmations and church fetes complete with charity tombola and cake stall. Being involved in an archetypal version of English life helped feed the illusion of being middle-class. Part of the torment of being dragged to the Church of England service each week as a young boy was enduring Sunday school. Possibly the worst least justifiable use of precious time and legitimised stifling of young minds ever created.

As a young boy I never considered my mum might be struggling with life, in need of answers or searching for deeper meaning. Her step-mum had practiced spiritualism and I see now the seeds of her own need to feel there was something else, something otherworldly and magical were sown at an early age. The fertile ground in the landscape of her earthly disappointments was all they needed to grow with vigour. I thought going to church was just something people did and All Things Bright and Beautiful was a song they sang when they came together. I was unconvinced the Lord God made them all. I couldn't wait to become old enough not to have to go to church as well as escape the tyranny of shorts. Before a short stint as a born-again believer, a period in my life I now view as an undiagnosed mental breakdown, I don't recall a time when I thought much about the existence of a god, any god.

One day, around the start of the eighties, a leaflet came through the letterbox of the council house we lived in on Pategill. The flyer offered answers to life's big questions from a large white tent set-up on the common fields in the middle of town, now a retail temple for Sainsbury's. I don't know if the same brochures were ever delivered to the middle-class parts of town, probably not. The rootless trees are the easiest to harvest and response rates amongst the less disaffected and more educated would doubtless be significantly less.

The outreach mission, a crusade as it was boldly called, had been arranged to support the launch of a new Pentecostal church in town. A Welsh pastor, smelted and twisted in the valleys where fire and brimstone was still preached by the messengers of a jealous god, had answered the Lords call to bring the gospel to Penrith, and his church was seeking new recruits to the cause. Mum and Alison read the leaflet and one evening they went to see what it was all about. I wish with all my heart that tent had never made its way to Penrith. I wish they had never left the house that day. I wish they had responded to a leaflet offering part-time work selling Tupperware, Pools Coupon collectors, Catalogue agents, money laundering, double glazing even. Anything but the false promises, ticket to heartache and self-imposed isolation and fruitless guilt they bought into.

Looking back, I see that point in time as one of those junctions in the journey of a family where everything changes. It's funny how our lives and our fates can spin so quickly on a moment in time. That evening, mum and Alison answered the preacher's powerful emotive plea for people to give their lives to Jesus and to become born-again. They were offered life afresh, happiness and joy, free from the suffocating baggage and disappointments of the past. Jesus loved them, he would hold them safe, keep them close and protect them from harm. An empty promise he would soon break. They stood-up in a tent full of people, acknowledged their sins, renounced their old lives and publicly devoted themselves to the service of their newly revealed saviour.

Visible public commitment is an important tool used by traders of radical religion. It ensures new apostles quickly identify and unwittingly detach themselves from former friends, peers and non-believing contacts at the earliest opportunity. Once isolated fresh recruits become more dependent on their new circle of fellow converts. Like vampires who need an invite to retain their powers, the bloodsuckers had been let in the door of 47 Pategill Road. Why, why did mum who seemed so self-sufficient, logical, and Alison who was so intelligent, clever, funny, and incisive, why did they feel the need to commit to a course of action so illogical, so unexpected. Their acts that evening are still a mystery to me. They threw a rock into the pool of our lives from which the ripples still emanate. Their unwitting decision to swallow the unscientific sorcery being fed to them changed everything.

Mum and Alison were conned by pushers of baseless hope, experienced in their art. Such dealers know that those who have already had a tough time are prime candidates for the product they are pushing. How is it we let these self-appointed prophets, people who display all the classic signs of schizophrenia; delusions of grandeur, a persecution complex and belief in a personal relationship with somebody famous, peddle their unevidenced beliefs, spreading guilt and shame, often amongst the most vulnerable in our communities?

Even the term unevidenced is wholly inadequate. What they offer are untruths flying in the face of all the overwhelming evidence to the contrary. But you can't tell them that. All logic is lost as the flock are encouraged to stand fast as they develop their unshakeable faith in the invisible.

Mum still insists going to the mission tent that evening was the best decision she ever made. I think she had been on the point of breakdown and needed something to believe in. She tells me I will always remain incapable of comprehending her decision, as long as I remain outside the brightly enlightened spiritual circle of born-again Christian knowledge. I would understand if only I would view the world through the spiritually renewed eyes of a true believer. The King is not in the altogether, I am just wearing the wrong glasses.

It is of course the ultimate collective delusion, there is no explanation. She and those like her are metaphorically in the altogether. But I have been kind, perhaps too kind. I have held back, using the excuse she is too near the end of her mortal journey for me to tell her what I really think. It is a difficult message to break to anyone approaching the end of their life, especially one who has been through as much as mum. Oh, by the way, you were fooled by all that baloney, the time, effort and money you gave, the guilt you felt, the pleasure you denied yourself, it was all for nothing and you won't get another chance on the roundabout. It's not the comforting final bedside death speech a well-intentioned mother deserves.

If you can deal with isolation, then life becomes easier when you commit to one of the more radical strains of religion on offer from the buffet of meaning and salvation. You no longer have to think about things for yourself. In fact, you are positively discouraged from the potentially dangerous act of engaging your mind, seeking new knowledge and applying logic. Strong religious beliefs become the disempowered persons dogmatic guide to life. The Bible states, the pastor said, the elders say, therefore it must be right. It also becomes easier because life amongst your newly acquired like-minded peers means you don't have to mix with people who hold different views. Which closet bigot wants the inconvenience of having their paradigms challenged by people with different views?

And of course, if God is on their side, they cannot really be called bigoted, they are simply right. Ill-informed judgemental attitudes are masked behind shields marked faith. Using the F word means nobody can argue with you. If only the poor heathens could see the truth.

Radical beliefs and cultures survive and thrive when people only swim with their own sort, reinforcing prejudices and quelling each-others doubts. The process of developing religiously fuelled bigotry is a powerful self-reinforcing self-perpetuating one. The previous pastor from mum's church claimed the catastrophic tsunamis of Christmas 2004 were a message to the unrighteous from God, the Christian one. Various Clerics, Imams and Rabbis said much the same, claiming it as a message from their god. The science of shifting tectonic plates under the Indian Ocean played little part in these ignorant deliberations.

Questioning people's faith, the right to believe and peddle whatever nonsense they wish, is not the done thing in politically correct diverse societies. I am unclear why we are still encouraged to respect other's faiths. What do we even mean by faith? It seems we use the word as a polite label to explain what we see as people's right to believe in the irrational. Surely faith is nothing more than a set of unfounded myths and wish-lists without evidence that defy all logic. Faiths entry into my family has been as a debilitating identity stealing and life robbing force, not an enlightening empowering one.

Do we need to preserve a hallowed space in our societies to accommodate the untruths of religious belief? To deny the true magic and mystery of our universe, to place the wonder and beauty of the human mind on hold, to put aside natural inclinations to love, to feel and be inquisitive in exchange for slavish adherence to something called faith, must rate as one of the worst deals ever made. If there was ever a role for Karl Pilkington's fictional superhero creation, Bullshit Man, to appear and call out the crap, then it's right here in the arena of unevidenced faith. Now that might be worth making time on a Sunday morning to see.

My experience of the damage unchecked religious belief and its salespeople can do has made me increasingly intolerant of our collective and utterly irrational tolerance of religion's intolerance. We let pastors preach damnation of the unwashed, threatening non-believers with impunity, we allow churches to erect posters and billboards inferring people, women, children, the infirm, the elderly, will burn for eternity in seas of scorching sulphur, screaming in agony and torment forever, unless they agree to live their lives according to the rules of an old book; the origins of which are sketchy to say the least. Why?

They prey on the vulnerable, the mentally ill, with their message of heaven or hell, and somehow, we think that's ok? Why should educated societies with the benefit of scientific evidence to call upon continue to pussy-foot around the fanciful notions of ancient and often brutish systems of thought control whose reason for existence has been superseded by consumerism and the advent of CCTV. There is no longer any need for the threat of the all-seeing eye in the sky watching our every move when we are filmed on every corner and tracked by every click. Google is the closest thing we have ever had to an omnipotent supernatural presence.

Radical religions also make life harder for their followers by isolating them. The path is narrow and difficult, the way is tough, nobody said this will be easy. Jesus died on a cross wearing a crown of thorns just for you, you, you! And yes, it can be tough, but suck it up and be thankful you were chosen for the challenge. This is the message believers are offered when things are tough.

This sense of existing in a difficult space, of being under siege for a worthy cause forms an important part of the persecution complex holding isolated groups of radical believers together. Pastors, preachers, the guardians of the faithful flock, play on this to reinforce the sense of belonging to something special that keeps the sheep safely together in the fold. Nothing unites like a common enemy. It really is them against the world.

The Pentecostal church mum and Alison became part of was a full on born-again happy clappy, speaking in tongues, dancing, singing, hands in the air, faith healing, shout Hallelujah, laying on of hands, praise be, Amen Brother affair. The only thing missing were some nuns, a conductor and Whoopi Goldberg. If I hadn't seen it with my own eyes and been part of it for a while, I'm not sure I would have been able to comprehend just how emotionally intense the whole thing was. Mum and Alison no longer went to St Andrews each Sunday, they attended the new church they had found. Twice on Sundays and at least once through the week. The pastor hugged each member of the congregation as they came and went. Sarah and I were actively encouraged, threatened with the fires of hell and ceaselessly hounded to accompany them.

Their enthusiasm and new-found concern for our spiritual wellbeing was unrelenting. Their minds had been well and truly hijacked. Their newly found messiah and his earthly emissaries had tasked them with bringing salvation to the whole family. Jesus was suddenly everywhere, wasn't Jesus wonderful, wasn't it brilliant he had died for our sins and wanted to save us. Our annual holidays turned from pleasurable and memorable visits to friends on the train into dutiful sodden Christian gatherings called Bible weeks, held in Wales or Yorkshire.

Looking in life's rear-view mirror I see the Pentecostal church was meeting their needs for security and certainty. Alison had found her missing father figure, one who would never desert her, and mum was finally being made to feel like a somebody. She was being told the creator of the Heavens and the Earth had time for her, accepted her and loved her. Now she was once again sitting at the highest of tables. She needed that.

Being involved with the Pentecostal church was more than just a mentally costly affair for my family. The pastor implored the faithful to give ten percent of their gross income to the cause each week. Surely the giving of a little money now was a small price to secure an eternity in heaven. Of course, the amount wasn't compulsory, just a guideline. But the congregation were left in no doubt heaven was watching and to short-change the church was to short-change the Almighty. It was a form of extortion. We were already as poor as church mice. Mum attempted to pay her dues at every possible opportunity.

Getting sucked into the machinations of the new church with its life of restrictions and insistence its congregation became missionaries on its behalf made my family even more isolated than we had been up to this point in time. Mum and Alison became advocates of a spiritual pyramid selling Ponzi scheme which meant sharing and selling their new-found beliefs to everyone.

They had not been recruited to a subtle religion to be practiced in privacy, this was a strident confident message that demanded its followers make it heard. The increasingly visible displays of their faith in the small town we lived in ensured we became the subject of ridicule and derision. Of course, the true believer's reply to these things is to say such responses are to be expected from the unwashed, who in turn deserve prayers and pity.

My mother seemed hellbent on ensuring any kind of life that could be labelled as somewhere near normal, remained constantly out of reach. Low self-esteem often comes with a self-destruct button. It feels as if she wished a life of exclusion, ridicule and hardship on us, because it was all she felt we deserved. Her lack of self-worth is the gift the mother who left her gave her.

I was approaching my teenage years and found the self-imposed isolation we were placing on ourselves increasingly difficult to deal with. I was discovering myself, I was starting to notice girls, I wanted to listen to the music my peers listened to, wear the clothes they wore and be where they were. The harder religion pushed on my door the harder I pushed back.

I recall the pastor trying to settle mum's anxieties about my emerging teenage rebellion by quoting scripture to her. He was not one to miss any opportunity to turn something natural into part of a grand battle against the forces of darkness he told her she was now embroiled in. He built her up by telling her she had been chosen for adversity because she was worthy. He would solemnly quote the gospel of Luke, telling her Jesus had not come to bring peace, but to divide, to set people against each other, to shatter households and tear families apart if need be.

Was I really to believe my teenage self was in the grip of demonic forces as I fantasized over posters of Debbie Harry or Kim Wilde? If so most of my generation are destined for hell. Had I become subject to dark harmful influences because I was listening to punk music? Some of it may have been bad, step forward the Anti Nowhere League, but it wasn't of the devil. I struggle to comprehend how anyone can still hold and advocate such ill-informed views.

Even though I know they are trapped in prisons they didn't build, I can't help wanting to punch every meddling mind manacling mini messiah I see on telly or hear on the radio, spouting their poisonous faith-coated shit. Get thee behind me, get thee behind us all.

The enormity of the impact radical born-again Christianity had on Alison would become clearer in the coming years. The timing of its entry into our lives was terrible. Right at a point where adolescents struggle with the transition to adulthood and seek the acceptance of their peers. Just when she started to show signs of needing professional help, the evangelical church arrived on the scene with quackery and fantastical thinking.

Alison was preyed upon at a time when she was vulnerable and mentally ill. The falsehoods she was fed skewed the thinking of a vibrant clever teenager. She became more confused, racked with guilt about natural teenage feelings and more estranged and isolated from the many young people around her who cared about her. If there was a mentally ill vulnerable young woman who needed protecting from the arbitrary black and white dictums of right and wrong and harmful self-flagellating labels of sin, Alison was it. The religion mum allowed into our lives would soon open the door for another wolf in sheep's clothing. One whose acts I believe, determined Alison's fate.

I remain at odds with my mum, angry about the role born-again Christianity played in splintering and destroying our already shattered little family. I struggle to comprehend her decision to embrace the medieval attitudes to mental health hastening her daughter's descent into darkness. Alison was being savaged by chemical imbalances, not troubled by demonic activity. She was entering the early stages of a severe mental illness that would come to dominate the rest of her life. But in the radical born-again believer's mind, everything has a spiritual root.

I feel deep rage towards the pastor and the other ignorant ill-informed peddlers of bullshit who promised heaven but stole devotion and money under false pretences. They delivered only isolation, turmoil, misery and conflict to our family. I see now the very fine line between the radical born-again Christianity my family became involved in and a cult. I count myself lucky I saw the light and escaped. Thank god, any god, for Dawkins.

I have a fantasy about the eulogy I will give at mum's funeral. I want to write and read a very un-English outpouring of honesty. A seething bitter stinging festival of cathartic blame apportioning candour which I want to savour slowly as the polite born-again squirm in their seats. I want the church doors locked so they must listen. I want them to know I love my mum, that she didn't need fixing and I hate what they have done to her. Many people have made decisions which changed the course of mine and my families' lives. On most occasions we didn't even know something had occurred or understand the consequences at the time. My mum's welcoming of born-again Christianity into our homes was one such decision.

The wicked side of me would like to believe in reincarnation, if only in the hope each and every leader, pastor and elder of the evangelical Christian church comes back as a member of the same troop of Bonobo Chimps. Constantly torn between desire and guilt as they fornicate ceaselessly, hopelessly predisposed to having inordinate amounts of gratuitous sex with each other, regardless of gender. And with each thrust, movement and moment of climax, suffering flashbacks of each other's faces from their previous human incarnations; thou shalt not, thou shalt not, thou shalt not...but I can't help it, I can't stop.

I used to feel ashamed that I had drunk the Kool-Aid and become an enthusiastic if short-lived part of the born-again Christian movement. I succumbed to the promise of security it offered at a low point in my life, I was confused, depressed and susceptible, ripe for religious picking. But I am now strangely grateful I went through this period. I couldn't have understood its pernicious destructive capacity fully if I hadn't been utterly immersed in it. Importantly, I remain delighted to be liberated from it. I am a harsh and increasingly knowledgeable critic; shaped by experience and therefore entitled to be so. I only wish Alison had escaped the clutches of the men and women of certainty who filled our minds with dogma and impossible inhuman standards.

Ignorance, along with the seemingly unstoppable rise of arseholes, must rank as one of the last ultimate remaining enemies to humanity's progress. I can't help thinking it is time to call time on our tolerance of the intolerant.

The Garden of Love

I went to the Garden of Love,
And saw what I never had seen,
A Chapel was built in the midst,
Where I used to play on the green.

And the gates of this Chapel were shut,
And Thou shalt not. writ over the door,
So I turned to the Garden of Love,
That so many sweet flowers bore.

And I saw it was filled with graves,
And tombstones where flowers should be,
And Priests in black gowns, were walking their rounds,
And binding with briars, my joys & desires.

William Blake

Chapter 6 – Who was Alison?

Alison, I know this world is killing you.

Alison; Elvis Costello

If the purpose of this chapter is to paint a picture of Alison that will do her justice, then I feel like a decorator's apprentice staring at the roof of the Sistine chapel, good intent in my head and a coarse industrial paint brush in my hand. I so want to give you more than merely a shadow image you can imbue with meaning, an entity to colour and contaminate with your own perceptions.

I can see Alison clearly in my mind's eye as I write this. Rightly or wrongly I've become practiced at blocking out memories of the acts and words of the person she became and the final manner of her death. I remember her full of life, of hope. I see her laughing as she tried helplessly to hit the ball in a game of rounders on the green outside our house. I see her marching upright, in full regalia and grinning broadly as she played the cornet for the town band. And I see her standing smiling in front the gas fire in the living room, dressed in the Brownies uniform she was so proud of. It seemed designed for her. The brown coloured fabric of the dress and the bright yellow scarf perfectly matching her red hair and youthful freckles. Freckles I used to tease her about, though I think I had just as many.

Alison was born on the fifth of May 1966, one day late for the force to be with her. She was kind, sensitive, humble, unaware of her own acuity. An intellectually gifted yet gentle light that shone warmly, brightly. Even through the clouds of darkness following her. She could be exceptionally clever and perceptive but sometimes left her common sense in a cupboard. Drying tea towels and socks under the grill was never going to end well. And she was overly trusting, a trait I understand fully. Her flame red hair reflected a fire of activity which seemed to burn continually in her mind. The life and joy that could shine from behind her eyes was mixed with no small amount of intelligence and often a great deal of mischief. Gifted with a quick wit she was the most academically able of her siblings by a country mile.

In the first picture taken of my two sisters together, my oldest sister Sarah is pinching rather than holding her sister's hand. Alison had her father's colouring but with more vivid auburn hair and stunning blue eyes. She had delicate fair skin and an understated Hollywood smile. She was her dad's favourite when she was little, and he made no secret of it.

The thought that haunts is thinking what Alison could have, should have become. Should have been allowed and helped to become. The longer I live the more strongly I feel this. She was worth a thousand of the people who damaged and ultimately destroyed her.

Alison was nearly five when mum and dad separated. She felt his absence most acutely and would be upset for days after his all too infrequent visits. Visits Alison eagerly anticipated. The anger and resentment she held for dad not being around was thrust onto mum. Blaming her for making him leave, for splitting up the family and for the situation we were in. Mum never told Alison it was dad who had chosen to leave us. Maybe if she had it would have helped. But for better or worse she never told any of us they had parted because of his affair. Perhaps mum didn't want people knowing another woman had been involved. Or maybe it was better for Alison to think mum had been unreasonable rather than acknowledge the father she loved had left her, left us all, by choice.

The most vivid memory I have of my sister's mischievous sense of humour is of a picnic by the river at Maulds Meaburn, a picture postcard village in the heart of the Eden Valley. I would be nine or ten. We were there with my childhood friend Johnny, his mum and his sister Sarah. I had been playing and fallen in the water, I needed to change into dry clothes. Alison offered to hold a towel round me while I took my wet trousers and pants off. Right at the point where I was most exposed, she threw the large orange towel she was holding to one side and shouted so everyone would look in my direction. Embarrassed doesn't get near.

Not long after we got back to the UK and were living with my granny near Appleby, I remember shaking a ladder Alison was standing on to pick apples. I was sure she had been up there too long and there would be none left for me. She fell into the greenhouse breaking her arm and leg. I never heard the end of it. I still feel bad about it. She was in hospital in Carlisle for eight weeks and when she came out, she spoke with a newly acquired Cumbrian accent. Every sentence followed by an, eh. Sarah and I went to visit her in hospital but were only allowed to look through the windows of the ward at the Cumberland Infirmary. I wouldn't blame Alison if she had told the nurse to keep me away from her.

If she was the sensitive talented Lisa Simpson, I was her annoying Bart.

Like good children we adhered to the job description issued to all siblings and fought like cat and dog. She was way too intelligent for me to argue with. With her sharp mind and quick comebacks, she could tie my brain in knots. Like a clever cat goading a simple dog. I would inevitably bite, and what started as lively discussion would descend into chaos as we started hitting each other, ending only when Mum's patience ran out and she stopped whatever she was doing to come and break us up. You children will be the death of me was mums most used phrase.

Sarah and Alison shared a bedroom. Sarah euphemistically describes this as both fun and tricky. Alison had her side of the room, the wardrobe, and dressing table, and woe betide you if you crossed or encroached on it. When Sarah started doing serious sessions of homework revising for exams, she had to move her desk into a corner of mum's bedroom as her books often straddled the sacred divide onto Alison's territory. Such hostile acts of space-invasion were not permitted.

Saran and I were dressed in hand me down clothes until early adulthood, but Alison refused as far as possible to wear anything that wasn't new. She tried to maintain a sense of style and became quite good at using a sewing machine to make and adjust her clothes. Anything to avoid wearing second-hand garments. We used to joke we had a hippo in the house because Alison hogged the bathroom for hours at a time. She would use all the hot water, this bothered mum and Sarah more than me. Like most young boys I wasn't overly concerned about my cleanliness.

Sarah was more of a lark and Alison something of a night owl who liked to sleep in. Sarah became very adept at getting up, dressing and getting out the house in the quiet, even on school mornings. Initially they had walked to school together, but Sarah hated being late for anything and waiting for Alison, who hated being anything other than late or just in time, drove her nuts. Mum was eventually persuaded to let Sarah walk to school and meet with her friends on the way. Looking back, Alison was probably suffering with depression even at a young age. Constant tiredness and a desire to sleep and stay in bed rather than face the world can be indicators of poor mental health.

Alison was caring as well as intelligent. She had a gentle soul and was loyal to her friends. The kind of person who didn't seem to have to try hard to get good grades in her exams. She started learning to read music at secondary school. The paper-thin walls of the house we lived in meant she drove us and our neighbours to distraction learning to play the violin. To ensure we got no peace she also played cornet for the town band. Alison loved the occasion of performing with her fellow band members in the procession on bank-holidays.

I remember her birthday parties each May. A broad circle of friends would be invited to our small house and when the weather was good, they would play rounders on the green across the road. We would find a tennis ball; a sturdy silver hoover pipe from the pull along vacuum was used as a bat. We had that hoover come rounders bat for years. Things were made to last then. Alison and her friends always insisted I joined in their game; I think this was because I didn't mind running after the ball. Mum and Sarah would join in as well. Alison couldn't hit a ball for toffee, but she didn't care. I remember the smile on her face, I remember the sound of her laughter, she spent most of the time giggling. Mum would hit the ball for miles, I think she practiced in secret, or maybe she imagined dads face on the ball as she swung the hoover pipe. She loved it. We all loved it. The true worth of those golden days has only become obvious with time. They will live with me forever.

Alison is remembered by many who knew her, especially before her teenage years, as a beautiful child, earnest and sensible as well as kind and sensitive. They also speak of her as funny, engaging and clever. She would stay at friend's homes, sleeping in a tent on the back garden and talking about anything and everything into the small hours of the morning. Her habit of placing a hand in front her mouth to stifle laughter when she thought humour was crude or inappropriate made her friends laugh hysterically. She became part of the treasured childhood memories of others. A close friend described Alison as a gift to all who knew her. I don't ever remember hearing her shout at any of her friends. They all miss her.

It was shortly after she became a teenager Alison was enticed into the snare of radical religion. Upon committing her life to Jesus and becoming part of the born-again Christian church she became lost in the Bible and books written by evangelical authors. The evangelical beliefs she had been sold provided certainty and purpose, a sturdy ship to sail in the uncertain seas she found herself on. The god they offered was the father figure she craved. She would spend hours listening to cassette recordings of sermons.

These speeches and life-lessons as they were labelled were delivered by English, Welsh and American preachers who applied a frenzied snake oil sales approach to the delivery of their messages. Their voices came out the cassette as if they were talking directly to you, you, yes you, can you hear me. Zealous in their beliefs, utterly unwavering in their views, and other than the Mercedes they drove and large homes they lived in, uncompromising in their contempt for all things earthly and transient. They taught the gospel of the end times and the coming of the rapture with all the fervency of religious fundamentalism we have come to be afraid of in the twenty first century.

She believed God had spoken directly to her and had taken to sitting in front the monument clock in the town centre each weekend with a sign hung round her neck telling people to repent and be saved. She was utterly convinced non-believers in the Christian faith were destined to a tortuous eternity in hell and thought it was her duty to save as many as she could. Her increasingly erratic behaviour, fuelled by belief in demonic possession and thoughts she was an unworthy instrument in the ultimate battle between good and evil that was coming, was punching ever larger holes in the fabric of her mind and all our lives.

Like many families facing some sort of mental health crisis we hadn't the faintest idea how to deal with or manage what was happening to her and to us. Her radical outlook was distancing her further from reality. Alison was breaking apart in front our very eyes.

Alison had first received help for what were described as moderate mental health issues around the age of nine and then again in her early teens. But as the perfect storm of parental abandonment, low self-esteem, inner turmoil, and chemical imbalance became fuelled by extreme religious belief, it's gathering momentum was unstoppable. Her episodes were becoming increasingly severe. Following a particularly bad period of mental illness in the summer of 1987, the local Doctor diagnosed Alison with Paranoid Schizophrenia.

She was pitifully pale and suffering with Anorexia which made her already delicate frame look spindly and fragile. Her beautiful flame red hair had become lifeless and she would often wear a headscarf to cover it. She had taken on a slight physical stoop and lacked the energy to do almost anything, mumbling her words. Her eyes had become darkened pools of tormented questioning confusion, constantly flitting back and forth as if on guard, ever watchful for something.

That summer, following the initial diagnosis, Alison was sectioned, forcibly admitted to the Garlands Mental Health Hospital in Carlisle. It was the nearest mental health facility and was just over twenty miles away from Penrith.

She was entrusted to the care of the NHS. We all thought, desperately hoped, she would get the professional help she clearly needed. If we had known then what we know now, we would have kept her away from there at any cost.

In early autumn of 1988, Alison left the Garlands hospital in Carlisle and went to live with mum who had moved to Doncaster. We were starting to get more used to her erratic behaviour, mood swings and outlandish ideas, like the time she decided to become a nanny in America. An entirely inappropriate action she would not be talked out of and which didn't go well. Alison's NHS mental health consultant at the time told mum that at least if her daughter had a breakdown in America, she would be more likely to get the treatment she needed. Not a ringing endorsement of their abilities or of mental health services this side of the pond. It turns out they were probably right.

Alison, utterly unprepared and ill-equipped, was thrust as a nanny on an unsuspecting American family by an agency who had clearly not checked or did not care about her suitability. It was an unmitigated disaster. Her baggage was lost in transit and her mental illness quickly resurfaced. The family asked her to leave and she came back to the UK in a matter of months, deflated, defeated, depressed.

Alison had become a constant source of worry, of palpable tension. None of us knew what frame of mind she would be in when we saw her. Would she be in a place of conviction and guilt, ready to preach and proselytize. Or be the kindest funniest most irreverent person in the room. Then there were the calls from police forces in other counties asking us if we knew Alison was in this place or that. These calls happened on the occasions we reported her missing. She would be found in a confused state, more than once having left a purse and coat on a park bench somewhere.

We were contacted by Interpol after Alison took a trip to the Greek Islands but didn't come back on the expected date. We reported her missing and shortly afterwards the body of a young white woman with red hair was washed up on a beach on the isle of Crete. Interpol informed the local police it might be Alison and while South Yorkshire police asked Sarah for photos and permission to access dental records to enable identification, Cumbria police sent two officers to visit mum. It wasn't Alison and to our great relief, and doubtless equal amounts of another families' distress, her death was delayed. She walked up the garden path of our home in Penrith while the local bobbies were still talking to mum in the front room. Blissfully unaware she was the subject of so much angst, she asked, what are the police doing here mum? Mental illness does this to families, it throws the comforting predictability of life as we know it in the air, rendering our often-narrow definitions of normality and predictability, completely irrelevant.

In the years preceding her death, whenever they met, Sarah recalls Alison would follow her round, clinging to her with a desperation Sarah couldn't fathom. She would need constant reassurances that Sarah loved her and seek assurances about her safety. Sarah didn't know what she had gone through. She still dreads phone calls after nine in the evening. They always presaged a crisis or trouble of some sort, where was she, what had happened, and made Sarah frightened for her sister and physically and mentally worn down.

Alison made huge efforts to get on top her illness and was making a valiant attempt to get her life on track. In an attempt to leave her past behind she changed her name by deed-poll from Bell to St James. She never explained the choice of new name to us and at the time we had only superficial notions of the things in her past she was struggling to break free from.

She was completing university work and studying sociology by distance-learning. She also enrolled on a writing course and created various fantasy characters including one called Ginger Bear. Ginger Bear was President of the newly formed Teddy Bear's Association. The TBA, as she referred to it was a member's only club for bears from all over the world. In her writing she created a series of fictional situations in which she used stories of Ginger Bear as a way of expressing herself. Writing allowed her to share her thoughts about the world and especially her relationship with mum, thoughts she felt unable to share directly.

The TBA had five rules, number three stated that a teddy should never be forced to do something they could not bear. I often wonder if she was talking about the situation she had been put in at the Garlands when she created these rules. Alison was a big fan of hugs, the TBA's central policy stated they were neither in favour of nationalisation nor privatisation, but CUDDLISATION. She capitalised the word in case their policy should be in doubt.

As well as being a compulsive doodler she saved up to buy one of the first versions of a new-fangled thing called a word processor. She used it to write articles including Sex and Self Respect, Women and Depression and Ready, Teddy, Go. These covered topics including self-esteem and mental health counselling and were well received by her tutors with whom she seemed to be building up a good relationship. Alison appeared to be getting much more focused support for her health and wellbeing in Doncaster. To the untrained optimistic eye, it seemed she was on the road to recovery.

Chapter 7 – The descent into hell

It is very tempting to take the side of the perpetrator. All the perpetrator asks is that the bystander do nothing. He appeals to the universal desire to see, hear and speak no evil. The victim, on the contrary, asks the bystander to share the burden of pain. The victim demands action, engagement and remembering.

Judith L Herman

Alison was a tormented young woman whose tortured mind became hostage to extreme beliefs. As conflict surrounded her every thought it became clear she desperately needed professional help. The Garlands Mental Health Hospital where she was sent to recover, gave her precisely the opposite. Garlands was an NHS hospital in Carlisle serving the population of North Cumbria. It was a classically outdated and foreboding mental health institution.

We did not know it at the time, but it was also a bubbling cesspit of barely concealed neglect. A hiding place in which it seems a number of desensitized people were allowed to behave as their desires dictated with impunity. In later years it would emerge the hospital had been a long-serving warm accommodating host to the harmful bacteria of insouciance, petty vindictiveness, poor-practice and abuse. And more, much more.

A couple of years ago I had the pleasure of meeting a courageous lady. Ann Dawson was a former inpatient of Garlands in the late 1980's, later becoming director of Carlisle Mind, the mental health support charity. Ann had been in the ward next to Alison's and had answered a call I made in the local press for people with information to contact me following coverage of Alison's case. We met twice and corresponded by email. She told me sex between staff and mentally ill patients had been commonplace in Garlands. Both male and female mental health nurses engaged in the practice. Management knew but simply turned a blind eye. In 2018 in an unscheduled and entirely unanticipated moment of candour, a former NHS manager who worked at Garlands in the nineties told me that along with illicit sex being a common occurrence, he had personally been made aware of numerous accusations of patients being raped by staff.

A former senior policeman who I respect, I count those on one finger, said that in his experience, mental health hospitals sometimes attracted the wrong sort of employee. Such institutions provide ideal settings for the depraved and duplicitous to locate and prey on the vulnerable. Another former Garlands employee suggested to me that some of the staff regarded sex with patients as perks of their job.

In a letter Alison sent the Garlands Mental Health Hospital after leaving in 1988, she talks about the horror of psychiatric institutions and refers to awful and shocking facts she doesn't want to distress herself or others talking about. She refers explicitly to the rape of a patient by a nurse, in which she says the patient was told no one would listen to them.

In statements given to Cumbria police in 2001, during the first discredited investigation into Alison's death, people spoke of an organisation so openly dysfunctional that the rules were observed being broken more than they were adhered to. Knowing what we now know, we can only imagine the levels of physical, mental and sexual abuse meted out and tolerated in the criminally chaotic and culturally broken hellhole Alison was admitted to. We had unwittingly placed her in danger, sending her to a place where the chances of recovery were not only minimal, they were positively decreased.

Following a series of damning internal reports in the late nineties, the contents of which eventually surfaced as the Kielder Report in the year 2000, Garlands was renamed the Carleton Clinic. It's fascinating to watch how public sector organisations once exposed as cultural basket cases, think simply renaming themselves will change their nature and address their problems. Its classic unicorn thinking, fuelled and perpetuated by an industry of well-paid consultants who do the rounds. These bringers of words without wisdom achieve nothing other than promising to sort out the shitstorm the last set of consultants created whilst ensuring they leave enough of a mess for the next lot.

Organisations and their cultures consist of the actions of the people within them, the same people who are then employed in the newly named institution. But a new name is so much easier to implement than any genuine attempt to change the behaviours of the people that have sullied it. Relabelling is a lazy surrogate for the hard work real change requires.

The perceptions of change the public sector sells are nothing more than thinly veiled slights-of-hand. Comforting illusions behind which the wrongs of the past can be concealed and a convenient opportunity to hide the paper trails which might lead to their discovery. Just change the name and while you're at it lose the records in the restructure.

When I left my doomed five-year stint in Cumbria's NHS in 2017, there were still numerous staff in its employment who had worked at Garlands since the 1980's. Continuity of service can be a good thing, but the shit also rises to the top in a stagnant pond.

Alison was shy, vulnerable, and obviously disturbed. Staff were shocked at how ill she appeared following her first admittance to hospital in summer 1987. She was described by hospital staff as severely mentally ill. Alison was not suffering a mild depression, as undesirable as that would be, she had entered the eye of a full-blown psychotic meltdown. She refused to speak. She would sit with a bible always within arms-reach, occasionally eating butter with salt poured on it. A tea towel was worn on her head which hid her long red hair.

She explained she was wearing a tea towel because she did not feel worthy of being seen. She was eating butter with salt on because although she knew she must eat, she said she didn't feel worthy of enjoying the taste of whatever she had. To say she was a mess would be a serious understatement. She was racked with guilt and convinced there was a problem with her relationship with God, for which she felt sure the fault lay with her. Alison captured just how depressed she felt in notes she made after leaving the Garlands.

I went from depressed to suicidal and then totally psychotic. I wanted to go abroad, because I knew that I would be quietly allowed to die, the only peace at that time which I could imagine. I pictured myself in my mind dying all the time.

Alison was in the hands, as will become clear care could never be the right word, of the NHS in Carlisle for over a year. Twice as an inpatient and between admissions as an outpatient. Unknown to us, on the 12th August 1988 Alison had an abortion at the City General Hospital in Carlisle. An older trainee mental health nurse working at the Garlands had been having sex with her on the hospital premises.

As well as a blatant contravention of NHS policy, these acts were illegal in the eyes of the law. Unsurprisingly, sex between NHS staff and mental health inpatients and outpatients on hospital premises was and still is a criminal act, punishable by imprisonment. Alison was an outpatient and still in the care of the NHS when the trainee nurse says he had sex with her.

Information we have discovered suggests she was being groomed when she was an inpatient, if not physically taken advantage of. Sexual abuse, some may even say rape, being less genteel descriptions of what was occurring. Alison was twenty-one.

The picture we can paint from the statements taken by Cumbria police in 2001 and only shown to us recently, is that the trainee nurse in question started to take an overly close interest in Alison when she was admitted as an inpatient. His actions were so obvious to some of his co-workers they recall him being warned about his behaviour. It has emerged one of the nurses on the ward went so far as to put their concerns in writing to hospital management and the nursing tutor from the nearby college. These concerns were ignored. He had taken to openly and regularly sleeping with Alison in his student quarters. An act which was against hospital regulations. Students were not allowed any overnight guests in their rooms, never mind patients in the care of the hospital's services.

NHS employees stood by and did nothing as he brazenly broke the rules of the hospital, the laws of the land, and the mind of a mentally ill young woman. Witnesses say Alison came and went freely from his accommodation, in full view of supervisors, colleagues and even the apparent approval of nurse Weston, his nominated nursing mentor.

We were blissfully unaware any of this was going on. In her mental illness Alison was convinced she was in love and that God had brought them together, guiding her to the trainee nurse who was showing such a keen interest in her. He in turn said he believed in the same god and held the same beliefs that were so dear to her. He told others their shared interest in born-again Christianity drew them together. It turns out his was a new novel interpretation of the faith in which unprotected pre-marital sex with younger mentally ill women was sanctioned by the Almighty, if not by decency, the law or the hospital's rules.

Alison's state of mind co-opted her to play an unwitting part in the unfolding deception. She was under the illusion she was embarking on a sincere and lasting relationship. She wasn't in the right frame of mind to understand that what was being done to her was unethical, unsustainable, unprofessional and highly inappropriate, as well as illegal. She led family and the social workers looking after her into thinking she was living in newly refurbished sheltered housing on the outskirts of town. This accommodation had been provided by social services as part of her recovery following her discharge as an inpatient. She would meet with us there to keep up the pretence. There would be flowers in a vase and the combined living and kitchen room had the look of being lived in. She never let on she was staying and sleeping with a student nurse in his quarters at the mental health hospital.

Records show that despite being warned on numerous occasions about his behaviour toward Alison when she was an inpatient, the nurse persisted in his efforts to develop a physical relationship. Most worryingly, though it can be difficult to know what should be worried about most in clusterfucks of such enormity, we were recently told by the Crown Prosecution Service that the consultant psychiatrist tasked with treating Alison was one of the many others who also knew what was going on.

Seriously mentally ill and with deeply held religious beliefs, upon discovering she was pregnant, Alison's mind would have been subject to one of two equally unpalatable choices. Childbirth arising from a crisis pregnancy resulting from sinful pre-marital sex, or a hastily arranged abortion to kill her unborn child. A baby her religious peers insisted was already a person, a sentient entity with an eternal soul and one of Gods precious creations.

Being placed at this emotional crossroads was anything other than the professional intervention she needed. Facing these impossible decisions was a recipe for a mental implosion Alison never truly recovered from. The torment, as a young woman of conviction, caught between the deeply entrenched born-again Christian guilts of illicit sex or the burden of taking a life, would have been unimaginable, unbearable.

Alison had been used for the gratification of a man in a position of great responsibility. He was entrusted to look after vulnerable people in his care, not have sex with them. When things became complicated, she had been cast adrift to fend for herself and deal with the aftermath. It was not something she was equipped to do. The medical oath to do no harm had not just been ignored, it had been kicked to the ground, tortured, spat on and then buried. They had messed with her body and messed with her mind. Alison emerged from the clutches of the NHS in Carlisle more damaged, confused and with more issues to deal with than when she had been admitted. Stripped of dignity and hope the weight of her woes had been exponentially increased. She was further from her god than ever and carrying even greater burdens of sin that would ultimately prove too much.

The implications for her state of mind would have been massive. The mental health traumas for young women enduring a crisis pregnancy and then abortion are well documented. The affect, on a young woman as mentally ill and vulnerable as Alison would have been far more significant. She should never have been put in this position by the negligence of an NHS Trust. She was in no fit state to make life shaping decisions without appropriate and impartial professional support.

Alison left Carlisle to be with mum in Doncaster shortly after the abortion in 1988. If the truth be known I imagine she was encouraged to leave. In a handover letter the Consultant Psychiatrist treating Alison sent to her new GP in Doncaster in January 1989, there is no mention of the significant events that occurred on his watch and with his knowledge only five months previously. He excludes any reference to the crisis pregnancy his patient was subjected to by a fellow NHS employee and makes no reference to the subsequent abortion we now understand he was party to arranging.

In his position, his choice to omit these important medically relevant facts about the life-altering events his patient had experienced is alarming and disturbing. The very purpose of handover correspondence between health professionals is to share information that helps their fellow clinicians provide informed appropriate care. In Alison's case she was a seriously ill patient whose ongoing treatment required coordinated efforts between all the staff treating her. For her former psychiatrist to withhold the most salient points from the summary he sent her new carers is the clinical equivalent of a dodgy car dealer passing off previously crashed cars as carefully driven vehicles with full-service histories. The NHS in Carlisle had turned Alison into a mental health crisis they were more than happy to ship elsewhere.

It now seems clear Alison's psychiatrist and his colleagues were desperately keen to ensure what happened was brushed under the nearest carpet. By not sharing information he put her future treatment at risk and neglected his duty of care, though it could be argued the horse had already bolted in that respect. The mental health staff treating Alison in Doncaster were denied important medically relevant information which meant they were placed at an immediate disadvantage. They were blissfully unaware of the events Alison had endured and therefore unable to understand the cause of the anxieties she displayed.

Alison's religious beliefs reinforced the shame she felt and precluded her from talking about the crisis pregnancy or abortion she had experienced. She could not confide in or talk meaningfully with the religious zealots of the church she attended. Their hard-line unforgiving stance on abortion was not a place from which empathy and understanding would have been forthcoming. Perhaps the trainee nurse who took advantage of her knew the shame of disclosure would shield his actions. Perhaps he encouraged her, implored her, begged her to say nothing to incriminate him? Did he tell her he loved her? Did he tell her if she truly loved him, she should stay silent and tell no-one? Did he tell her that her born-again peers would not forgive her for what she had done?

The attempt to rewrite Alison's medical history makes me wonder if pregnancies were terminated frequently to deal with the aftermath of the intercourse which seemed so prevalent between staff and patients at Garlands hospital. The use of abortion to hide evidence of wrongdoing was highlighted in operation Yewtree, the police investigation into the predatory behaviours of Jimmy Saville and other high-profile celebrities. Was abortion a commonly used way to hide what may have been going on at Garlands Mental Health Hospital in Carlisle?

What is clear is that Alison did not get the support to deal with or even understand what she had been subjected to. The abuse of power, the sexual exploitation of her vulnerability, the manipulation of her beliefs, the breaking of trust with those treating her, the crisis pregnancy, the abortion she had undergone, the child she felt she had sacrificed and the unbearable weight of her sins. Perhaps her faith in the healthcare system to even treat her professionally, objectively, had been irreparably broken. Who could blame her for feeling that?

On the 13th December 1991, during the ongoing battle with her mind we naively thought she was winning, Alison took her life at Rotherham Railway Station. The date was around what we later found out would have been the third birthday of the baby she aborted. Anniversaries of significant events are often trigger's for women who have had pregnancy terminations. She took off her coat and placed it on the nearest bench, she put her handbag on the station platform and walked down some maintenance steps onto the tracks in-front an oncoming train.

Station staff and passengers on both platforms watched in helpless horror as the trains warning whistles went unheeded and tragedy unfolded in front their eyes. The train driver, like many who experience such unforgettable events, was traumatised. At the time she took her life Alison had been a voluntary inpatient of NHS mental health services in Doncaster. She seemed to have been looking forward to an imminent move into assisted accommodation which was seen by most as a welcome step toward independence. It was something she said she was excited about.

Her suicide was a vicious curved ball twisting out of left field. It took us, and everyone involved in her treatment by surprise. She had seemed to be getting better. She was in good spirits the last time Sarah and I saw her.

Mum recalls a nurse from the psychiatric unit at Doncaster Royal Infirmary ringing her early that fateful Friday evening. Alison had not returned to the ward and the caller asked if mum knew where she was. Mum said she didn't, the nurse shouted at her, accused her of hiding her daughter and told her she was not doing Alison any favours by keeping her at home. If only. However, hospital staff were not unduly alarmed, they did not see Alison as a suicide risk and had not expected her to take her own life. Like us, the NHS in South Yorkshire were unaware of the burdens Alison was carrying.

When she was first admitted to the NHS mental health hospital in Carlisle in 1987, Alison was a young twenty-one. I can't imagine how she was feeling. A deeply troubled mentally ill young woman who found herself confined in a grim looking Victorian Style Asylum. Alison was miles from home, scared, alone, confused and highly vulnerable in an era when matters of the mind and mental health hospitals were only spoken of in hushed tones.

She should have been a safeguarding priority. That an older nurse took an unhealthily close physical interest in her was bad enough. Today we call such behaviour grooming. Alison needed help, not sexual interest from the lustful unrestrained. That supervision for trainees was so lax he did what he did under the noses of managers and colleagues is almost unbelievable. That it was known he was sleeping with a patient in student quarters, in which the overnight entertaining of any guests, never mind patients, was forbidden, is beyond words.

Vulnerable patients are placed in mental health hospitals because they need protecting from themselves, as well as from those who might prey on them in the outside world. Surely no civilised person can think it ok for nurses to have sex with patients. The condoning and facilitating of illicit sex by randy trainees with patients whose illnesses and conditions they do not even fully understand is beyond wicked.

In short, a vulnerable young woman in the care of an NHS mental health hospital was singled-out by a nurse who then had unprotected sex with her on numerous occasions on hospital premises. She became pregnant and had a hastily arranged abortion. Information about the crisis pregnancy and termination were then withheld from her medical notes and three years later the same vulnerable young patient took their own life.

When Alison stepped in front a train on a cold Friday in December 1991, it is my belief the trainee nurse who took advantage of her, the consultant psychiatrist, the staff, managers and mentor who turned a blind yet knowing eye to what was happening, they all had their hands on her shoulders. From a safe distance they had pushed her into the train's path.

There are so many good reasons why professional boundaries should exist and be adhered to in the world of health and care. They should not be crossed, they must be upheld and enforced. The consequences of them being broken can be disastrous for patients. The impact on those left behind lasts a lifetime. I did not know of the events leading to Alison's death for almost ten years. I am still unsure whether knowing has been a good thing.

In 2017, almost three decades after committing his offences, and in the face of damning evidence, Cumbria police finally obtained a confession from the man in question. He admitted having sex with Alison on multiple occasions in his student quarters on hospital premises. He also acknowledged knowing about the crisis pregnancy and helping arrange the abortion. He says that though he knew what he was doing was morally wrong, he didn't know it was illegal in the eyes of the law.

If ignorance is ever a valid defence, which it seldom if ever is, and he is to be believed, the same excuse cannot be used by the psychiatrist treating Alison. As a senior clinician he would have known the law regarding sex with patients on hospital premises. I wonder what his excuse for not exposing what happened is? The police say they tried to interview Mr Singh the psychiatrist in 2017, but he said he couldn't remember anything. I don't buy it. What happened to Alison would have been a significant occurrence in his career. How many tall striking young redheaded patients can a psychiatrist forget they've arranged abortions for?

During the writing of this book, former employees of the NHS in Cumbria have shared many stories with me. This is England's largest small county; we may be spread out, but everyone knows everyone. One former NHS manager told me that during senior management team meetings, a previous Chief Executive of the mental health hospital in Carlisle referred to the patients in their care as, those nutters over there. This was in the year 2000; just over fifty years since the Universal Declaration of Human Rights. It has become increasingly obvious that the treatment of mental health in the NHS has been so slow to catch up.

I shudder to think what the culture was like in earlier decades when Alison was a patient. When attitudes towards vulnerable people are so dehumanising at the leadership level, it creates a toxic climate in which patients are viewed as less than human. This lack of compassion and disregard for humanity is an abuser's mandate, a green light to do whatever takes your fancy, however misguided. It leaves the vulnerable open to abuse by the less scrupulous.

When things go wrong in hospitals and healthcare services it is often assumed, as I wrongly assumed myself for many years, it was just one bad apple, that the reality for the majority was still positive. But my experience shows the fish rots from the head and the rot spreads quickly, especially when such derogatory inhumane language is used to set the tone.

Garlands hospital in Carlisle was the first in the UK to be subject to a report and inspection under the government's new regulatory regime. When the Commission for Health Improvement, a forerunner to the Care Quality Commission, inspected the hospital in 2000 following reports of patient abuse and neglect, they found a culture had developed within the Trust that allowed unprofessional, counter therapeutic, degrading and cruel practices.

It's interesting to note use of the word allowed, which I think really means NHS employees and managers knew what was going on. By ignoring it they condoned it. But using the word allowed is so much less pointed than saying they were complicit, but less accurate I feel. After all, if the Chief Executive thinks the patients are just nutters and employees view sex with them as a perk of the job, is anyone going to make a fuss if they see colleagues making patients sit on the toilet while they feed them?

Or depriving them of blankets and bedding when they get awkward? Or bathing them in soiled water? Or having sex with them?

In their report into the Garlands the Commission for Health Improvement identified a culture of collusion, describing it as closed, inward looking and insular, a description still ringing true. Hospital employees were so undermanaged that staff in the occupational therapy department were able with impunity, to construct a crude wooden board and harness which they used as a restraining device to keep patients on commodes. Sometimes while being fed.

Just think for a moment if you will what a lethal combination and recipe for abuse this was. An isolated mental health institution located at the northern tip of England's most rural county, with a chief executive who thinks the patients are less than human; no-one will know what you're up to and managers won't care if they find out. It's a predator's dream.

What is most disturbing about the Commission for Health Improvement report, is that as soon as it was published it was ridiculed by staff and managers. They said it was a storm in a teacup and the government had overreacted in their search for scapegoats. The culture was so poor they had become institutionally blind to their own shortcomings. Unable to even see what others could clearly see, and quite rightly called out, as cruel and degrading.

The lives of the staff who made the original allegations, so called whistle-blowers, were made as difficult as possible.

With hindsight I can see why some staff thought the report of November 2000 was a storm in a teacup. Let's face it, the instances of physical abuse highlighted were most likely the lessor of the many evils doubtless being practiced. The regulators only scraped the visible tip of a large iceberg containing many forms of abuse.

Sadly, the story of healthcare regulation in the UK continues to be that of the drunk looking for their house keys under a streetlight. A passer-by offers to help but is also unable to find the keys and asks the drunk if they are sure this is where they were dropped. The drunk replies that he does not know but is only looking for them under the lights because it will be impossible to find them in the darker places. Healthcare regulators like the Care Quality Commission are the key losing drunken fumblers of the public sector, looking where they always look, for what they always look for, in the places they can most easily see. In all the reports highlighting malpractice at the Garlands, it is lamentable not one of the inspectors highlighted the obvious potential for sexual abuse, a poison clearly thriving in such an obviously contaminated culture.

Some former employees I have spoken to over the years tell me it's pointless revisiting the past. They hide their insouciance behind the phrase, that's just the way it was. The former manager who told me about the reports of rape, said such abhorrent behaviour was simply an inherent feature of what he referred to as the dark ages of mental health. I pointed out rape has been a crime since medieval times, and to suggest the raping of patients could be viewed as acceptable behaviour by publicly funded employees of the NHS in the eighties and nineties, seemed a little odd. His response was, we did things differently and we didn't recognise it as a problem at the time.

I have also asked some of the people who used to work at Garlands why they didn't share knowledge of what was happening with the police. They just keep repeating that they don't want to make anything of these issues now and they continue to say, that's just the way it was. That's just the way it was, that's just the way it was. It is a mantra they feel compelled to use to defend their inaction, their choice to do nothing. I find it incredible people can sit on knowledge of serious sexual offences, justifying the rape of vulnerable patients by the very people supposed to be caring for them, all under the hollow meaningless mantra of, that's just the way it was. I want to scream at them, no it wasn't, it was the way you allowed it to be. But people who turn a blind eye to such things don't seem to have the courage to acknowledge and own their complicity. It's always easier to say you are stuck in traffic rather than acknowledge you are part of it.

There is seldom if ever a compelling reason to cross the professional boundaries that exist in healthcare to protect the vulnerable. To do so in situations where patients are vulnerable and mentally unwell is an inexcusable abuse of power and position, whatever the motivation of those involved.

Boundaries are broken by the unaware, the unscrupulous, the inexperienced, the ignorant. And in places where boundaries are not recognised or respected, the opportunist. Vigilant principled management is vital to stop those who commit acts with significant and long-lasting consequences, simply because they lack morals, self-awareness or judgement.

The impact of the abuse of power by health professionals on patients leads to a breakdown of faith in the system and those within it. Trust is lost and patients, now victims who have been taken advantage of, become less treatable, less cooperative. They are trapped, locked within a healthcare system telling them the answer to their problems is more exposure to the things that have let them down. More of the same will fix you; really?

Some people who have been taken advantage of or abused experience heightened feelings of inadequacy or inferiority at having been used in this way. Perversely, they also believe it was somehow their fault and lose self-esteem and whatever remaining trust they may have had in their own judgement. Alison already felt she had let us down. In her notes she wrote, *I am sad to be in a psychiatric hospital, but I know things will turn out well one day, as they have done in the past. I have hurt my family by being admitted as well, which is terrible.* The last thing the person writing these words needed was any further emotional trauma. What was done to Alison in the Garlands was the building of a burden that destroyed her.

The inquest into Alison's death was held in early 1992. Like many families who have lost someone violently and unexpectedly we were in complete shock, both before and for some time after the inquest. We were, and in many respects still are in that category of average Joe's; people who don't know what they don't know. We didn't know what type of inquest should be held. We didn't even know there were different types of inquest. We had no idea what to expect and we saw it as something to be got through and endured rather than a chance to find anything out. We did not know there was anything to find out. We were not offered any support or guidance by any of the agencies involved in Alison's care. Most importantly we were unaware we were not in possession of the facts leading to her death.

We did not know and were not told what the responsibilities of the statutory bodies involved was or to what extent they should be represented. The Mental Health Trust from South Yorkshire submitted a letter rather than attending in person and there was no representation from the NHS or Social Care Services. Alison was officially in the care of the state at the time of her death. South Yorkshire NHS and other public sector services were not present as they should have been. But we didn't know what we didn't know.

People like Alison were ideal prey, manna from heaven for anyone intent on satiating their sexual desires inside the thick protected walls of a culturally dysfunctional mental health hospital. Miles from home with a distant disinterested father, not a man to beat a path to anyone's door seeking vengeance for his wronged daughter, Alison was exposed and highly vulnerable. She should have been safe and secure in the compassionate confines of a caring institution, instead she became someone's desired fish in a heavily polluted barrel.

I have read documents and reports on what the hospital was like years after what happened to Alison. The experiences of my own family and what I have seen and heard combine to paint a tragic yet unsurprising and still evolving picture of the behaviours and practices enabled and tolerated in Garlands Mental Health Hospital. The perception I now have of the hospital she stayed in is so grim, that I wonder if sex with an errant trainee nurse was a price Alison paid for protection from the unwanted advances of others? It's disturbing to think she may have attempted to secure her safety by aligning herself with a man she could say she belonged to.

That she took her own life speaks volumes about the utter darkness of the place Alison ultimately found herself in. Suicide is even less talked of in born-again circles than the red-hot potato of abortion. It was the strength of her heavenly convictions and their stark contrast with earths realities that were the source of so much of her angst and confusion. The intensity of her religious beliefs and her mental illness meant everything she did and everything that happened, no matter how small, was viewed and interpreted through the unforgiving lens of radical Christian belief. Little things, tiny things, things you or I wouldn't think twice about, were constantly questioned in Alison's head. Will this please the Lord, is this allowed, is this sinful, right, wrong.

I look back now and think perhaps Alison never really stood a chance. She was a precious delicate flower tossed into a hurricane. Cast adrift to the fates by a thoughtless father, brought up by a well-meaning mother who was unwittingly co-opted to seek meaning in quackery. Dad had left his beautiful blue-eyed little girl behind in the pursuit of his own pleasure. She had adored him and suffered severe separation anxiety. Fathers are supposed to protect their children, where was he?

Perhaps Alison felt the act of suicide was the only means left of exercising any control over her life. The loving networks that sustain us all in times of need, the supporting pillars of her world had collapsed. The empty promises from men who told her they cared for her had evaporated, and now her keen mind was turned in on itself. Its capacity for sharpness was toying with her, destroying itself and its host like a rogue antibody.

And when she took her life, had she reached a point where she realised there was no grand plan for her, that it had all been an elaborate scam? Or did she do so, believing an eternity in heaven or hell awaited? Did she scream fuck you at the skies, did she tell God she couldn't take any more of life's disappointments or his empty promises, or did she cry out for forgiveness, seeking the arbitrary mercy of the twisted dictator at the last moment?

I can't bear to think of my sister, tormented lost and alone, standing in front the irresistible path and solid unfeeling steel of an oncoming train on a cold dark December day. I sometimes watch their passage as they trundle along the West Coast main line through Penrith. I cannot even begin to imagine how someone summons the courage to stand in front of one, knowing there will be no doubt about the outcome. Nor, until recently could I fathom the state of mind that feels this course of action is the best one to take at any moment in time. To anyone who would say suicide is a coward's way out; what would you know.

Before stepping onto the railway line Alison wrote on a small brown envelope, she placed in her coat pocket. British Transport Police recovered the note. On one side she had written her address in Doncaster, on the other she wrote, I Love You, Mum, Sarah and Thomas.

Chapter 8 - Living with the fallout

Welcome to the club nobody wants to join.

Survivors of bereavement by suicide.

Mental health is without doubt the least understood most widespread medical phenomena of our time. It was even less so in 1991. People suffering mental illness seldom receive Get Well cards. The thought Alison would take her own life had never been on our radar. I don't know if that makes us sound stupid. Of course, with the benefit of hindsight we should have been more vigilant to the risk, but we simply didn't think it was something Alison would do or would ever be inclined to do. Death by suicide was a needless shambolic tragedy that happened to the less fortunate, the dispossessed we were brought up to believe we weren't.

I can only describe Alison's death as like a bomb going off in a small room. An emotional grenade lobbed through the unsuspecting window of the warm and homely living room of our lives. You cannot jump behind the sofa or shield your eyes from the blast. There is nowhere to hide from the shockwaves. Suicide in a family strikes the very epicentre, the safe and treasured space of your world. Everything is thrown in the air, the ground you stood on, the things you once held true, the certainties you had, the aspirations you had, the mental lens you use to view and make sense of the world shifts irrevocably. It is truly a What the Fuck moment.

Try if you will. Close your eyes and imagine you have just been told someone close to you, dear to you, someone you love, has taken their own life without warning or notice. There is no lengthy suicide note of explanation. They did not text you with an outline of the logic leading to their decision. There was no dark brooding obviously ominous post on Facebook. You have not had the chance to talk to them recently, but you recall the last time you did, and they seemed fine. Go on, try.

Suicide is most definitely not painless for those left behind. And who else can you blame but yourself for not seeing it coming. My family and I were largely ignorant of the potentially lethal consequences of mental illness. To talk openly of it in the eighties and early nineties was almost unacceptable. Use of the word suicide, the S word, was beyond the breaking of taboo in polite circles. People died suddenly; they didn't take their own lives. Suicide prevention training wasn't even yet a glimpse in the eyes of public health officials, charities or government departments.

When suicide takes someone, you cannot hunt down their attacker, the assailant or drunk driver. You will not get to look your loved one's killer in the eyes across a court room, or shout at the cancer or fundraise to search for a cure into whatever malevolent medical condition is responsible. In the privacy of your own mind you can only keep asking why. Why, why and why, again and again. Why didn't she talk to us? Why couldn't she see how much she meant to us? Why didn't she realise things were going to get better? Why did she choose the one option that closes all the other possibilities down? And of course, why didn't I make more time for my sister, why couldn't I see it coming?

Early in 1992, when the Coroner delivered their open verdict into Alison's death, it was not only made in the absence of information, the open verdict they recorded also reflected the laws bluntness and inability to keep pace with the times.

Until recently coroners were compelled to record open verdicts in cases like Alison's, they were not allowed to record a verdict of suicide based on the balance of probabilities alone. Until 1961 suicide in the UK was classed as a criminal act, self-murder, hence the term committing suicide. Therefore, the standard of proof applied in coroner's courts had to be the same as a criminal act and provable beyond doubt. This meant there had to be certainty a person intended to kill themselves before a verdict of suicide could be recorded. For many years, the only evidence generally accepted by coroners as unequivocal proof of this, was an unambiguous suicide note. Thankfully, the law has now changed, and verdicts of suicide can be recorded on the balance of probabilities. Alison may not have left the archetypal neat handwritten letter, but if actions speak louder than words then she scrawled goodbye cruel world on life's canvas in bigger and bolder letters than any graffiti artist has ever used.

After mum and Sarah had spent the Christmas of 1991 with friends in South Cumbria, every Christmas thereafter seemed a fraught confusing and guilt-inducing affair, veering between mum's fervent born-again celebrations of Christ's birth and an annual period of mourning. Mum had lost one of the few people in her life who could poke fun at her and still make her laugh. She had also lost someone who had needed her, depended on her.

Mum's religious beliefs gave her a way of coping. She clung tightly and with great certainty to the belief Alison was now in heaven. To her this was all that mattered. She surrounded herself with people who reinforced this belief and somehow, she kept going. What many would see as tragedy, she attempted to see as Alison's passage to a better place. I'm sure the truth of how she sees her daughter's death lies somewhere in a grey area between grief and celebration. Her doctor prescribed her sleeping tablets, which she stopped taking after a month.

Sarah missed Alison terribly. She had looked out for her little sister. Having grown up sharing the same bedroom in their formative years, they were close. She saw her sisters untimely and horrific death as the extinguishing of bright promise. She felt she had failed her sister and didn't fully grieve until getting bereavement counselling some years afterwards. Sarah's doctor also gave her sleeping tablets. She took these for eighteen months until she reached a point she describes as noticing Spring for the first time since Alison died.

My memories of the Christmas immediately after Alison's death are opaque. There were so many thoughts and emotions running amok in my head I think they cancelled each other out. Sadness and disbelief turned to numbness. How should a young man feel after his sister has taken their own life? Where is the rule book, where are the life lessons for such things? Was it ok for me to feel angry, with myself, with Alison, with God, with everyone or no-one?

I remember wrestling with feelings of guilt and of even being ashamed of my sister for what she had done. Stupidly and naively I prided myself on my positive outlook. My life was just beginning, I told myself I would never kill myself. I would never allow my mental health to get so out of control. Suicide was such a taboo, why had she left this legacy on us. I would be known as the uncaring brother of the girl who took her own life. I would be seen as one of the people who should have known what was going on, who should have helped her.

In my ignorant grief I was holding my sister to account for the state of her mental health. I had no right to do that. I don't even know if grief counselling would have been available to any of us back then? It may sound strange but the religious beliefs I had bought into at the time made me question my right to sorrow. If everything was part of a plan, then who was I to feel sad because I had lost my sister? Wasn't that just self-indulgence, a pity party I had no right to participate in. Alison had gone to a better place. My duty was simply to move on, to live and make the most of my life. I look back now and realise just how far under the spell of the charismatic born-again Christian preachers we had all fallen. The contempt I have now developed for these, life robbing beauty stealing fuckers, knows no bounds.

Debbie and I tried to behave as normally as we could. We were still young and struggling to understand our own emotions. We never saw the need to make time to gather our thoughts and talk meaningfully about what had happened. And what had happened? We didn't have the mental tools to interpret the events which had unfolded. I didn't know how to begin a conversation about it and Debbie didn't know what to say for fear of upsetting me. We put on a veneer of normality as we attended the festive gatherings we had been invited to that Christmas and New Year. One of the features of living in a small town is that everybody knows everybody else. In happier times it's a great upside. Some looked, whispered and kept their distance, some were polite, offering their condolences. But most were just plain awkward, obvious in their discomfort.

In the timescales of the universe the early nineties are less than the blink of an eye ago, but in terms of the average person's attitude towards mental health and suicide, it was another era. The idea of a government suicide prevention minister would have been thought to be a liberal indulgence at best. The fact the UK has one now is nothing to shout about, but it does at least reflect a shift in the right direction of our collective awareness if not our understanding. I spent the holiday season hiding behind Debbie. I stuck to her like glue, clinging onto her tightly as I tried to hide my six-foot frame behind her petite stature, avoiding eye-contact and conversation.

The Christmas holidays ended, and in January I went back to the small family owned firm in Carlisle I had worked for since the previous summer. I didn't expect or was offered any extra time off work. I didn't talk about Alison's death or the funeral. My workmates behaved as if nothing had happened. Aside from the boss they were a good bunch and I don't know if their avoiding of the topic was part of a deliberate effort to help me move on or just a reflection of the times.

The ten of us would sit round the table with our packed lunches and talk about the usual trivia. The overly demanding customers, the deals in the pipeline and whatever was in the local

News & Star. In those days work was work and I had always been encouraged to leave my personal life at home. What nice clean crisp misguided thinking that is. As if we can leave a part of us somewhere else at will. All I was doing by hiding within myself was storing up an emotional atom-bomb, waiting for the right trigger to explode it at some yet unknown but inevitable point in the future.

Alison had died in the care of the NHS and perhaps it would have been appropriate, useful, compassionate, if we had been offered some emotional support following her suicide. It's sad, but nearly thirty years later the NHS is still blind to the impact on those left behind when mental health patients take their own lives in its care. The needs of the families of the bereaved are largely ignored by NHS Trusts. Now there are charitable organisations, CRUSE Bereavement Care and SOBS (Survivors of Bereavement by Suicide) who provide much needed help and peer support to those left behind. Once again, the state fails and charity steps in to clean up the mess.

After Alison's funeral, the already small dysfunctional family, fate had made me part of became even more fragmented. We had no shared knowledge of the wrongs that had occurred to galvanise our anger, no common enemy to harness our collective energies and fight. I think to some degree we turned on each other. In the absence of the facts that would later emerge I blamed my father almost entirely for Alison's suicide, her loss of hope, for leaving her behind when he knew she adored him. For chasing his own dreams of pleasure and grinding hers under his heel. I called him out in front of his close friends and family, openly accusing him of being the main protagonist in Alison's poor mental health and her decision to take her own life. I think I will always believe his actions had a role in the demise of her wellbeing, that seems obvious. But I know now to accuse him of being the lead actor in the tragedy of Alison's death was utterly unfair.

In turn, my dad's side of the family, who up until this point had been happy to sit back and watch the chaos in our lives unfold, now started to apportion blame on mum and on the radical isolating beliefs she and Alison had been coerced to adopt. Though I thought their accusations misguided at the time, they were probably nearer the mark than I had been when I was busy blaming dad.

Mum had now lived in Doncaster for three years and became even more immersed in the born-again Christian church she had moved there to be part of. She threw herself into any available opportunities to proselytize, spreading the gospel of Christ to the unsuspecting residents of her newly adopted hometown. The church and its apostles doubtless felt they were doing the right thing by keeping her busy. The irony of her attempting to peddle the harmful guilt and shame inherent in the deal God offers the dispossessed and emotionally vulnerable is beyond tragic. Damage to the world and the people in it usually comes dressed in attractive parcels delivered by people of certainty. Mum held tightly to the open verdict the Coroner had delivered. She clung to the belief Alison did not take her own life and had been able to pass unhindered from this world to the glories of heaven that await all true believers.

I love my mum dearly, you can feel a "but" coming can't you, but my love is not entirely blind. I wish we'd had the presence of mind after Alison's death to sit down as a family and have an honest conversation about what had brought us to this point. But we didn't. I don't think mum would have ever asked herself if the radical religious beliefs and mental restrictions that had become part of Alison's life had played a role in her death. Mum was living her life in a bubble of mind-control in which those around her protected from any views that might contradict their shared beliefs.

Mum was unwittingly and shamefully encouraged by the faithful to see what had happened as a test of her faith. Believers see and interpret every act, every event, through wildly distorted spiritual lenses. To question the acts, the intent or competence of the Almighty is not condoned in the born-again circles her mind had become hostage to. Questioning the course of pre-determined history, our inevitable destiny known only to God, remains tantamount to heresy.

The pastor and elders of her church told mum the Lord would not have given her the burden of Alison's death to bear if it was unbearable. If she held fast, she would emerge stronger and more worthy of the rewards awaiting her in heaven. Radical religious beliefs take the people we know and love from us as surely as moving them to a foreign land. Dad had left, Alison had died, and mum, once humorous and fun-loving was now even further in the hands of the ill-informed men and women offering spiritual certainty and alienation.

My older sister Sarah, a rock to Alison in life, now became a pillar of support to mum. Sarah had been studying at Sheffield University and was working in London and living in York. Her faith in God, though no longer the radical bigoted born-again version, has remained largely intact. Sarah had been the closest of us all to Alison and like me she did not know how to interpret what had happened. She has wrestled with more than most will ever have to. Fortunately, she has many good friends who have helped her on the journey.

As time passed, I continued to do my best to live, love and work. My motivation to succeed in the material sense, which had never been in doubt before, waned. I found that as hard as I tried, I couldn't get as excited about selling things and making money as I once was. I was a good salesman. I had made decent money and won numerous trips abroad including flights to Madrid on Concorde. All I used to want was a nice detached house with a black BMW parked on a neat red gravel drive. That seems incredibly hollow now.

I was still conscientious, hard-working and self-starting, but I was aware I was not as driven to achieve the same things anymore. I would go through periods where I just felt empty. If I was out on sales calls prospecting for orders, I would sometimes park the company car and sit for a while. I don't remember what I would think when I was doing this, I just recall feeling I needed to zone-out, to switch off and be alone. As I approached my thirties, I knew I needed to engage my mind in other ways, so I started studying with the Open University.

It really is true you can pick your friends and not your family. And one of the good parts of my life, a part that plays a significant role in keeping me afloat when things get shitty, and things have got really, really, shitty these past few years, is my wife Debbie's family. My disappointment in parts of my own has been fed by becoming part of another wider family. It's only when you have something to compare and contrast your experiences with you recognise the patterns of the life you had led were entirely untypical, dysfunctional even. The low-esteem I have grown to hold my biological father in has been shaped by the more life-affirming behaviours demonstrated by my adopted father-in-law. He has been more of a dad and parental example to me over the years than my own was ever willing or attempted to be.

It's surprising how quickly life rolls on, a phenomenon that only seems to accelerate with age. As the new millennium approached, we had settled into our lives. Mum continued her mission to spread the word in Doncaster, Sarah now had a good job in the picturesque city of York, living within sniffing distance of the Rowntree Chocolate factory and I was still in Penrith, working for

Carlsberg. My mother hated me working for a global corporation selling alcohol, she thought it was ungodly and reminded her of dad. She would tell her friends in church it was only a temporary job until I could find something more suitable.

The truth be known, I'm not sure I have ever found a more pleasant job. I was selling beer across Cumbria and the Lake District and I loved it, what wasn't to like? Debbie and I had moved from the half-buy half-rent house we started our married lives in to the first home we fully owned, a house we still call home. And I was attempting to regain the very many miles of educational ground I lost in my youth. I had passed my second postgraduate diploma on the way to an MBA; master of bugger all as I now call it. But most importantly, I had finally shaken the remains of any shackles of religion from my life. God and I had parted company, and I was happy.

I rarely visited Alison's grave in Doncaster. As time passed that period of my life seemed more and more like a fantasy. None of us had achieved closure, whatever that is meant to be, but we had all got used to life without Alison. Things were about to change.

Chapter 9 - What did you just say Mum?

Three things cannot be long hidden, the sun, the moon and the truth.

Buddha

After mum left Penrith and moved to Doncaster, a life decision I have never understood, agreed or come to terms with, Sarah and I would visit the small terraced house where she lived, 79 St John's Road. We have been visiting her in Doncaster over thirty years now. I still shake my head in disbelief when I think she chose to leave Penrith. Swapping the safe if insular parochial comfort of the rural shire and the warm reassurance of its feel-good weekly paper, to live in the bruised heart of a fatally wounded town. A place held together by pride, echoes of importance and the paper-thin shedding skin of a once glorious industrial past.

Doncaster's free newspapers, filled with adverts for double glazing, soulmates seeking each-other and premium rate chat lines were a far cry from the Cumberland and Westmorland Herald. A bit of me understands and acknowledges mum's desire to escape Penrith. It was and is, a place with lots to offer, but like many small towns it can mistreat what it doesn't understand.

Penrith could be mean, at times offering little more than misplaced snobbery, nosey neighbours and the petty-minded bigoted perceptions of people who know little and have seen less. I see now mum needed help and understanding, she wanted to belong to something, to be around people who would not judge, who would treat her with the unconditional respect she had earned. She deserved a medal, not the patronising pity and disdain of the rural middle-class. They weren't fit to tie her shoes, but I think she had such low self-esteem she sought their acceptance.

Since leaving Cumbria and gradually losing affinity with nursing friends and former colleagues and being unceremoniously jettisoned by dad's side of the family, mum had given herself completely to bringing her family up. She hadn't a moment to breathe. A social life was a luxury she had neither time nor money for. She was treated very poorly by dad's side of the family and had no confidante to turn to.

I think the warm welcome she, and the ten percent of her already small income she was willing to contribute, had been given by the evangelical church, was the first time in many years she felt she belonged to something. She was told she could place her cares at the feet of Jesus and put her future in his hands. She was told she mattered, she was the apple of Gods eye, that Jesus died and rose again for her. She was assured the master of the universe was in her corner. I wish they had been. She was offered a way of being free of all the worries and mortal regrets she had because now every situation could be seen to be simply part of a bigger plan under the safe and sure control of the Almighty.

It's a reassuring message for everyone, a kind of don't worry be happy with a twist, and it found a welcome home in mum. I can say now with the certainty hindsight brings that the radical strain of born-again Christianity she became involved with was divisive and ultimately harmful, but it dug her out of a hole at a point when she needed help. And such was the zeal of the faithful, they all seemed so driven by passionate beliefs, they would do almost anything for each other.

They were led by people who modelled themselves as un-stuffy opposites to the self-righteous vicars from the Church of England, who offered no help at all. They made themselves available, providing lifts, meals at their homes and even coordinated the giving of financial assistance, generally relying on other members of the congregation to provide the money. They may have been peddling a lie, but like all zealots they did it with the courage of their convictions.

It was the summer of 1988 and the small band of born-again religious fanatics and their charismatic pastor mum had become so enmeshed with, had left Penrith to set-up a new mission in Doncaster. They said God was calling them. Numbers of the already small flock in Penrith were dwindling and mum decided she should follow the faithful few on this new leg of their journey. She had found something she could believe in and people she wanted to be around and wasn't prepared to let this go.

I was told afterwards it may not have been the Almighty calling the pastor to Doncaster, the hierarchy had got wind of an affair with one of his flock. Rumour has it he was asked or told by his overseers, a humbly titled body called the Assemblies of God, to find another place to preach. This has a familiar feel to what happens in other religious and public bodies when a senior figure drops a clanger. They are simply shipped off elsewhere and the problem is moved for someone else to deal with.

I don't visit mum as regularly as I could or should, but I have my reasons. Through no fault of its own Doncaster became the holder of my worst memories. Her timing, moving further away from Cumbria when Alison was hospitalised in Carlisle, was terrible.

I may never understand and I'm not sure I forgive the religiously driven self-inflicted descent into urban decay she undertook, and the worry she imposed on us as a result. But she was convinced it was where the Lord wanted her, perhaps in his absence. I will always associate Doncaster, Donny, with the loss and burial of Alison and the estrangement of mum. I lost dad to the desires of the flesh and now mum was becoming more and more distant as she became inextricably tied to what seemed increasingly like a cult.

St John's Road is a long almost straight street of terraced houses sitting just off one of the main dual carriageways leading to Doncaster town centre. It was a stark contrast from Penrith's views of High Street and the Pennine Hills, but on bright sunny days it felt friendly and the people were warm. Ten years later Doncaster would be unceremoniously proclaimed the Aids Capital of Britain. Grim news for most but emotional affirmation for followers of Christ who use such facts to justify their need to be present to address the iniquity and sleaze. The greater the sins the greater need for the presence of the god-fearing and devout was mum's view. Now, in 2019, St John's Road looks and feels well and truly like another world from the place she moved to in 1988.

Once a prosperous town surrounded by mines and the industry that went with them including a significant locomotive and carriage building works, Doncaster's industrial history and its shadows loom large. The National Mining Museum is just a short trip away in Wakefield. St Johns Road would have been one of many streets formerly full of people gainfully and proudly employed, miners, engineers, tradesmen and the like. How things change. In the nineties it became one of the first streets in the UK to operate private security patrols in the wake of escalating crime and anti-social behaviour. Thatcher's legacy in the flesh, but not many Tories round here to see or feel the impact of their ideology.

When mum first moved to Doncaster the street was clean and with the odd exception the houses well maintained. Residents had an obvious pride in the appearance of their homes. Mum bought a classic two up two down with a cellar and stairs like a climbing wall between the downstairs rooms, steeper than any I have ever seen. In recent years she needed a stairlift as her long-serving pedestrian knees could not cope with descending them. The kitchen was a small add-on that overlooked the back garden and the bathroom was directly above the kitchen with access through the spare bedroom being the only way to get to it. There was a tiny single-bed sized flower patch to the front and a small lawn leading to a garage on the back. She rented the garage out to a neighbour who didn't have one and wanted somewhere secure to park his vintage Rover.

The last time I walked down St John's Road it was full of For Sale and To Let signs. Unkempt gardens, peeling paintwork, cracked slipping slates, crumbling brickwork, ageing cars, the taxed, untaxed, insured and uninsured, some on their last legs or blocks, and all manner of litter. The atmosphere had changed, friendly exchanges tempered with suspicion. The residents have heard all the political rhetoric you can imagine, they understand now that the cavalry of economic regeneration will not make it over the hill, if it was ever coming.

And if it ever does arrive it will bring no real change, only the symbolic flags of hollow press releases which accompany all such projects. Initiatives trumpeted in the minutes of local council meetings which go unnoticed on the streets where they are supposed to have an impact. There is no obvious sense of community anymore, not even a collective belief of being underdogs together. Just an air of powerless isolation and a heightened sense of the need for self-preservation in the face of increasingly uncaring change.

UKIP has held it biggest national conferences at Doncaster Racecourse and in 2016 the town had the highest proportion of Brexit leave voters in Yorkshire. Having watched the Eastern Europeans living opposite mum, leisurely pissing out the front window in broad daylight as the sound of loud pumping music filled their house and much of the street, I can completely understand the desire of some communities to take back control.

I thought about playing the role of strapping concerned son, without the strapping, being a responsible citizen and engaging them. But they didn't strike me as the kind of people I could approach to politely explain we don't do things like that in England unless we're at a music festival. I also feared for what might happen after I played the part of crusader, briefly imagining streams of chemically infused urine pouring through mum's letterbox all times of day and night. More selfishly I was also aware my car was parked very obviously across the road. The rusting Vauxhall outside their house was parked on blocks. I turned from the front window and discreetly adjusted the curtains. Ever the optimist, mum suggested they would only be urinating out the window if their toilet was broken.

In the last couple of years mum has needed to use a walking frame to steady herself. She could just about manage around the home, with the adjustments, grab-rails and staggered steps we arranged. But the thought of her walking to the shops for a pint of milk or going to the bottom of the street to post a letter became increasingly worrying as the change in the nature of the neighbourhood became more obvious, palpable and visible.

Mum had to move into social housing last year, her home was sold to cover the costs of care. It was bought for a song on a street few with choice would now choose to live in. She was incredibly proud of the house she bought, the first she had owned. I found watching her frail and stooping frame as we sat on the dining room floor, sifting and sorting the trinkets of a life into categories, utterly heart-breaking. Items were picked-up, looked-at, caressed, discussed and mentally classified as practical or emotional; the must have, the can't do without, the, there won't be any space for that, the when was the last time you used that, the I've had that forever and, I've had that since I was a child, and the, you can't get rid of that it was given to me by such and such. You remember them, don't you?

Many of the things we kept or discarded that day were part of my childhood. I was unprepared for the wave of emotionally charged memories that flooded my senses. I found an old battered circular Nabisco biscuit tin that had followed us all the way from Barbados. I had not seen it since ratching in the shed of our council house in Penrith decades earlier. I was almost moved to tears when I looked at it. I think it was the first time I have been close to understanding what the Japanese mean when they talk of mono no aware, the pathos of things. I recalled the future was full of promise and hope when I last saw that tin. Lives and adulthoods better than our childhoods were eagerly awaiting. So much has happened since then. That tin holds so many memories. I kept it.

Mum's house was probably one of the best maintained and well kept on the entire street and despite her dippy beliefs, her next-door neighbours on both sides, the old friend and the new young couple, were both sorry to see her go. Her house was bought to let.

The fast food outlets and betting shops that always thrive in climates of want, have sprung up around St John's Road with greater intensity since the crash of 2008. The gambling shops look prosperous, their frontages well maintained, sat within a spit from the pay day loan outlets. Always fresh sets of promotional posters advertising new and novel ways to speculate on the sport or occasion of your choice. Your future might have been stolen but there's always gambling or scratch-cards.

I've always hated visiting Doncaster. A heaviness I can almost grasp descends on me as I approach the town on the A1, the same heaviness I feel lifting as I drive away, getting nearer Scotch Corner and the final leg of my journey back to Penrith. I have always tried to make the journey there and back in one day as a matter of principle. I don't want Doncaster to have any more of me than I need to give it. But on this visit my mind would be stretched beyond anywhere it had been, and I would experience levels of anger, confusion and disbelief I had not known. This trip to Doncaster was the start of a journey I could never have imagined. It turned out to be the commencement of a quest that has consumed my time, attention and energy, almost without mercy ever since.

It was coming up to Christmas 1999. The artist formerly known as Prince was doubtless getting increasingly excited and ready to party, Sarah and I were sat in mum's living room. We had both made our way to Doncaster to see her before Christmas and the three of us were drinking tea. Mum had been earnestly wittering on about Y2K and the imminent arrival of the end of times, as radical fundamentalist born-again Christians are prone to do over a cup of Earl Grey. Sarah and I had been exchanging that exasperated rolling eye look siblings get so good at, the let her get it out of her system and don't get involved approach to family diplomacy.

A new Millennium was on the horizon and mum and the decidedly strange group of evangelical Christians she had regular fellowship with were unusually merry and more than a little excited about the possibility of the arrival of the end of times. They were looking forward to Christ's return, the salvation of the righteous and the coming of the rapture in which they would be taken to heaven. A place from which they could gloat at the great unwashed sea of non-believers and doubters left behind, as we flailed in their own filth destined for unpleasant painful deaths in a world run by Satan.

Realising we were not engaged in this pressing topic of conversation, and most likely having seen the faces we were pulling in the mirror, mum changed the subject. Do you remember the man from the Garlands hospital in Carlisle Alison had a relationship with? she asked. Sarah and I said we did vaguely recall somebody friendly being on the scene, a trainee nurse. I remember being curious about mums use of the word relationship. Sarah then recalled feeling that she felt he had tried to get inappropriately close to Alison during her time in the mental health hospital in Carlisle. She sensed something was amiss at the time but had no idea the extent of what had occurred. Almost indifferently, mum then said, you know Alison got pregnant with his baby and had an abortion, don't you? We didn't.

It's strange to look back and recall how those few words were uttered. Spoken casually, delicate rose bone china cup of tea in hand, almost as a throwaway. As if she was saying, it looks like rain again. The words she uttered that day, changed so much, opening wounds, turning our worlds upside down and reopening secrets buried long ago in other's lives. There is great power in words.

At this point the looks and wry smirks Sarah and I had been giving each other changed from amusement at mum's outlandish religious statements to disbelief at what she had just said. Looking back, I think one of two things led her to share what she knew with us that day. Either the bombshell she had just landed tripped unconsciously off her tongue, or her need to tell us was driven by the belief she may not be here much longer. She was absolutely convinced the new millennium would trigger Christ's return to rescue the righteous. I think it was the pre-rapture equivalent of a death bed confession, something she needed to get off her chest before she left us. Either way, the genie was now out the bottle.

Mum could tell by the change in atmosphere in the room what she said had had impact. Oh, I thought you knew all about it, she stuttered a little sheepishly. I looked at her, catching her eye as she tried to make her escape back to the kitchen. I felt sure I had misheard. Just say that again I said, in my best business-like fashion, as if I was now chairing a meeting. Tell us everything you know about what happened. In an Oscar worthy understated response, mum said, well, there's not much to tell really. We insisted.

Sarah and I listened, trying to suppress shock, occasionally interjecting for clarity as mum told us of a relationship that developed between a trainee mental health nurse called Robert Scott-Buccleuch and Alison when she was a patient of the NHS in Carlisle. She said they had become close through the religious beliefs he professed to share.

Mum went on to tell us he had taken an interest in Alison when she was first admitted to hospital in the summer of 1987. Alison had initially warmed to him. Mum explained that though she knew they were in a relationship she assumed it was purely platonic, and as a fellow Christian she had naively trusted his adherence to his faith. From the medical records we have since recovered it seems Alison was not enamoured with him for long. An entry in her GP notes refers to a clinging needy boyfriend.

There is evidence he also accompanied Alison to appointments she had with her consultant psychiatrist. Snippets and accumulated brushstrokes of information we have unearthed over the years have combined to paint a potentially unhealthy picture of coercive control; not a mutually loving relationship and certainly not a situation in which the power bases could ever have been equal. He was older and with a professional duty of care; she was a vulnerable mentally ill young woman. Alison's story acts as a grim reminder of the importance of boundaries between patients and professionals in mental health settings.

As mum continued to speak, I found myself going back to that time. I had met the trainee nurse on one of the occasions Debbie and I visited Alison in hospital. He had seemed like a nice man. As a nurse, albeit a trainee in our cherished NHS, I had portrayed him in my mind as a caring employee who was being friendly, going the extra mile to make Alison feel human in a dehumanising place.

Like many mental health hospitals of the 1980s, Garlands was a horrid unwelcoming place. A haunted castle like frontage with odd unevenly placed windows set in deep damp brown stone, sheltered from storm as well as scrutiny by a dark Lakeland slate roof. Staff referred to the management building as Fortress Coppice; looking at pictures it's easy to see why. I can understand Alison wanting to get close to someone, anyone who could make her feel safer in such a strange and harrowing place.

The tales Alison told when she was alive of the way staff mistreated patients were difficult to listen to. Her recollections of the nurse who called her a silly girl, woke her with cold water and removed her mattress as soon as she went to the toilet to stop her laying back down, remain with me. This individual remained on my mental dark alley hit list for many years, until I realised, she had been one of the lessor transgressors in the story of Alison's care. It was against this backdrop of brutish behaviour I had originally welcomed the thought Alison had found someone who seemed compassionate. A caring professional giving her the time and help she needed. How wrong I was.

Mum told us the relationship (sic) had become much more than platonic and much less than professional. As a result, Alison became pregnant and had had an abortion at Carlisle Hospital. Relationship in this context is a word which sets my teeth on edge. It was not a relationship, it was a profound betrayal of trust, a flagrant misuse of power. A crime. Nothing less than institutionally sanctioned abuse; physical and mental.

Finally, mum told us Alison had confided in her only once about the pregnancy and abortion; they never revisited the topic again. Mum hadn't known how to respond and had parked the conversation in a box in her mind marked, too difficult to deal with.

Sarah who was two years older than Alison and spent a great deal of time and energy supporting and encouraging her, was completely floored by what Mum was now sharing. My head was about to explode. The nascent thin business-like demeanour I was trying to develop in my early thirties was slipping as I moved swiftly past curiosity, steamed through anger to incandescence, before finally hitting confusion.

I have spoken to mum many times about what happened since the day she first told us. Mum admits she withheld what happened to Alison because she was ashamed. She hadn't even felt able to tell the people she had left Penrith to follow, the born-again believers and the pastor she had placed so much faith in. She was, without reason, deeply ashamed of what had happened, the act, its consequences, and her inability to stop it. But on this day in 1999 her attempts to justify why she hadn't shared this information with us before now, were not cutting the mustard.

Mum kept saying she was putting her faith in God, that he was the only worthy dispenser of justice. There was no point digging up the past she said, the trainee nurse would face justice for what he had done in the afterlife, at the pearly gates, or in some post death pre-entry to heaven interview he would face. She hadn't thought it through. Mum had buried her head in the sand and sat on it in the hope it would never raise its head again. She hadn't allowed herself to consider the possibility that the impact of what he had done had contributed to, perhaps even been directly responsible for the final choice Alison made to take her own life.

I asked mum if she had thought about the possibility the nurse in question might have acted inappropriately towards others? Was Alison the only patient he developed an interest in and had sex with on the hospital premises? Hadn't she thought of her responsibility to share what she knew so other vulnerable patients might be protected? What would Mum do if he was found to have acted inappropriately with other patients while she had been sitting on knowledge that could have stopped it, how would she feel then?

But mum hadn't allowed any of these scenarios to take root in her mind. She seemed to be using the possibility of eternal justice as rationale for doing nothing in the here and now. I tried explaining the purpose of a justice system, a police force, courts and judges, was to deal with just such things; or so I thought at the time. And I asked Mum to explain why we were paying taxes to maintain a justice system on earth if everything was ultimately going to be resolved in the courts of heaven. She had no answer, but she wouldn't be swayed. The Good Lord was in charge and he would ensure that all would be well.

Amongst the many people whose hands I see on Alison's shoulders guiding her into the path of an oncoming train, are the religious zealots whose baseless bigotry shamed mum into silence. Mums inability to process and talk openly with Alison about what had happened to her, was a lessor one of the many disparate winds combining to become the perfect storm defining her daughter's fate. Mum had also had a chance to share what she knew at the original inquest, to tell the Coroner of the crisis pregnancy and discreetly arranged abortion; but said nothing. She was a trained nurse, and in her heart, I think she knew what had happened was wrong. In many respects, I feel mum was as vulnerable as Alison. Despite her protestation's Gods view was the only one that mattered, I can't help wondering if concern for what her spiritual brothers and sisters might think and say was haunting her.

If further proof were needed that our parents really do fuck us up, then mum's status conscious, appearances are everything stepmother, laid the foundations for the fear of shame that has followed her all her life, even after spiritual rebirth. Mum bitterly regrets not letting Alison talk more openly about what happened.

Radical strains of religion are welcoming homes for disillusioned penguins of all shapes and sizes. The disenfranchised, dispossessed and disillusioned huddling together for shelter against life's many storms. For mum to share what she knew of Alison's abortion with those huddled around her was to invite disapproval and risk alienation from the only group of people she had really felt at one with. It was also to admit just how badly things had gone wrong in her life. She followed her stepmother's advice to keep quiet rather than acknowledge uncertainty.

I sometimes wonder how different life would have been if mum had not said anything to us that day. It is not true that what you don't know doesn't harm you. What we hadn't known had harmed us all, and Alison beyond repair. But now we had knowledge and sitting on what we collectively knew was not an option.

But doing something was not made easy. Mum remained steadfast in her desire to let sleeping dogs lie and in her insistence the perpetrator would face justice in the afterlife. Rationale which never made sense to me. Sarah and I knew something had to be done but we wanted to present a united front to the authorities, and we did not want to alienate mum; our family is small and fragmented enough. It took a year to convince her the right thing to do was to allow me to report what had happened to the NHS and the police.

Early in 2001 I sent a letter to the Chief Executive of NHS mental health services in Carlisle. I had no idea of the hornet's nest I was about to kick or of the incredible mentally destructive journey my simple one-page letter would send me on.

Chapter 10 – When is an investigation not an investigation?

It is difficult to get a man to understand something, when his salary depends upon his not understanding it.

Upton Sinclair

My plan was simple, so I thought. On behalf of my family I would approach the Chief Executive of the NHS Trust in Carlisle to outline our concerns and seek his cooperation in unearthing the illegal acts we thought had occurred in 1988. Once the NHS Trust agreed to look into the matter, I would then approach Cumbria constabulary. We would ask the NHS and police to work together to investigate the actions of the individual in question as well as the behaviour of the NHS managers on whose watch events had occurred. What could be more straightforward? After all, a serious crime had been committed. Surely, they would move mountains to unearth the facts, discover the truth and hold those responsible to account; wouldn't they?

In January 2001 I wrote to Nigel Woodcock, then the acting Chief Executive of North Lakeland Healthcare NHS and soon to be appointed Chief Executive of the snappily retitled North Cumbria Mental Health and Learning Disabilities NHS Trust, recent scandals having triggered the need for the obligatory restructuring and change of name. Woodcock seemed on the upward trajectory of a career in the NHS at this point in his life. He would later become better known to many as the overpaid public servant who tried to extract a further £700,000 from the NHS in 2012, following what he said was his premature departure in 2006. He had apparently been made redundant at the age of 49 and was only given £225,000. For various reasons he felt he should have been entitled to more. Most of us will never know what such an amount looks like.

He was supported in his role at the time by an HR Director called Shirley Chipperfield. She would later also become nationally infamous when a report found her, and her colleagues produced tainted evidence in efforts to protect the NHS Trust they worked for from legitimate claims of racial discrimination. Chipperfield had sent a subtle memo to colleagues suggesting the claimant may "play the race card". A report into the matter said the Trust had been self-serving and obstinate. A tribunal judge went further saying they acted in a highhanded, insulting, malicious and oppressive manner.

Unfortunately for me, I had no idea at the time what fine upstanding characters I was attempting to deal with. And we are told its benefit cheats who drain the public purse.

I didn't know it then, but in the best traditions of my family the timing of my approach could not have been worse. Just days before my letter hit Nigel Woodcocks desk, the Trusts poor treatment of its patients had been the subject of discussion at the highest levels.

The same week my letter went to the Chief Executive, members of Parliament had been discussing the content of a report compiled by the Commission for Health Improvement published three months earlier in November 2000. This was the same report in which Trust staff were described as using degrading cruel practices. It referred to vulnerable patients being tied to commodes. Stripped of dignity and rights and fed while forcibly held in a homemade restraining device.

Patients had routinely been fed while sitting on the toilet. They had been manhandled, flicked on the genitals to encourage compliance, their faces washed with the same flannels used on their genitals. They had been deliberately left outdoors in the cold and their normal diets withheld from them.

It would appear however, that the fallout from this report had been significant only for some. The Chair of the NHS Trust, Mary Styth, was summarily dismissed by the government health secretary. Alan Place the Chief Executive was sacked after a period on sick leave and the director of nursing took early retirement ahead of a disciplinary hearing. Changes were made to the board and some staff were disciplined. Whatever the consequences for one or two individuals, it is noteworthy nobody was ever prosecuted.

It is still an unfortunate feature of our NHS that what passes for criminal behaviour outside the hospital doors, when inflicted on patients, especially in mental health settings is often treated with relative indifference by the police and regulators of healthcare services. Mary Styth went on to become Mayoress of the City of Carlisle. In 2014 the previously disgraced Chair of the Garlands was given an honorary fellowship by the University of Cumbria for what it called her lifelong and outstanding contribution to public service, education, health and social care. I'm not sure this sends out the right message to the recipients of ill-treatment and those with damaged testicles who were subjected to cruel and degrading treatment on her watch. Or the families of the neglected and abused who were left to pick up the pieces. The victims have received no such recognition or awards.

I can only hope Mary was forced to accept her award as she sat exposed, humiliated and vulnerable on a specially installed toilet situated on the stage. Writhing and muttering confusedly in a medically altered state whilst safely restrained in the clutches of a homemade wooden device. I feel a new reality TV show in the making, public sector payback. I think the ratings would be pretty good, and the format could easily be franchised.

The Kielder report as it became known, named after the ward the incidents occurred on, focused on mistreatment and poor care that happened in the 1990s. I can just imagine the face of Woodcock the aspiring chief executive, when he opened my letter at the start of 2001. Just as he thought the dust was settling, as his feet were starting to feel comfortable under the executive desk. Just as he felt they had done what they needed to demonstrate they had addressed the issues of the previous decade and move on from the past, along I came with an accusation of illegal sex acts, occurring on hospital premises in the 1980s.

He and his newly reshuffled hospital management team probably shat themselves. But then I think they quickly, coldly and calculatingly, shifted into reputation defence mode. They had just swept the decks clean and they were not going to let me the piss on their parade or their careers by raising such a trivial matter as the state sanctioned sexual abuse of the mentally ill.

There were many other things it turns out I didn't know at the time. One being that a former senior police commander happened to be on the board of the NHS Trust I was about to engage. With the benefit of hindsight this seems a clear conflict of interest, and something we as Alison's family should have been made aware of at the time. Directly or indirectly, his presence on the board is something I think would have had a significant impact on the desire of the local bobbies to really investigate what had gone on. I understand we may never be able to prove the investigation was hampered or scaled down on orders from above, my hard-earned cynicism may be doing Cumbria police a great disservice. However, I can't help thinking, such a senior police presence on the board of the NHS Trust they were supposed to be investigating would dampen the appetite of junior officers to really get their teeth into the case. Such conscientious behaviour can easily be career terminal wherever you work in the public sector, but even more so in Cumbria.

The police have not been a brand embodying honesty and openness for many years now; ask Stephen Lawrence's parents or the Hillsborough families. Knowing just how poorly the now discredited first investigation regarding the offences committed against Alison was conducted, it is difficult to ascribe every mishap to incompetence when they are more logically explained by deliberate interference.

Soon after my first meeting with Nigel Woodcock in February 2001, I was informed Alison's medical records from her time as a patient at the Garlands hospital had been destroyed under the Trusts medical records destruction policy. Just weeks earlier I had been told her records were still intact. Medical records destruction policies allowed NHS Trusts to remove and destroy records following a minimum period of eight years following the death of patients who had been in their care. If I had been thinking straight at the time, I would have asked how they even knew Alison had died. Hindsight is great, and very, very unforgiving.

Another thing I was unaware of at this point was that the person we suspected of having sex with Alison when she had been a patient, was still working at the hospital in an administrative role. They were not even suspended following the serious allegations we made, they continued to work in the hospital with full access to medical records. In the post-scandal reputationally sensitive environment the hospital was then in, it suited everyone that what happened to Alison should never come to light. In 2018 I learned from a former NHS manager that a records destruction policy was not officially implemented at Garlands until at least 2003. It appears Alison's records were singled-out for destruction in 2001.

It's easy for me to be wise now. Having spent time inside the NHS I think I understand just what their reaction to my unwelcome revelations would have been. But at the time my family and I were blissfully unaware of both the insular culture of the NHS and the unfortunate timing of our approach. All we had was a legitimate concern which we assumed they and the local police force would help us get to the bottom of. We had no idea about the reputation management measures doubtless being implemented behind the scenes. Could these measures have included the deliberate destruction of Alison's medical records? Were the junior investigating officers assigned to the case by Cumbria police told to back-off by their former senior commander, to suppress the truth and let the Trust try and rebuild its tattered reputation? We may never know the answers to these questions, but I wouldn't be surprised if our thoughts accurately reflect the reality of what was really going on.

Not to be outdone in my hunt for Alison's medical notes I contacted the records department of the City General Hospital in Carlisle. This was a separate NHS Trust to the mental health hospital and was where an abortion would have taken place. They would have their own records. I explained Alison had died and I was a family member seeking information about a pregnancy termination which occurred in the summer of 1988. Again, I was assured over the phone the file existed, and so I sent a letter on the 16th February 2001 formally requesting access.

Within days, in what I know now was an incredibly over-efficient response, I received a reply from the medical records supervisor saying Alison's records, you guessed it, had been destroyed under the Trust's destruction policy. Within a matter of weeks, I had been told by two separate NHS Trusts Alison's medical records had conveniently been destroyed. I was sent a copy of the medical records destruction policy to justify their action and reassured they were only doing what they were allowed in law to do. They protested to much. The policy was twenty pages of gobbledegook I had not asked for and which made little sense.

Policy or no policy I asked why I had been told only weeks earlier the records existed and was now being told they didn't? I never got a straight answer from either hospital. I did get a letter informing me that even if the records existed, Alison would need to request access to them herself. Something about Alison being dead had clearly got lost in translation. We were now in a strange position where all the NHS organisations involved in Alison's care in Carlisle were telling us they had destroyed her medical records. At the time I just thought they were incredibly poor at their jobs; I should have realised there was more to it.

Sarah and I had no reason to doubt what mum had told us about the sex and the abortion. But now it was starting to look like we had no information to prove any of it. We had made serious allegations without any real evidence. I was feeling almost as exposed as when Alison had whipped the towel away from me in childhood, and it was not a comfortable place to be. It was June and in the absence of any hard evidence the man we were accusing of committing illegal sex acts with Alison had still not been interviewed by the NHS Trust he was working for. The tone of the letters I was receiving from the Chief Executive had changed from earnest intent and concern to questioning the very occurrence of events.

In one letter from early June 2001 they explain in finest weasel words that they haven't yet spoken with the individual in question as it has been difficult to speculatively raise such issues. Speculatively, the word got under my skin and set me on edge. The tone of his letter still irritates me now. They were treating the serious concerns we raised as nothing but unfounded speculation. Their approach was becoming less sympathetic and increasingly obstructive, defensive and frustrating. What they appeared to be saying was that in the absence of evidence or documentation to support our accusations, they had no intention of even raising the subject with their employee. They were circling the wagons to hide sex crimes their colleague and employee had committed.

You could be forgiven for thinking we had raised a petty issue like stolen stationery or theft of a patient's slippers, rather than the illegal amoral sex acts of an NHS employee committed on a vulnerable mentally ill patient. I could not understand why they simply didn't ask the man in question whether there was any truth in our concerns. I would later be told the trainee nurse who had sex with Alison had been stopped from completing his training because concerns had been raised about how close he was getting to female patients. Why hadn't they simply looked at the records from his time as a student to see why his training had been curtailed. Again, with hindsight I see they were sitting on their hands and holding back information, hoping we would run out of steam and this messy inconvenient situation would quietly go away.

The almost amusing thing about finding out he had been stopped from completing his training, is that it was told to me with a sense of, didn't we do well, and shouldn't we be congratulated. However, in what seems accepted public sector style, he was not appropriately dealt with by any reasonable measure relative to his actions. They just moved him sideways and found him another role in the hospital. Amazingly, one that still enabled contact with patients and access to medical records. I remember thinking if they had known what he was like he should have been disciplined, dismissed and the police notified. We should also have been informed.

Moving someone who likes having sex with patients into an administrative role seems a bit like giving Peter Sutcliffe an office job to keep him off the roads and out of trouble. I would later find out to my cost, it's not harming patients that gets you hounded out the NHS, it's telling the truth.

At this point things were not looking good. I was beginning to think what happened to Alison would never be investigated and the thought of living with this injustice was utterly infuriating. I realised if any of Alison's medical records still existed, I was going to have to do the legwork to find them and so I took on the role of amateur sleuth. I started to locate and contact NHS Trusts in Doncaster where Alison had last been treated. This was a pre-internet nightmare and unfortunately, they seemed as helpful as the NHS in Cumbria. I wouldn't be at all surprised if they had been contacted by colleagues in Cumbria asking them to destroy any records they held relating to Alison.

Then I struck lucky. I contacted the GP Surgery around the corner from mum's home on St Johns Road where Alison had registered as a patient. The Surgery receptionist listened patiently if curiously to me explaining what was going on and what I was looking for. She seemed genuinely shocked and said I could come and obtain copies of whatever records they might have. I cancelled my appointments, drove to Doncaster immediately and didn't spare the horses. I was not going to let this opportunity pass me by.

And there it was. The evidence of wrongdoing the NHS themselves said they couldn't locate. Tucked between photocopies and dog-eared notes in an old file was a crisp clear copy of a pregnancy termination certificate. I think it must have been sent from Alison's GP in Carlisle as part of a larger set of notes and I don't think it had ever been looked at. The headed paper was from the Gynaecology department of the City General in Carlisle. It was dated 15th August 1988, two days after a recorded consultation with Dr T M Singh. He was the NHS Consultant Psychiatrist from the Garlands Mental Health Hospital who had been appointed to look after Alison. Curiously, Dr Singh's record of the consultation refers to a change in Alison's mood yet makes no reference to the abortion we are told he knew was about to occur within days. Had Dr Singh already started covering tracks when he wrote that note?

The copy of the pregnancy termination certificate was the cast iron evidence needed to prove what had gone on. It revealed unambiguously that what happened occurred while Alison was in the care of NHS mental health services in Carlisle. I remember just staring at the document. I had believed mum without hesitation when she first told Sarah and I what had happened, but here was documented evidence. It was real. Alison had been taken advantage of and we had been kept in the dark.

Now surely the Chief Executive of the NHS Trust in Carlisle would have to pull his finger out and deal with the serious allegations we had raised. This was no longer a speculative issue. I also thought at the time what we had found would be all the evidence Cumbria police needed to secure a successful criminal prosecution. Again, I was being far too trusting and far too logical. Perhaps the fact neither the NHS or Cumbria police had found this evidence, or as it later emerged, had attempted to find it, should have told me all I needed to know about their desire to properly investigate Alison's case.

I faxed the records I had found, including the copy of the pregnancy termination certificate to North Cumbria NHS and Cumbria police. I was precise and sent a cover note outlining the contents in numerical order. I also sent copies to the Coroner's office in Doncaster who had undertaken the original inquest into Alison's death ten years earlier. After the open verdict the Coroner recorded, I felt it was important to let them know there had been issues at play we had not known about at the time of the inquest. Issues which probably had a significant detrimental impact on Alison's state of mind and her decision to take her own life. The coroner sent me an immediate reply, thanking me for the information I had shared and agreeing with my thinking. The Chief Executive of the local NHS also thanked me for sharing the information I had sent, though it would later emerge he did not share it with Cumbria police. I rang Cumbria police to confirm its receipt, they acknowledged it but gave me nothing in writing. The significance of this would only become clear years later.

I sensed an immediate change in the tone of the letters from Nigel Woodcock. The word speculative was no longer used. I was thanked for bringing this important sensitive issue to their attention. I was offered an apology if I had been given the impression, they were not treating the matter as seriously as they should. Only now was I informed of the large amount of work they had undertaken in their efforts to obtain copies of Alison's medical records. Efforts I had curiously not been made aware of before. I was also asked to clarify how I had been able to obtain the information I had shared with them. Here was the Chief Executive of an NHS Trust asking me how I managed to obtain the same information he said they had been unable to locate. I wondered how hard they had really tried.

In a separate letter to me from the Trust in November 2001, I learned the Chair had only been receiving updates about this matter from the Chief Executive since June, after I had placed the irrefutable evidence of wrongdoing under his nose. It appears Woodcock did not think our allegations serious enough to warrant the attention of his Chairman or the board. Had he been trying to brush our concerns under the carpet hoping he would never have to raise them? Was the thought of his upcoming appointment to the permanent post of chief executive influencing his thinking about what to share with his influential peers?

If I were the Chair or member of the board, I would be livid he had not thought fit to tell me about the serious concerns we had raised five months earlier, even if only for the purpose of risk and reputation management. I remain convinced to this day, if I had not turned amateur sleuth and located Alison's medical records, effectively doing the work of Cumbria police and the NHS for them, the horrible truth about Alison's time in the Garlands would still be hidden. The guilty would never have been identified.

So, there we were. It was Autumn 2001. We had provided Cumbria police with the evidence to support what most right-minded people would see as an open and shut case. Our concerns were no longer seen as speculative, we had been vindicated. We were informed by the chief executive that the former trainee nurse had now admitted during an internal interview having sex with Alison on hospital premises, that he knew about the crisis pregnancy and was also involved in arranging the abortion. The NHS told us they were in the process of disciplining him. We were assured he would not work in a patient-facing healthcare setting in the NHS again.

The truth was finally emerging from inside the guarded walls of the Garlands, all we had to do now was wait for Cumbria police to do their thing. We waited, I chased them, no news yet. Christmas would soon be here. I kept chasing them. My calls went unanswered. Christmas came and went and still no news from Cumbria police.

At the end of January, I received a letter from the Chief Executive of the NHS Trust offering an unreserved apology for the behaviour of the employee in question. In the letter he also apologised for the totally inadequate management supervision that allowed the events to go unchecked. The Chief Executive informed me verbally the employee had resigned from the NHS, apparently on the advice of his union.

I forwarded a copy of the letter to Cumbria police thinking it would support the solid case they were doubtless busy building. It was after all a clear admission from inside the hospital that a significant wrong had occurred, and it named the person responsible. This coupled with the copy of the abortion certificate would be gold dust for the inevitable court case we were sure was about to commence. Justice for Alison was around the corner. We waited.

It is mid-March 2002 and a letter arrives from Cumbria police. The letter, signed by officer Kirkbride who holds the title of Decision Maker, is short. Too short for the issues it relates to and the disappointment it contains. It says in half a dozen lines that a person had been interviewed in connection with the offence of indecency. It goes on to say the criminal courts demand a high standard of evidence and it is considered there is no realistic prospect of conviction in this case as the evidence available does not meet that standard.

We now know Cumbria police not only applied the wrong charges, indecency was a lesser offence, but officer Kirkbride's reference to interviewing a suspect was untrue. Amazingly, the suspect was never interviewed by the police in connection with the allegations. A fact only recently admitted. They now call the lie they told me an error; this is just semantic gymnastics. More importantly, and something we did not know at the time, is the police had mysteriously mislaid all the key evidence, the information and medical records we had sent them.

Cumbria police had effectively submitted an incomplete casefile to the Crown Prosecution Service, one which excluded the most relevant information and potent evidence. The CPS were not given copies of the pregnancy termination certificate, medical notes or the letter of apology from the NHS. Cumbria police should have known, must have known, that the allegations we had made would be rejected by the CPS without evidence to support them.

In our blissful state of trusting ignorance and deference toward the institutions involved, we had no reason to suspect that people we trusted to do their jobs were letting us down or misleading us. We had been royally screwed over, and we did not even realise it.

If I had felt elated and vindicated when I found Alison's medical records months earlier, I was now the polar opposite. I rang officer Kirkbride, he said little. The call was filled with silent pauses as we each waited for the other to blink first. I politely expressed my disappointment, too politely. He revealed nothing.

I licked my wounds and wrote a letter to Cumbria police at the end of March. In it I referred to what I had thought was the cast iron evidence we had given them. I received a short reply saying the Crown Prosecution Service had made the decision not to pursue the case, and if I had any question's I should contact them. I sent the CPS a letter, they never replied. I knew very little about the CPS at the time, I didn't really know what they did. I still don't.

I spoke with my sister Sarah and mum and we reluctantly agreed to accept the vacuous apology the NHS had given us and drop our efforts to bring a prosecution against the trainee nurse. This was because we were under the impression the police had done their best, why wouldn't they. We convinced ourselves that obtaining the apology from the NHS was an adequate result.

We thought we had done all we could and now we needed to get on with our lives. I look back now on the decision we made then, a terrible decision it has taken me years to stop beating myself up about. I understand now the apology from the NHS essentially meant nothing and I wonder what we were thinking. Why did we let the NHS and police fob us off? Why did we let the CPS ignore us?

The truth is I think we still felt awkward about exercising our right to revisit the past. A perception the police were happy to fuel. Cumbria police always made us feel they were doing us a huge favour looking into Alison's case. When I first contacted them in 2001 to highlight what had happened, they had questioned my motives, making me feel small and stupid for attempting to deal with a crime that occurred over a decade earlier. They asked me why I had waited so long to bring the case to their attention. They were dismissive of my explanation that I had only recently become aware of it.

With the benefit of hindsight, I see that in 2001 the police were just not bothered about investigating allegations of historical sexual crime, especially if they occurred in the confines of an NHS hospital. They had, and still appear to have, an unwritten hands-off policy when it comes to investigating crimes committed against patients in the NHS. During the non-investigation, they maintained an aloofness and distance which did not reflect the serious sensitive nature of our allegations. Their attitude, one they have maintained to the present day, is that they thought we were wasting their precious time. I only recall meeting the officers twice, they didn't go out their way to be available or respond to queries and questions. What would emerge in 2015 is that for some reason, they had not treated Alison's case seriously at all.

Looking back, I don't think it would have mattered what evidence I uncovered in 2001. If Cumbria police were prepared to lie about interviewing the suspect, then by hook or by crook they were determined Alison's case would never make it to court. During this time, a period in which on reflection I realise I was doing the job of the NHS and Cumbria police, I had also been holding down a demanding fulltime job and studying for the final part of a Master's Degree in whatever free time I could find. We had all expended a lot of emotional energy revisiting the past. We had relived Alison's death for a second time and more harrowingly discovered the awful events leading to her suicide. The process had been emotionally costly and mentally painful.

I was also conscious I had not been the husband, friend or employee I should be. My attention had understandably often been elsewhere. My employer Carlsberg had been as accommodating as they could be, but I was under no illusion that like every salesman I was only as good as my last set of results. My wife's family and our friends had been broadly supportive of what I had been trying to do, especially when the facts of what happened finally emerged. But in truth I don't think they did or could understand the significance of what we had just gone through. If I had told the people around me, I was playing amateur detective, chasing all and sundry and driving up and down the A1 in search of medical records they would have questioned my sanity. Let the police do their job would have been their response. If only they had. If only they could be trusted to.

It's worth remembering Jimmy Saville's crimes did not come to light until 2012. Attitudes even at the start of this bright new millennium, were markedly different to the present day.

Investigating historical crimes of a sexual nature did not garner the attention or understanding they deserved. People were far less willing to even acknowledge them, let alone discuss the implications for victims and their families. In 2002 at the end of what would be the first of two investigations into the events leading to Alison's death, I remained angry at the outcome of our efforts. I could not understand or come to terms with the decision Cumbria police and the CPS had reached. But I also felt everyone around me just wanted me to put up and shut up, and I was completely knackered. It was time to paint on a happy face and look forward to the future. I had no idea this was just one leg of what would become a much longer journey. And I still had no idea how duplicitous people can be and just how fucked up the world can be. I think I do now.

Despite the assurances given by the chief executive of the NHS in Cumbria that the trainee nurse in question would never again work in a patient-facing setting, Scott-Buccleuch spent the next twenty-years as a volunteer hospital DJ at the NHS infirmary in Carlisle. For many of these years under Shirley Chipperfield, the very same head of HR who knew what he had done during his time at the Garlands. Sleeping with patients was clearly not a big deal.

It's said you should not ascribe to malice what can be explained by incompetence. But there comes a point when even ineptitude blushes. As much as I would dearly like to be proved wrong, I remain convinced Senior Executives at North Cumbria NHS and Cumbria police conspired and perverted the course of justice.

Chapter 11 – A gateway to the past

You should never meet your heroes lest you discover they have feet of clay.

Various anon

In January 2012 I went to work for one of almost everyone's heroes. I joined the National Health Service. I had been made redundant the previous autumn from a wonderful job and separated from what I can honestly say were the best bunch of people I have ever worked with. I had been working for an organisation called Business Link helping small companies and supporting people who wanted to start their own venture.

I felt I was doing something incredibly worthwhile and I excelled at being involved in something that created opportunities in Cumbria, the county I live in and place I love. In my earlier years I was one of many who looked outside Cumbria for work and education. It was enterprising individuals and employment that helped lift me from a hopeless unqualified future in bedsit land to owning my own home, not the careers service. It is evolution, enterprise and innovation that has taken humanity from sitting round the campfire disputing the spoils of the hunt to living in the relative comfort we now enjoy. Policymakers, civil servants and public sector planning departments have been bit-part players in the economic revolution catapulting mankind to where it is now.

And I know it's not rosy for everyone, capitalism as with all things is still very much a work in progress. But few would deny the life expectancy we enjoy now is a marked improvement on pre-industrial times. It is enterprise which ultimately generates the funding our public services need. Enterprise and endeavour will always be needed. I was extremely happy and up to this point satisfied and fulfilled in my work. I thought I had a career in the making.

Then austerity, or more accurately greed and banking mismanagement happened, and public funds became scarce. With the stroke of a misguided minister's pen, the Business Links were scrapped, and my career was no more. Our demise was announced in the House of Commons to applause and cheers from Tory MPs. My job along with thousands of others was cast onto a bonfire of quangos, in part so the government could fund the new fur coat it planned to parade on the international catwalk of credibility. The legacy of the London Olympics has certainly had a lasting impact on me.

After losing my job, I thought I would take some time out, kick back for a couple of months and look at my options. Debbie and I have no kids and I used the redundancy I received to settle the small amount left on the mortgage. But I had underestimated the power of habit and like a hamster running on a wheel I had become so used to working I started to suffer anxiety attacks in the absence of regular work. I picked up the local paper one day and there it was, a job working for the local NHS. The role description looked as if it had been written especially for me. The only thing I was lacking was existing experience of working in health services, which the advert said was not essential.

It's a quirk of fate I come from a family with a tradition of working in the world of health and care, pre and post the creation of the NHS. As well as a nurse, health visitor and a matron in the family, my great grandfather was a public health official in Gateshead, and I'm told his grandfather had been a bonesetter for the pit ponies and miners of the North East. For me, joining the NHS seemed like the only avenue open that provided an opportunity to exceed the satisfaction and fulfilment I had felt in my previous job. If creating wealth and a prosperous economy was important, the delivery of healthcare was vital.

I believed then, as I still do now, Ruskin's dictum that there is no wealth but life. The chance to be involved in improving health and care services in Cumbria was just too good an opportunity to miss. Surely, I thought, surely there can be no higher purpose than being involved in the provision of health? I prepared diligently for the interview, reading tome after tome of NHS documents and I sailed through. I felt privileged to have the role I had been offered. I had prepared myself and I felt my time had come. What a sucker I turned out to be. It was in my new role I discovered just how broken and dysfunctional many parts of the NHS were and still are, and in the process, I unwittingly opened a door to the past.

I was formally offered the job of Stakeholder and GP Engagement Manager with Cumbria Partnership NHS Foundation Trust on the 13th December 2011, the twentieth anniversary of Alison's death. I was welcomed into the very heart of the NHS Trust in whose care she had been abused over twenty years earlier. If I thought I had left Alison's death behind, she had no intention of letting it go.

This is the bit where I tell you getting a job inside the NHS was part of a cleverly executed plan, hatched and refined over the years, to infiltrate the organisation that wronged my sister in my unrelenting efforts to get to the bottom of what really happened. It may have been fate, the universe forcing me into a position where I would be compelled to revisit history, but it wasn't design. I'm not that smart.

My induction into the NHS was just the first of many disappointments I was about to encounter. At this point in my life I was still annoyingly optimistic, viewing setbacks as merely opportunities for improvement. I would soon reach a time in my employment with Cumbria NHS where it was simply no longer possible to hold onto this illusion. But I still remember the embarrassed face of the Chairman of the Trust as I applauded enthusiastically after his speech at the induction. I understand now that clapping is not the done thing on such occasions. Being the only person slapping their hands together like a demented seal in a room of fifty unmoved glowering people was a tumbleweed moment to cherish. I didn't care, I was so proud to have joined the British National Health Service.

The Chairman who I later worked with in my role, referred to jeeringly by directors behind his back as Captain Mainwaring, would subsequently reveal himself to be more interested in my opinion on the quality of leaflets for his recently renovated Bed and Breakfast venture than dealing with the absence of printed information for patients.

I think I understand now that when he looked strangely at me as I applauded, it was because he himself was not excited to be there. Perhaps jaded and no longer enthused to be part of this wonderful concept we call the NHS. Maybe people in such positions know the facade of togetherness and harmony is an illusion and eventually even they grow tired of hollow cheerleading.

The induction itself was a tick-box exercise. My induction into Carlsberg in 1998 lasted for about three weeks. My induction into the NHS was a bland half-day sheep-dipping, vanilla for everyone present, regardless of whether they had previous NHS experience or were being employed into patient-facing roles or administrative posts. After being introduced to someone forgettable who was the warm-up act for the Chairman, we were shown how to wash our hands, not something the son of a school matron needed. We were told who to contact in the unlikely event the press wanted to know something, which turned out to be more likely than I had ever realised. And we were reminded of the need to keep patient information secure, at that time the Trust was mislaying about one bag of patient records each month.

Finally, after enduring what I can only describe as one of the most boring men I have ever encountered presenting a set of PowerPoint slides on the importance of health and safety, finishing with a bizarre video clip from the eighties of a Christmas tree setting on fire, we were introduced to the obligatory well-rehearsed carefully chosen and highly scripted service-user. This unwitting individual was wheeled out to tell the audience their story of how well the Trust had looked after them when they needed their help. Apparently, they had been ill, and the local NHS had helped them. Not newsworthy I felt, but they seemed excited. Have you noticed that anybody who has had a truly terrible experience is never invited to speak at such events? They should be, it would be much more informative.

And where else would my induction be held than the Carleton Clinic. The renamed site of the former Garlands and scene of Alison's abuse all those years ago. As I applauded the Chair of my new employer at the beginning of 2012, I had no idea about the culture of the organisation I had joined. I had been brought up to extend trust as my default position. I thought when Alison had been taken advantage of it had been the act of one misguided individual, tolerated by a few weak and inept managers, not the inevitable product of a healthcare system that too often remains wilfully blind to the worst of itself.

I had never considered for a second so many other people in the NHS had known what the trainee nurse who took advantage of Alison was doing and chosen to say nothing. And I had not even entertained the idea people would knowingly collude to cover-up his crimes. But that was all to come. I was officially inducted into the nation's largest employer and most cherished organisation. I had a lapel badge saying, Proud of the NHS, and I was relishing the challenges to come. If I knew then what I know now.

Chapter 12 - Inside the Fortress

Expectation is the root of all heartache.

All's Well That Ends Well; Shakespeare

Jesus H Christ I thought to myself; I have only gone and joined the NHS. The N bloody H bloody S. I can't begin to tell you what this small achievement meant to me. The young man I can still remember, the one written off by his teachers, despaired of by the probation service, had worked hard and made his way from sleeping rough on park benches to securing a responsible role with the countries best loved institution.

Working in healthcare and the NHS is surely the ultimate revered employment for anyone seeking a purpose bigger than themselves. If there was a place where ethical driven able people with life experience could thrive, it had to be here. I thought my future looked fantastic.

My new boss called me the most positive optimistic person they had ever worked with. It didn't last. Within a few short tumultuous years, I would become like a suicidal battery hen, sat at a sterile workstation trapped in a tiny cubicle. I took to jamming a pencil across my mouth to mimic a smile in a vain attempt to replicate facial movements that would fool the chemicals in my brain into thinking I was happy. I would reach a point where just sitting in my work booth, a horrible bright lurid red cube clearly designed by a sadist to rob its inhabitants of calm, became an endurance test. My time in the NHS would reduce me to trying almost anything in increasingly desperate attempts to maintain my sanity.

As well as the pencil in mouth trick, I bought a book called the A-Z of Positive Thinking and another book that told me if I started each day with a recap of the things that made me happy, I could cheat the misery now shrouding me. I chewed through a box of pencils as I sat in my anger inducing booth with an inane false smile on my face.

The five years I spent inside the fortress would see me bullied, humiliated and belittled in front my peers. Deliberately and systematically drained of self-belief. A tall outwardly confident once proud man and the only male member of the team I was in, I would be reduced to sobbing openly in full view of my co-workers. I recall the day I was brought to tears in an open meeting in the main reception area as one of the lowest and loneliest points of my adult life. My employment in the NHS would ultimately take me to a point where I questioned my very place and desire to remain in the world.

The irony of ringing the Samaritans from the carpark of an NHS Mental Health Trust makes me laugh now. I wasn't laughing at the time. Crying uncontrollably in the driver's seat of my car I realised how much my emotional state had changed during my time in the NHS. Thank fuck for the Samaritans, the voluntary sector rides to the rescue again.

Despite all its protestations to the contrary, that it needs innovators, that it needs driven motivated people with private sector experience, that it needs new blood and fresh thinking, the NHS I joined was an unwelcoming place for anyone with views and an ethical backbone who wanted to make a meaningful difference.

Working for the Cumbria Partnership NHS Foundation Trust became a hell. It was the most divisive duplicitous environment I have ever been employed in. I had experienced bureaucratic office settings before, but this was a whole new ball game. When I joined the NHS, I made the mistake of thinking I was entering a slick well-oiled machine which would treat its employees well, whilst maintaining a laser like focus on the patients it is publicly funded to serve. I could not have been further from the truth. The needs of patients or the need to understand their needs are seldom discussed in senior NHS circles. The needs of patient-facing staff do not feature highly either. Analysis of the people receiving treatment for work related stress and depression reveals a disproportionately large amount of them work for the NHS.

I felt working in the NHS and being paid for by the public purse was a privilege, an opportunity I was not going to waste, and I threw myself wholeheartedly into it. Within months of being in post I was taken aside and advised to take my foot off the pedal and not move so fast. My propensity for action, for doing, for making things happen, for trying to make a difference was making others uncomfortable. I ignored the advice. Why would I sit on my hands when there was so much that needed doing and I was being paid for by the taxpayer? Since Alison's death I had never been ambitious for material wealth, but I wanted to make a small difference. I had joined the NHS thinking I would have the opportunity to do that. Not change the world, just make my part of it a little better.

The first real indication the culture of the Trust was seriously broken was its response to the results of a survey. On joining the NHS, I was told my team were to undertake an annual survey of local GPs. It was apparently one of the most important parts of our role. The Trust said it was so keen to obtain feedback from GPs, the local doctors who referred patients to its services, that the requirement to undertake an annual survey was written into my job description. The results of the first, and only survey we were ever allowed to undertake, were alarming.

The Trusts response to the survey was not to acknowledge the problems it highlighted; it was simply to change the colours on the charts to make the results look better. After seeing the results my director made it clear to me, I was not to repeat the exercise. If as the adage goes, improvement begins with understanding, I asked how we might improve services if we couldn't ask the questions that would tell us what was wrong with them? My director said he needed to make an urgent call and asked if I could shut his office door behind me as I left. I did, and once again ascended to the red rage inducing chicken-coup I occupied on the second floor, shaking my head trying to make sense of what I had just heard.

The Trust was not interested in listening if it involved any degree of challenge or change. Directors were keen to create the perception they wanted views from all sources, patients, GPs and voluntary services, but this was a deceptive hollow act designed to create the illusion of meaningful concern. The Trust had no intention of acting on what it heard.

My small team and I continued in our roles for just under three years. In that time, we had thousands of conversations, meeting and talking to hundreds of different people and organisations with an interest in local NHS services. GP Practices, Doctors and their Practice Managers, voluntary and charity bodies, patient groups, public health teams, social care staff, district councils and the various hospital Leagues of Friends who rattle buckets in town centres to support their respective community hospitals. The notebooks I kept of the meetings I had make fascinating reading.

In November 2014, a new piece of legislation came into force. It was called the Fit and Proper persons requirement and was part of something called the Health and Social Care Act. It would signal the end of the role I held. The act aimed to address the increasingly visible ineptitude and amorality in NHS management, which various ongoing scandals were so clearly highlighting. The fit and proper persons requirement for NHS directors was a well-intentioned idea which arose following the national outrage and highly publicised incidents of patient neglect and unnecessary deaths at Mid-Staffs Hospital.

Though the legislation was broadly welcomed by patient groups, healthcare regulators and the upper echelons of government, behind closed doors it was feared by the directors of many local NHS Trusts. They were concerned they might now be held accountable for failings occurring on their watch. The idea behind the act was to stop the regular swapping of underperforming directors that frequently occurred between NHS Trusts. The act meant that if a person proved themselves unfit to be a director of an NHS Trust in one part of the country, they couldn't simply move with impunity to another NHS Trust elsewhere. Just like failed directors in the private sector who are struck-off centrally at Companies House, poorly performing directors could now be deemed unfit to hold senior positions anywhere in the entire NHS.

So far so good, the act made sense. Up until this point underperforming, unscrupulous, sometimes unsafe directors had simply been tossed like the bags of excrement thrown across the roofs of Nairobi's slums to become someone else's problem. These toxic transient flying bags of expensive executive level shit were never dealt with, they just landed on other's doorsteps doing the rounds until finally disappearing in a heavy downpour of retirement with a golden handshake and a fat pension. I initially thought the fit and proper persons test was a great idea. Like most of the taxpaying public I have had enough of watching highly paid public servants being rewarded for failure and walking away from the messes they have made without any accountability.

Why should the directors of the publicly funded institutions we finance be more immune from sanctions than their counterparts in the private sector; that's lunacy. And Cumbria, hazard county, has seen more than its fair share of incompetent public sector rejects and defects promoted here to see out their days in a rural idyll where their opportunities for ineptitude are minimized and inevitable fuck ups more easily hidden. In my naïve enthusiasm for what I saw as a positive development, I completely underestimated the mendacious capacity of the NHS Trust I worked for to find a way around this new legislative hurdle in its path.

Up until this point I and my small team, now officially tiny as it consisted of only two people including myself, produced regular monthly and annual reports. These drew on feedback from meetings and contained insights taken from a broad swathe of people. The reports were a mix of the good, the not so good and all things in-between. Each month they were compiled and circulated to directors, the board, chairman and senior management teams. The reports often showed that as far as external health professionals and their patients were concerned, many of the Trusts services were underperforming. The reports consistently contained a sizeable chunk of the not so good.

Of course, it's great to know what you are doing well, I believe in praise where praise is due. But in a healthcare setting its more important to know what you are not doing well, so you can fix it, if you want to. It seems pointless telling someone the vegetables on their plate look delicious if you can see the meat is rancid.

Unfortunately for my colleague and I, the fit and proper persons requirement contained guidance about how directors should use the information they came into possession of. The act suggested that if directors were found sitting on information about unsafe situations or risks and had not acted on this information, they could be deemed unfit. Hurrah, I hear you say; seems fair. Why should directors of NHS Trusts be allowed to ignore information about risks to the safety and wellbeing of the patients in their care? This was precisely the problem at Mid-Staffs. The logic behind the act seemed undeniable, however its implementation proved highly fallible.

That October, one month before the fit and proper person requirement for NHS directors came into force, I was taken aside and informed my team was to be disbanded. In finest David Brent style, I was earnestly told there was no need for the work we had been doing anymore because the activity I had been leading was so valuable and important, it was going to be incorporated into every managers role. This is bullshit speak for, we're knocking it on the head. Anyone who has been in the world of work for more than a day knows that when something is everyone's responsibility, it becomes no-ones. I was told my colleague and I were to be absorbed in a newly structured communications team. The consultation process was to start immediately, and we were to wind up any activity we had started.

The timing was not a coincidence. Directors understood the introduction of the new act posed a risk to their friction free careers, their long-term employment prospects in the NHS and their pensions. Rather than stepping-up to the plate and dealing with the many issues we were highlighting in our reports, the Trust's directors decided it would be best to simply close the channel by which any negative information might reach them. After all, they could never be accused of sitting on information on which they had not acted, if they did not possess any. Can there be any finer example of the let's run round with our fingers in our ears I can't hear you style of management, ruining the public sector and our NHS?

I tried to share my concerns about the removal of our roles with members of the board and the chief executive, to no avail. I explained that in a large rural county like Cumbria if you had no means of listening to peoples experiences you could be making services more unsafe. If you removed the bridges, we had spent the last three years establishing you would become increasingly out of touch with the GPs who referred people into services and the patients who used them. Unfortunately, the chief exec was a product of the NHS graduate trainee scheme and thus immune to principles or logic from outside planet NHS.

It's a sobering thought many FTSE listed companies are now more open and transparent than the NHS Trusts we collectively fund to provide healthcare services. What set out as legislation to make the NHS a safer place in which to receive care, has made parts of it less safe. After the team I led was disbanded, the database of information containing the feedback, concerns and insights from the hundreds of meetings we had attended was destroyed. The Trust buried the evidence of our activity. Nothing was left to chance.

Working in the NHS in Cumbria was a rollercoaster of great expectations and dashed hopes. Initially I felt engaged, welcomed, stimulated, developed, fascinated, joyful, excited, energised and part of something genuinely fantastic. But these feelings were quickly becoming less of a reality and more a memory. The occasional blips of optimism and encouragement from people who worked in the services had kept me afloat, but my moral compass was making me less and less welcome. My naive belief in honesty, my conviction that publicly funded employment was a privilege and my wages came with responsibility, along with my desire for openness had made me persona non grata in an organisation so culturally broken it confused the ability to lie and deceive with resilience.

As the bullying ramped-up and the gap between my character and that of the people I was working for widened to a chasm, I felt my mental health deteriorating and I was increasingly kicked as I was down. I needed help. The stress and depression I experienced as a result of being bullied and asked to work in ways I couldn't agree with, was viewed as weakness. Bizarre indeed, in an NHS Trust tasked with providing care to the mentally conflicted.

To add fuel to my emotions, Voreda House the office I was based in, used to belong to Social Services. The Trusts head office was the same building in Penrith I collected a daily homeless allowance from many years ago. When I started work for the NHS in January 2012, I felt a huge sense of personal accomplishment. I watched with glee from the upper floor windows as the old courthouse across the road was demolished. I had been convicted there as a teenage tearaway and the symbolism I was finally conquering my past was tangible, I felt elated. Being in that building in a responsible role was a hard-won victory. I was replacing old painful memories with a sense of achievement. I was doing something worthwhile with my life.

However, as my honest behaviour made my presence less bearable to my new employers, they became more explicitly hostile to me. Each day became more of an endurance test. Feelings of dread, the sense of powerlessness, memories of having nothing, of being cast-adrift, came to the surface each time I entered the building. The process of claiming a daily allowance, of filling out a form each day in exchange for three pounds had been personally humiliating, as I think such things are designed to be. When I joined the NHS, I thought I had travelled a long way since my fate and future were discussed and decided by privileged panjandrums, yes men, and women who viewed the world from behind their desks with little desire to understand real life and less desire to experience it. But here I was, being humiliated again in the same building. Perhaps I hadn't come as far as I thought.

By Spring 2015 I was struggling to keep it together. The Trust had unleashed a new attack dog in the form of a smiling sadistic line manager who seemed to relish the task of bullying me. I was in what can best be described as an abusive relationship with my employer. I was covering five people's roles, I was openly undermined at every opportunity, and being asked to carry out increasingly meaningless tasks which clearly added no value to anyone.

I had nearly three decades of experience gained in multiple work settings at every level, and more qualifications than I could remember, yet I found myself being treated like a child. I was deliberately and obviously marginalised, the whispers of the pack, the willing weak, just loud enough to hear. I was demoralised. I was physically and mentally run down, and it became more than I could take. I went to see my GP and was signed off for a month with stress and depression. I needed help with my mental health and so I sought counselling from a private sector psychologist. The waiting list for NHS services was way too long.

By now my faith in the NHS Trust I was working for was shot to pieces. My confidence in myself was just as low. I felt like I was losing a game I hadn't even known I was playing against an unknown number of invisible opponents. The NHS has little time for jagged pegs shaped by experience that won't fit neatly into the holes and target chasing roles they are assigned. As the Trust tried to push me out, I sought support and called on the assistance of the Union to help me. Surely, the champions of working people would stand up for the conscientious and the principled?

In a strange yet peculiarly typical Cumbrian twist of fate, it transpired my union representative had worked at Garlands hospital when Alison was a patient in the eighties. When the issues around Alison had first been raised with the NHS in 2001, the same union, Unison, stepped in to support the trainee nurse who had sex with Alison. Needless to say, they didn't help me now I needed their support. Of course, the union said all the right things to keep me appeased. But when the rubber hit the road they stepped back and looked on as I was hounded from the NHS in the most obvious fashion. If the proof is in the eating, then my experience suggests Unison worked with management to oust me from the NHS. I think the emerging attempt I was now making to get justice for Alison was making everyone involved in the local NHS, including them, a little nervous. Hazard County strikes again.

I don't think anyone can really understand an organisation unless they have worked in it. I was eventually forced from my employment in Cumbria Partnership NHS Foundation Trust at the end of March 2017. Shortly after leaving the Trust I was sent a letter by the director of Organisational Development and Human Resources. It says:

"...Cumbria Partnership NHS Foundation Trust acknowledges you were put in an untenable position due to behaviours of directors and senior managers. The Trust fully recognises this, and we regret that this happened."

Yet I'm the guy that's out of a job?

They had sacked me on the grounds of my poor mental health under the benevolent banner of being concerned for my state of mind, now they were acknowledging their role in destroying it. It's almost funny isn't it. The NHS I had been so proud to become part of had turned on me. Not content with abusing Alison, they were now taking me to the brink of sanity as I uncovered the sins of their past.

Before I left, I was thanked by a colleague for being the best NHS manager they'd ever had. Coming from an NHS Employee it may not be the greatest endorsement, but I'll take it.

Chapter 13 - Turning over stones

Losing an illusion makes you wiser than finding a Truth.

Ludwig Borne

In January 2013, a year after I joined the NHS, a young lady called Helena Farrell tragically took her own life. Helena hung herself in woods on the outskirts of Kendal, the well-known lake-district town she and her family lived in. Helena was just fifteen. In what has sadly become an all too familiar story, this talented teenager full of promise fell with disastrous consequences into one of the many growing cracks in our fragmented health system. As a result, she had not received the help from the NHS she desperately needed and was entitled to receive.

The circumstances surrounding the death of this gifted photogenic troubled schoolgirl quickly attracted the attention of the national media. Seeing Helena's face and reading about her reminded me of Alison. Helena, like my sister, had been an academic high-achiever and was musically talented. Like Alison she suffered with an eating disorder. And because of her striking red-hair she had also been the subject of taunting by her peers.

Helena had recently experienced an unwelcome incident which precipitated the need for help with her mental health. Within the last months of her life she had overdosed, self-harmed and written several letters which after her death, the coroner observed appeared to have been suicide letters. Such insight! Following talk of taking her own life, she had been referred by a school nurse to NHS Child and Adolescent mental health services. The referral had been made almost a month before her death, but services did not meet her until the day before she died. Christmas can be such a busy time can't it? The person who eventually saw Helena decided she was not suicidal and posed no immediate risk.

It baffles me why NHS services have such long response times for dealing with young people who have openly talked about taking their own lives. Is there anything more worthy of a speedy response? When people ring the Samaritans, they are not placed on hold, patronisingly reassured their call is important, or told to call back a month later. Surely talk of suicide should be the mental health equivalent of a physical emergency requiring immediate attention. Being asked to wait a month before someone will see you is like turning up at a hospital Accident & Emergency department with a suspected life-threatening brain injury, only to be told to go home and wait, they will get back to you as soon as they can. Your suspected brain injury is important to us, you are in a queue and will be dealt with shortly, in the meantime you might want to look at our website as many queries can now be dealt with online.

In their report following the inquest into Helena's death, the coroner noted referral systems were not working adequately and staffing levels in Child and Adolescent mental health services were inadequate. Everyone working in Cumbria's healthcare services already knew this, except patients and their families. Nobody within the system was surprised the referral processes were not working or that services underperformed when they could be reached.

I was a year into my employment in the NHS and my team members and I had already spoken with many GPs as well as each of the mental health support charities operating in the county. They had all lost faith in the Child and Adolescent mental health services run by the NHS Trust we worked for. During our visits to GP Practices around the county, as well hearing countless tales of woe and worse, we had identified well over a hundred and fifty different referral forms relating to the Trusts services. GPs were unsure which one to use, where to find them, how to complete them even if they could locate them, or where to send them once they had been completed. Many were so poor the contact details and fax numbers (remember them) were often incorrect. The Trusts inconsistent approach was essentially making it harder for GPs and their patients to access the services they needed.

I shared my findings with the Trust's directors. I pointed out the obvious potential risk to the safety of patient's that poorly managed referral processes could create. Nothing was done. Getting to grips with the basics of administering a business, doesn't seem to feature highly on the radar of many managers in the NHS. They would rather focus effort on constructing meaningless reports, developing sets of values nobody asked for or launching vacuous strategies to generate publicity and keep regulators happy. Anything other than improving the processes that enable patients to access services. It's no surprise a great many people working in management and administrative roles in the NHS have never worked, a term I use very loosely, in any other environment. They wouldn't last five minutes anywhere else.

The coroner at Helena's inquest identified numerous blindingly obvious shortcomings and then made a series of recommendations to the local NHS and County Council who ran school nursing services. The question the coroner did not ask, a question few coroners seem to ask before dispensing their platitudes, is why? Coroners may say this is not within their remit, they would argue their role is only to establish the cause of death. But if coroners are going to make recommendations, they should be apprised of all the facts. They should seek to understand the forces conspiring which shape and influence the events they are looking into. If they don't understand the context against which their recommendations are being made, they are pissing in the wind.

It seems strange to me that when a Coroner makes recommendations, there is seldom any follow-up and they are often not apprised of any actions taken to implement the recommendations made.

It seems that the way many coroners work is like establishing that a car has crashed without understanding why. Knowing death was caused by the crash is fine but often glaringly obvious. Knowing the crash occurred because the brakes failed is a step forward. But if you are going to make meaningful recommendations and add real value to the debate, you need to establish why the brakes failed. By not adopting a wider approach and asking the NHS why the systems it was supposed to have in place had not worked, the coroner was letting them off the hook. Allowing them, in time-honoured public sector tradition, to waffle their way out of any accountability or responsibility for what had happened.

The coroner conducting the inquest into Helena's death was the same coroner who led the inquest into my childhood best friend Johnny's death the previous June. It alarms me that the coroner did not think to join the dots. These revealed clearly, unambiguously, that the shadow of the same culturally broken NHS Trust was hovering behind both these horrific avoidable tragedies.

What the coroner was not told was the extent to which services were understaffed and unsafe. There were simply not enough clinicians to provide safe levels of care; and the Trust knew it. This was in no small part because directors in NHS Trusts nationwide had been given direction from the government and their regulators to prioritize the building of cash reserves over the provision of safe services. When I joined Cumbria Partnership NHS Foundation Trust in 2012 it was sat on tens of millions of pounds yet providing some of the worst mental health services available.

The governments ill-informed drive to encourage NHS Trusts to behave like businesses, an idea akin to asking your granny to train for a decathlon, meant that diverting funds coming from unsuspecting taxpayers to build a money pile at the bank, became more important than spending it on patients. It also produced a new and uniquely strange mutated breed of arrogant and amoral management. People with no private sector experience were all of a sudden convinced they had not only been tasked with running large real life corporations, engaged in the cut and thrust of commercial markets, but with the cocksure arrogance of the ignorant, were also sure they knew how to do it.

I have met too many NHS directors and senior managers who in their obsession with developing plans of activity at the expense of real achievement, are convinced they are vintage entrepreneurial champagne in cut crystal glasses. The aftertaste of their track-records and trails of destruction suggests more warm flat complacent lager from thin plastic cups. I would go so far as to say some are deluded; unemployable in any setting where impact would be valued over the creation of fruitless plans and endless grand strategies that hover and disappoint like empty rainclouds over a desert.

If there is a list of government initiatives with obvious unintended and catastrophically negative consequences which could easily have been foreseen, the setting up of NHS Trusts to mimic competing businesses must rank in the all-time top three. Asking the most lumbering lethargic institutionalised hierarchical organisations in the public sector, administered and managed by the most cosseted, to think and act like innovative commercial companies, was never going to end well. Paying for NHS managers to get commercial management qualifications is like equipping people who work in a smelting shop with tools of ice. It was said many years ago, culture will eat strategy for breakfast. In the case of the NHS the strategy didn't even make it to the table.

I have been at senior NHS team meetings where managers decided not to advertise and fill vacant nursing posts because the cost of the salaries would take them over their budget. Despite all the talk of values, of patient centred strategies and cultures, the needs of patients and their families did not feature in these decisions or the conversations leading to them. Many NHS Trusts, in their attempts to behave like commercial businesses and obtain hallowed status as something called a Foundation Trust, deliberately withheld resources from the frontline where they were needed, simply so their reserves could remain at an artificial level to please the regulator.

Alarmingly, the Trust I was working for was building up its reserves with absolutely no idea of how it was going to spend them. Amongst the very many mistakes I made in the NHS, one was asking the director of strategy for a copy of, you guessed it, the business strategy. There wasn't one. Like a spoilt kid who cannot eat anymore but hides all the sweets to stop anyone else having them, the Trust was sat on a pile of cash with no idea how it would use it.

I see now the fundamental mistake I made upon joining the NHS was forgetting to park my morals at the door and place my balls in the jar provided. Employees are not supposed to question, challenge or query. Rather than tell directors that their services were dangerously under-staffed, managers said nothing because they were afraid of going over budget. They just wanted glowing annual appraisals and promotion through the ranks.

The true cost of not filling vacant clinical posts was brought horrifically to light in Helena's case. Unfortunately, the practice of deliberately running services below capacity to enable budgets to be met, was and still is widespread. I would be the first to acknowledge recruiting and retaining healthcare staff for any profession anywhere in the UK is an uphill challenge. But I would add in my experience some try harder than others and many NHS Trusts only have themselves to blame for becoming unattractive employment options.

What I and the small team I headed up were hearing did not make comfortable listening. The picture being painted was not a pretty one and should have been a much greater cause of concern for the board, directors and chief executive of the Trust. But they seemed more preoccupied in point-scoring and spying on each other to secure their own roles than in using the feedback we were giving to improve services to patients. My own director was one of three who asked me to spy on my senior colleagues and his fellow directors, each saying the other could not be trusted. Of course, my wannabee spymaster's surname was Smillie; what else would it be? My refusal to be one of his people was another nail in the coffin of my NHS career.

Watching the response of the Trust unfold around me following Helena's death, was eye-opening and disturbing. During the period of the inquest which ran until summer the following year, I was involved in many conversations about what was happening and what the Trust was planning to do. It became abundantly clear to me during this time that senior executives and managers in the Trust did not regard what happened as a personal tragedy for Helena, her family and friends. They viewed what happened only as a reputational risk to the organisation and themselves. The communications and public relations machine lurched clumsily into life to ensure the Trust managed its responses to an interested national press and avoided any adverse publicity. Staff were briefed on how to respond to anyone who asked questions and were told to direct any queries at the communications department.

The Trust worked hard to ensure anyone who might be deemed off message could not be accessed by the press. A report from the previous October which highlighted serious concerns about the quality of Child and Adolescent Mental Health Services was closely guarded. This report specifically referred to a lack of connection between services and culturally inward-looking teams who were rudderless, understaffed and lacked leadership.

To the best of my knowledge this report, an extremely revealing document paid for from the public purse, was not made available to the coroner or anyone else involved in Helena's inquest. In amongst all the reputational management activity which seemed to be animating the executive floor, I didn't hear anyone talking about the needs of the family. The head of our department would tell me of the Sunday afternoon phone calls they had fielded from the chief executive asking if everything was in-hand. Reputation was everything. The truth, if different to the required message, was simply an inconvenience to be managed.

It was around this time, I started to wonder what I had got myself into. I think I knew but didn't want to believe it. The behaviour I was watching, agreeing, unchallenging, obsequious and sycophantic, all in the face of a growing evidence base showing the Trusts services were unsafe, did not sit comfortably with me. I thought a lot about Alison and started to join the dots in my head. I figured if the NHS Trust was so quick to hide its problems and put its own reputational interests ahead of the people in its care, then I wondered if my family and I had fallen victim to these same tactics when we sought the truth about Alison in 2001.

I realised our situation would not have been viewed as a personal tragedy worthy of justice but managed as a reputational threat to the Trust and its directors. We had not been viewed as a grieving family seeking the truth, but a line of text to be entered on a risk register. I've never been the sharpest knife in the drawer, but the penny was slowly dropping. What if the people involved in Alison's mistreatment had been protected by the same defensive management culture? After all, it would explain why the trainee nurse in question had never been prosecuted for what he admitted doing. This conundrum had troubled me for many years.

Have you noticed following events like Helena's death, every public body, be it the NHS, police force, CPS or a council, say lessons have been learned? Words are cheap.

The seeds of my dissatisfaction with the way the NHS in Cumbria was being managed were taking root. There is something deeply disturbing about watching well-paid publicly funded servants focus all their effort on creating an illusion of concern in the wake of a young person's death. But at this point in time I still had optimism. I was clinging to a belief that the NHS and its purpose was bigger than a few duplicitous people and their petty politics. I still thought there was a chance to influence it for the better from within.

Chapter 14 – Should we do this, again?

The present is the past rolled up for action, and the past is the present unrolled for reasoning.

Ariel Durant

What is justice? What is its pursuit worth? How long should we hold people accountable for the unanswered crimes they have committed and does justice have a best before date? How many of us are placed in a position where we must answer these questions for ourselves? Where we are stripped of the luxury of holding onto an ideology we will never stress-test, a soundbite, an unproven theory to lazily fall-back on as we vicariously pontificate over other's tragedies, glass of wine in hand.

It is late Spring 2015, and I am sat in the consulting room of a private psychologist on the outskirts of Penrith. I have been driven to needing help with my mind by the NHS Mental Health Trust I work for. A well-presented woman in her fifties welcomes me in a friendly firm fashion. She exudes warmth yet manages to maintain a confident no nonsense air. The surroundings are orderly, functional and well-appointed, not ostentatious, I feel comfortable.

Unlike patients of many NHS mental health services, I am not left sitting in an open waiting room as I am viewed suspiciously by fellow patients or reception staff still struggling to recognise and break free from their own prejudice. Talk of removing the stigma of mental health remains just that, even in parts of the NHS. I have experienced the joys of using NHS mental health services. Waiting to see a counsellor while sat next to someone agitated and distressed is all the reason most people need to force them to seek private help or not bother at all. Services for the mind are the poor relation in our NHS. Having tried to access help from mental health services run by the NHS Trust I was working for I had initially been disappointed to find the waiting lists too long. Hindsight suggests they did me a favour.

Having reached the point where I could no longer deny I needed help, even if that meant paying for it, I parked my socialist principles and put my hand in my pocket. I was now heading into the eye of my own mental health storm. Work was being made unbearable on many fronts and doubts about how my family had been dealt with in relation to Alison were growing.

Strangely, or perhaps not, after years and years of blocking out what happened to Alison, I had started to dream about the moment of her passing. Of the physical impact of the train, the point of death and the injuries to her face and body. I had never discussed her death in depth with anyone. I thought I had done a good job at wrapping up these dark images and thoughts in the loft space of my mind to be hidden forever. But now horrific images were leaping without notice across my consciousness and I was struggling to sleep. I had started worrying that harmful indescribable things were about to happen to the people I love. The evening stroll to maintain my wellbeing, a walk which takes me under a bridge carrying the West Coast railway was becoming an ordeal. I was in a dark place and sinking further.

We made our introductions and I recall running through some basic breathing routines. Then I started to speak. I could immediately feel a sense of selfish relief that came with unburdening my mind on someone who listened without judgement. I talked like a novice firing a machine gun for the first time, indulgently, rapidly, spraying thoughts everywhere, messily, unstructured and unstoppable. My allocated appointment time was over before I knew it and I booked myself in for the following session. The advice I was to be given when we next met would send me down a path, I thought I would never tread again. We had started talking about the clash of values I had been feeling at work. My own values are important to me. I take myself to work, my whole self. Life is way too short and precious to spend it pretending to be someone else. I think too many people confuse sociopathy with professionalism.

I told the psychologist what happened to Alison and then feeling quite foolish I hesitatingly, almost apologetically, shared what I thought were irrelevant concerns about the lack of justice we experienced. How it still troubled me, how I couldn't understand why nobody had ever been held accountable for what we knew had gone on. I explained how stupid I felt having these concerns. I told her I hadn't shared them with anyone else. The people close to me seemed worried enough about the declining state of my mind without me airing doubts about the quality of an investigation that happened nearly fifteen years ago.

She listened and homed in quickly on what I was saying. She asked a simple question. Could I live with myself if I didn't try to find out what had really happened to Alison and understand why no-one had been held to account?

What you need to do becomes so obvious when you hear it from someone else. I realised at this point that whatever the journey I was about to embark on might hold, the alternative, sitting on my arse doing nothing, was not an option. If I didn't explore all the available avenues and try to reach the truth about what happened, why nobody had been held accountable for what they did to my sister, I would live and die with this regret hanging over me. I was not my father; I wouldn't put my head in the sand in the face of conflict. Who wants to live life in the knowledge they never really tried their best for their own?

My wife's family had shown me the importance of loyalty, sometimes flawed but always there. I would take my responsibilities as Alison's brother seriously. But I still felt incredibly self-conscious and stupid. How was I going to broach this with Debbie, my sister Sarah and my mum? How do you tell the people who care about you that you are about to reopen a Pandoras box of painful memories, when you are already clearly struggling to cope under the weight of depression? How do you explain that you think part of the solution to your current situation is to dig up the hurts of the past so you can inspect and try to understand them? To those around you it can look like self-indulgent self-destructive behaviour. Navel gazing while smacking yourself around the head with something blunt. It's not an easy sell.

After sharing the course of action, I was determined to embark on with my family and close friends, to what could best be called a mixed reaction, the biggest mental hurdle I faced turned out to be contacting Cumbria police. I recalled how dismissive they had been when I first spoke to them in 2001 about what we thought had happened in 1988. What was I going to say to them now, fifteen years on from the first investigation and nearly thirty years after the events in question? Surely, they would be even less pre-disposed to act this time. But sometimes doing the thing you don't want to do is easier than you thought it would be.

In August 2015 I plucked up the courage to contact Cumbria police and asked if they could locate any records relating to an old case, they investigated in 2001. I gave them the details and waited for a response. They got back to me a few weeks later. A file had been located at a storage facility in the north of the county, they would look at it and come back to me. I waited for over three months and eventually received an email from an inspector who said he would like to come and see me in person. I bet he still wishes he hadn't.

In late November 2015, Detective Chief Inspector David Pattinson and a colleague from Cumbria police came to see me. I welcomed them to my home and made the obligatory teas and coffees. Though quietly determined I still felt stupid, as if I may be wasting their time. I thanked them for coming to hear my concerns, misgivings I explained I was still unsure of myself. We sat in the comfy chairs in the small conservatory at the back of our house. They had brought the file relating to Alison's case. I was prepared and had my file on hand. The officers listened patiently to me outlining what had been going on in my life that had led me to this point where I needed answers from the past. I told them again I was grateful for their attention to this matter and then attempted, poorly, to give a concise overview of the doubts I had about the outcome of their original investigation in 2001.

They appeared attentive. Then in measured balanced and meticulously rehearsed tones, the lead detective assured me he understood my concerns. He told me there was nothing to worry about; generally, a sure indicator there is lots to worry about. He said that in relation to Alison's case they were sure the original investigation of 2001 had been of a good quality. In an effort to close the deal quickly he then went on to vouch for the character of the officers who had undertaken it, offering his own personal seal of approval to their efforts and their wider conduct and character as fellow police officers and former colleagues.

We talked casually about the surprising decision the CPS had reached not to take the case to court and I wondered if he could shed any light on this. He couldn't, and he then added that in his opinion there was nothing to be gained from revisiting the investigation. His advice to me was to let it go, to move on and stop torturing myself. I could rest comfortably in the knowledge Cumbria police had done their best, for Alison, for us.

Move on, move on, don't look back to the past. Like a blinkered racehorse just keep surging forward, your eyes focused on the elusive horizon of the future. It's the message offered to us all from a still growing plethora of half-arsed books, motivational training coaches, gurus of positive thinking as they prop-up their tyranny of relentless and thoughtless positivity. Our leaders and politicians don't want us to look back, understand and learn from history, or take time to inspect the mistakes of the past too closely. The world seems to want us all to just keep running forward, faster and faster in an unthinking sprint to some point in the future in which we will all be happy, fulfilled and content.

Yet whilst we all know humanity demonstrates an almost infinite capacity to repeat the mistakes of its past, it still seems unfashionable to look backwards. Whether riding high on the shoulders of giants or struggling under the yoke of oppression, physical or mental, we are where we are because of the decisions and actions of yesterday. I am increasingly convinced that understanding the past is key to interpreting the present and shaping the future. I have become wary of people who tell you there is no benefit in looking backwards, there is often a reason why they would prefer you not to do so.

I commented that the folder containing the file the detectives had brought seemed very thin and asked if I could see what was in it. I could not. They said it would contravene data-protection legislation as there would be information about individuals in the file. I said I understood and offered to play a game of evidence top trumps. I suggested that if I produced a document from the records already in my possession, they could then simply confirm or deny whether it was in their file. This would mean they were not sharing knowledge from documentation I did not already have and it would allow me to ascertain if the information I had given the police in 2001 was in their file, without the need for me to see it in person. He agreed.

I started high. The first document I pulled out was the ace card. A copy of the pregnancy termination certificate confirming Alison had an abortion when she was a patient of NHS mental health services in Carlisle. He looked surprised, shifting in his seat and shuffling awkwardly through the thin set of papers from the blue card folder on his lap. He replied in a stuttering defensive tone that it appeared this particular document wasn't in their file. His colleague exchanged glances, obvious, unsubtle, alarmed. One at a time I then produced the remainder of the thirty documents I had retained in my possession, holding each aloft in the air with my left hand so he could see them, and calling their title out so he could check them against the content of his file.

There was a copy of a letter from this person, a copy of a letter from another, evidence statements from family members, further medical records from Alison's GP in Doncaster, copies of faxes sent to the police, and crucial correspondence from the former Chief Executive of the NHS Trust Nigel Woodcock and its Head of HR Shirley Chipperfield. The list went on. Not one of the documents I produced was in their case file. By now the detectives had stopped looking at each other, the confidence they entered my home with had melted, turning to embarrassment in front my eyes. I had welcomed them into our house, they had come to my private cherished space and attempted to mislead me, to placate me with sweeping assurances and Arthur Daley style endorsements of their former colleagues. The penny was dropping on each of us in the room. They had come here to bullshit me, and now they knew I knew. They had been found out.

The letter I received from the CPS early in 2002 telling me they would not be pursuing the case because they did not feel there was enough evidence to support a conviction, now made sense. All the damning evidence I had gathered and given to Cumbria police in 2001 had not found its way into the case file and therefore never made its way onto the desks of decision makers in the CPS. I was shaking, part disbelief, part anger. I sat up from the comfy chair I was leaning back in. Steadying my voice, I asked the detectives who were sat in my home if they still felt the investigation, they had so unambiguously defended half an hour earlier was of a good quality? I was almost embarrassed for them. There was a shaking of heads and low grunts of acknowledgement.

Slowly starting to stand and make their exit, they explained that they needed to re-evaluate the situation and would get back in touch. Just how poor the original investigation had been would soon emerge; the detectives who came to see me already knew. These crisp shirted public servants who oozed empathy and understanding were aware their former colleagues, the same ones they personally vouched for, had not even created a basic investigation plan. Their own records showed this. The sense I had not been taken seriously in 2001 turned out to be nearer the mark than I could ever have imagined. I showed them out. As they left, they offered me warm sincere assurances that they would look further into the original investigation at the earliest opportunity. Even this turned out to be a lie.

After sharing my evidence with the detectives and thinking their parting comments had been made sincerely, I expected to hear from them almost immediately. I didn't and stupidly I was surprised. I had shown them documents which clearly suggested the passage of justice had been denied. Surely, they would be keen to progress the matter. After months of chasing the detectives who came to see me, I was informed over the phone they would not be taking any further action. I was told the only way Cumbria police would consider reopening an investigation would be if they found the quality of the first investigation to be sub-standard. In turn, to do this, they would firstly need to conduct an internal review. I was then informed that an internal review of the first investigation would not commence unless I raised a formal complaint about it. To further compound my frustration and presumably discourage me from doing anything, I was told that because my complaint related to incidents which occurred over a year ago, the police had the right to disapply my complaint, this being official polite police speak for ignore, unless I could provide compelling evidence to the contrary.

Cumbria police had swiftly and unashamedly changed their face from friendly responsive approachability to high-handed officialdom. They had embarrassed themselves and it seems they were now erecting every barrier possible to avoid reopening the investigation into the events leading to Alison's death. I think this was deliberate. They knew what they would be forced to acknowledge would not show them in a good light. Rather than put their hands in the air, admit their mistakes and take the opportunity to right a wrong from the past, they did what most public sector organisations do; they tried to bury it. I had shown them, their own records and the absence of them had clearly revealed, that they failed to investigate Alison's case properly, if at all. Yet here they were, placing the onus on me to force them to address their own shortcomings.

I had no other option but to jump through their hoops and duly submitted my complaint to Cumbria police in January 2016. They disappointedly if predictably attempted to exercise their right to disapply it, to ignore it. There was however a right of appeal which could succeed if I was able to provide compelling evidence to support it. I constructed my response and copied all the letters and records I could find, delivering it to police headquarters by hand, taking time stamped photos as I arrived and left. Now they were in physical possession of copies of all the key documents I possessed, which not only made it clear a significant wrong had been committed in 1988, they also highlighted the absence of these same documents from their own records.

The content I shared with them could not be ignored. In March 2016, the police were begrudgingly forced to acknowledge my complaint and an internal review of the original investigation they had undertaken in 2001 was launched. I was promised a copy of the final report once the review was completed. I was still a long way off getting an investigation reopened but the launching of the review was a vital first step. If this showed the first investigation to have been sub-standard, Cumbria police would have to consider reopening a second investigation into the events at Garlands hospital. There was of course a risk they would falsify the internal review and hide the shortcomings of the first investigation to avoid reopening a new external investigation.

We had nothing to worry about. Though Cumbria police attempted to hide their incompetence behind a wall of public sector double speak, the utter ineptitude of the officers who undertook the original investigation was too great to be hidden, it shone through. The findings of the internal review were so bad that despite their original promise to provide me with a copy of the report, I was denied access to it. It took two years of trying and a formal instruction from the Information Commissioners Office for Cumbria police to finally provide a copy. Though I was annoyed they tried to withhold it from me, I can see why they and the CPS did not want me to get my hands on it. The first investigation had quite simply been a complete, and utter shambles. It did not pass any official definition of what constitutes an investigation.

The revelations of poor practice and sloppy policing contained in the internal report were such, that Cumbria police's professional standards department were forced to apologise. They admitted in writing the investigation had been flawed and acknowledged they had let us down. A far cry from a good quality investigation conducted by two upstanding officers. The internal report revealed what I had been sold as a solid investigation by the snakes in suits I had welcomed into my home, was in truth no more than a series of cosy chats and cups of tea between Cumbria police officers and staff and executives of the NHS in Carlisle.

It emerged the police had not even interviewed the suspect, then having mysteriously mislaid the evidence I gave them, proceeded to hand an incomplete file to the CPS. NHS executives had also failed to share key information they were in possession of with Cumbria police, and police officers in turn did not actively seek records from any organisation involved in Alison's care. Even an optimist would be tempted to say they had put their heads together and made sure the whole affair was brushed under the carpet. In June 2016, under the glaring light of their own incompetence, Cumbria police were forced to reopen a second external investigation into the events leading to Alison's death. I had stuck to my guns, navigated the lies and misdirection and jumped every hurdle they had put in my path.

If I had not kept all the documents in my possession, quite how badly we had been failed by Cumbria police would never have come to light. These documents were the compelling evidence needed to make them acknowledge my complaint and forced them to launch the internal review which ultimately reopened the investigation. I have lost count of the number of times I considered throwing out the old files relating to Alison's case. They had been sitting in the corner of the loft in a disorganised pile for fifteen years. During that time, I have had countless clear-outs, I don't know what kept me from shredding and disposing of them.

One of the most telling pieces of information the internal review into the first investigation revealed, was a handwritten entry placed in the flimsy case notes the police filed at the time. Written by one of the investigating officers, it reads; *there are family members who can testify to a relationship between Alison and the suspect, but I don't think that fact is in dispute. Mr Bell would like you to consider whether or not the Garlands establishment ought to be investigated as opposed to just the suspect. If so a large amount of work would need to be done.*

I wondered how many times serious cases had not been pursued by police officers because they might involve a large amount of work. How many other cases had the officers who mishandled Alison's case fudged, fucked-up or dismissed as unworthy of their time? How many times had they decided who mattered and which laws should be upheld? And how many other families of the victims of serious crime had been placated over the years, assured they had been well-served, but in reality, let down by lazy policing and indifference?

The growing misgivings I had about the quality of the police investigation in 2001 and the potentially collusive role the NHS had played were being proved right. Family and friends no longer thought I was barking mad. They were starting to share my sense of disbelief at how casually an investigation into the events leading to a young woman's death had been handled.

I felt vindicated. At last, the facts could come out. The stage was set, the police and Crown Prosecution Service were now in possession of the evidence they needed. Surely this time we would get the justice we and Alison deserved.

Chapter 15 - Surely this time!

There is no scandal so serious that trying to cover it up won't make it worse.

Anon

My family and I were about to start living Alison's death for the third time. We had buried her in December 1991, we had reopened her grave in 2001 and now it seemed we were prizing the lid off her coffin again. But we felt that success, a word which feels strangely inappropriate, the truth, accountability and justice we needed, and that we could almost see emerging over the horizon, would be worth it.

Truth, accountability and justice. TAJ, as in Taj Mahal, the global icon of enduring love, beauty and constancy, seemed an appropriate acronym to sum up the objectives we were setting ourselves. We realised truth would have to emerge before accountability and justice could follow. We knew we may not get everything we wanted but we at least wanted the truth. We felt we all deserved that. Whatever happened after the truth surfaced would be in the hands of the police and the CPS.

Our task was never vengeance. We were clear from the start that should the perpetrator be found guilty we would like the option of applying restorative justice. We thought the use of this, a process in which we could physically face and tell him of the damage he had done and the impact his actions had on Alison and we her family, would give us the nearest thing to that elusive beast closure we could hope to get. His crimes had far-reaching consequences and it was important to us he was made fully aware of them.

Restorative justice would enable him to avoid a custodial sentence and continue life as a father and grandfather. If, during the new investigation it emerged he had committed other related crimes, then restorative justice would not be appropriate, and decisions would be taken out of our hands. And yes, there have been many times I have dreamed of kicking him in the balls, hard, repeatedly, and worse. His acts afford him status beyond my fictional dark alley list. But tempting as it is and though he may have treated Alison like an expendable rag, justice by Doctor Marten is no prescription for a sustainable civilized society.

Once more we had to place our faith in Cumbria police, what choice did we have. Make no mistake, if we could have chosen another police force to conduct the investigation it would have been any other. However, we committed ourselves to working with the officers assigned to the case and Sarah and I agreed to maintain regular contact and keep a close eye on things. This time we would endeavour to ensure they left no stone unturned.

The first sign we might be heading into another fine mess, other than the names of the officers tasked with leading the investigation being Lauren and Marty, was a refusal by the police to broaden the scope of the investigation. I felt very strongly if Cumbria police were going to do the job properly this time, that any new investigation needed to look at the behaviour of NHS managers and supervisors who allowed the events of 1988 to unfold as well as the individual who committed the acts.

To us it did not make sense to view what happened as the isolated acts of a single person. His crimes were committed under the noses of and with the knowledge of managers and peers. Though I have always felt he was entirely responsible for his own actions, I have also always thought those who looked on, who condoned and colluded as he broke the law and destroyed Alison's mind, are as culpable. Especially if not even more so the psychiatrist who was tasked with her care and recovery.

The fact an unqualified trainee was so freely and brazenly allowed to break the law and flout hospital policies was a stain on those responsible for training staff. And an even greater blemish on those tasked with safeguarding vulnerable patients in the hospitals care.

Cumbria police disagreed. They heard our protestations and appeased us by saying they would initially focus their efforts on the trainee nurse. Then, having got him to court they could start uncovering the role others had played. Foolishly we bought it. They say you live and learn. In relation to who I trust I seem to learn at a slower pace than most. I don't think Cumbria police ever had any intention of looking further than the nurse in question. And I'm not sure they even wanted to do that. I think the passage of time will clearly show they did all they could to avoid the messy inconvenience of lifting a lid on the serious issues occurring in the Garlands Mental Health Hospital at the time.

The second signal we may be getting lost in bureaucracy were the multiple points of contact we were given within Cumbria police. None of whom seemed able or willing to respond to simple queries and questions. I can now see that despite our efforts to keep close to the officers and the investigation itself, history was being repeated. Once more we were being kept at a deliberate distance. The police have a great knack of making the mundane seem mysterious and have mastered the art of reporting on the nothing they are doing.

In response to requests for information and updates we received bland meaningless responses. They would say they were collating records, verifying this or that, or waiting for a bit of information from an unspecified source. Emails were awash with phrases like;

"I can assure you the matter is being given the attention it should", or

"files are being reviewed for quality purposes", and the best one,

"third party records from partnership agencies are still being collated."

I have it on good authority from the one former senior detective I trust, such phrases are generally bullshit speak for sitting on your arse or doing something else. If it takes a week to make a sandwich in the public sector the police are the organisation driving the average up. They were incredibly and inordinately slow in everything they did. Unfortunately, their slow pace did not equate to rigour.

It took months to even agree a date on which they would take our impact statements. We kept up our constant queries and requests for updates, occasionally we would get a snippet of information. They dressed up inaction as thoroughness and always blamed other organisations for delays in making any progress. Sometimes they were just plain old unavailable, attending a seemingly never-ending stream of training courses which took them out of circulation.

It was nearly Christmas 2016 before the police met the CPS to show them the evidence they had and assess the merits of moving the case forward. In truth I don't think they obtained anymore evidence than the documents I gave them, the same ones they "mislaid" in 2001.

Finally, after what was beginning to feel like an eternity, on the 16th of February 2017, eighteen months after I had raised the matter, Cumbria police sent an email confirming they had arrested a man in relation to the investigation. Almost thirty years after committing his crimes, the nurse who abused his position of trust finally admitted to Cumbria police he had sex on numerous occasions on hospital premises with Alison.

To say my sister Sarah and I were utterly elated would be understatement in the extreme. I can't begin to think of ways to accurately convey to you how I felt. I was utterly overrun with endorphins. I imagine it must be somewhere between a huge lottery win, great sex, smoking a good spliff, cycling up a fell on a beautiful day, bungee jumping, watching Joe Strummers trademark guitar throw, preferably at Glastonbury, the greatest tastiest curry ever, cold beer, Leeds winning the premiership, unlikely, England winning the world cup, less likely, bossing an exam, crossing an ocean and seeing a tiger in the wild.

Vindicated is simply not a powerful enough word to express my emotions. I felt I had completed a journey, a quest from hell and back. I had fought and overcome the odds and was about to prevail. If injustice was the foe I was fighting, I had wrestled it to the ground and was standing over it resplendent, looking it in the eyes and savouring the moment as I decided where to place the last decisive blow.

This was it, the start of the outcome we had dreamed of, an outcome we had never been able to understand being denied. All the frustration and hurts of the past didn't matter anymore. I thought about the lies I had been peddled. The incompetence of Cumbria police. The shortcomings of the CPS. The slithering NHS Executives whose honeyed words concealed the cunning mendacity they applied to ensure their reputations and careers remained intact. I thought of how this course of action was costing my career, and none of it seemed to matter. We had reached what I thought was an invincible position, our quest for justice was now unstoppable.

Yes, yes, fucking yes, I leapt up and down, punching the air and screaming at the heavens. Fucking yes, yes, yes, we've only gone and fucking done it. A man had been arrested; he had actually been arrested. The trainee nurse who used his position of trust to take advantage of my sister when she was at her lowest, her most vulnerable, had finally been arrested. How long I had waited to read or hear those words. The selfish bastard had got away with his crimes for long enough. We had suffered Alison's loss for nearly thirty years, now it was his turn, his turn to be made to understand and answer for what he had done. To be held accountable in the eyes of the law for the wrongs he had inflicted on my family. I collected myself, I could barely contain the sense of triumph and optimism I felt.

A lot of water had passed under many bridges, an ocean of tears, anger and loneliness had preceded this moment. I couldn't believe we had finally reached this point. I gathered my thoughts and started to ring and email people. I notified the journalists I had become acquainted with to let them have the latest update. I wanted the acts committed in secret behind the darkly cosseted walls of a dysfunctional mental health institution made as public as possible as quickly as possible. I wanted the world to know I had been right. I don't recall posting onto Facebook and Twitter, but I probably did.

The police had concluded their investigation and presented a file to the CPS. We were now in the hands of the Crown Prosecution Service. They would apply something called a two-stage test and inform us of their decision at the earliest opportunity. The two stage-test is the simple if imperfect guidance the CPS apply to all cases. The test consists of two relatively straightforward questions designed to establish if cases are appropriate for prosecution.

The first question is, what is the evidence to support this? Prosecutors must establish the credibility of available evidence and be satisfied it provides a realistic prospect of conviction. If a case fails to pass this first stage, it is usually deemed unsuitable for prosecution. This seems logical, why waste tax-payers money pursuing cases that won't stand up in court. It also allows the CPS to go back to the police and advise them on what they need to do for a case to move forward.

The second question, which is generally only applied after a case has passed the first stage is, is it in the public interest to bring this case to court? The second part of the two-stage test as outlined on the CPS website says if the first question can be answered satisfactorily and the evidence stage is passed, the case will pass to prosecution unless the public interest factors against prosecution outweigh those in favour. In normal speak, once a case passes the evidence test it will be prosecuted unless there is a bloody good reason not to.

We were aware of the two-stage test; and had no fears about the outcome. We knew by now the man in question had admitted what he had done, and even if he changed his story now, to deny the evidence we possessed would make him look a fool and a liar. As for the second stage-test the CPS would apply, we were sure this was a formality. I was convinced our case would be welcomed through the second stage of the test like a conquering hero through the city gates, showered with rose pedals as it rode a sedan chair on its unstoppable path to court. This was an open goal for the CPS, a gift-wrapped prosecution.

The evidence was watertight. The police had obtained a formal statement and would later tell us he had admitted committing his crimes with Alison on multiple occasions. The case also seemed to provide a golden opportunity for the police and CPS to gain political capital by showing they were serious about dealing with historical sex crimes. The message they seem keen to spread and have been repeating for some years now is that victims of historical sex crimes and their families will be taken seriously if they come forward. We had come forward with allegations as well as the evidence to support them. We had given them a conviction on a plate, a sure and certain slam dunk they could toss in the basket then showboat in the glory of the victory we handed them. I felt safe in my certainty we would be going to court. I wanted our day in court. I was relishing the prospect of watching the parties involved squirm as they cowered under the probing bright hot light of justice.

How could a case involving illegal sex acts committed on a patient by an NHS employee in a mental health hospital, not be in the public interest?

How could a case in which a vulnerable disturbed young woman, a patient in a mental health institution, who had a crisis pregnancy and subsequent abortion resulting from the illegal sex acts committed by an NHS employee, not be in the public interest?

How could a case in which knowledge of the events was withheld by clinicians, omitted from medical notes and concealed from other healthcare professionals and from the patient's own family, not be in the public interest.

And how could a case in which ward managers, supervisors and colleagues of the accused knew about the illegal events occurring around them, not be in the public interest?

By now we knew what had been done to Alison contravened at least three pieces of legislation. Section 128 of the 1959 Mental Health Act forbids sex on hospital premises with mental health patients. Section 127 of the 1989 Mental Health Act suggests what happened could be classed as wilful neglect. The Criminal

Justice Act of 2003 lists what occurred as a specified sexual offence. Any one of these on their own would make copy in a national paper. Not for one second, one nano-second did I think our case would, or indeed could by any sane minded person in the CPS, be seen as anything other than in the public interest.

In May 2017 I was on holiday with family in Kefalonia. It is somewhere we have visited many times. A beautiful quiet and incredibly relaxing place, I feel at peace. The people are warm and welcoming, the food is fantastic, and the weather is normally great. Lying under the early summer sun watching buzzards ride the wind and listening to the gentle clanking bells of the sheep herd and the occasional bark of the dogs that accompany them as they pass the lane end, is the perfect antidote to life's busyness and bullshit.

I was reading on my Kindle, lying by the small pool overlooking the meandering valley that winds its way down to the picturesque little town of Argostoli. An indicator on my screen flashed to show I had incoming email. I had promised myself I wouldn't think about the investigation while I was on holiday, but this was from the detective leading Alison's case and I couldn't resist opening it. The email said the CPS had reached a conclusion and the detective wanted to meet Sarah and I to inform us of their decision. I replied instantly asking him to share the outcome now, why wait? He refused my request and wouldn't deal with me on the phone. Was he adding to the mystery, building his part, or in true public sector style, arranging meetings to fill his diary and make work for himself? It all seemed very cloak and dagger. I had been waiting for what seemed like an eternity for this moment. We had lifted the lid on so much and pushed so hard to reach this point. I was beyond frustrated, angry with myself for looking at his email and annoyed with Cumbria police for exploding my peace of mind in this sacred space of serenity. Why wouldn't they just tell me?

I had expected a feeling of incredible victory when news of the decision came through. After all, the nurse had now admitted having sex with Alison on hospital premises when she was a patient. He had admitted knowledge of the crisis pregnancy and acknowledged his role in helping arrange a discreet abortion. Surely this case had gone straight into the tray marked no-brainers for prosecuting when it hit the CPSs desk?

But my gut knew this was not good news. Like young pups seeking approval the officers dealing with our case had already shown a desire to share positive developments as soon as they occurred. Look what we've done, look how clever we are, but were nowhere in sight when awkward questions needed answering. I recalled how pleased with himself the senior investigating officer had been when he told me they had finally made an arrest and of the confession they obtained. I hadn't the heart to piss on his parade and ask what had taken so long. Now, I sensed their insistence on meeting us could only be a bad thing. I was right.

We arrived back home. I remember the headlines from the local papers. No prosecution for former nurse over historic sex with patient allegation. Garlands Sex Nurse will not be charged. Family devastated to learn male nurse won't be prosecuted. Behind every headline and soundbite there are people and their lives. Seeing my dashed hopes of justice emblazoned across the billboards outside the newsagent is something I will never forget.

We had entered this process with such high hopes. We felt the wind was at our backs, we had all the information and evidence needed to prove our allegations beyond doubt. We were convinced the police and CPS would throw everything they could at this case. The failings emerging from the previous investigation meant their reputations and credibility were on the line. This had been a cast-iron opportunity to redeem themselves and right wrongs of the past. But the scandal of what happened to Alison was again being covered up and the only people it seemed to be making things worse for, was us. It's the hope that kills you.

Chapter 16 – We got fooled, again

And the world looks just the same, and history ain't changed.

Won't Get Fooled Again; The Who.

Small towns have an ability to concentrate memories. Cumbria police arranged to meet Sarah and I at the old police station in Penrith's town centre. It is just across a small carpark from the headquarters of the NHS Trust I had recently been ousted from, in whose care Alison had been abused. I had become very familiar with the local copshop in my teens.

The two officers involved with the case, I wish I could say dealing with it, greeted us cordially at the side-entrance to the police station. They guided us toward a room, a less than salubrious space previously used to interview suspects. After all these years I recalled it well. Some of the same familiar police faces were still wandering the corridors.

The old police station was being prepared for sale; the room we were guided into no longer deemed fit for purpose. People suspected of breaking the law in Penrith and the surrounding areas are now taken to a new modern facility twenty miles away in Carlisle. Offenders have standards the families of victims of sex crimes are not deemed worthy of. The space was soulless and grey with uncomfortable seating and little natural light. A classic police drama setting. I began to wonder if we had done something wrong. This didn't feel like an appropriate place to break sensitive news to people seeking justice, people like us, victims in our own right.

Afterwards Sarah said she felt they used the dismal interview room to disarm us, to make us feel small and uncomfortable and specifically to remind me of my place in the universe. To the police I was probably still the former local juvenile offender who outran Penrith's unfit coppers even with the bondage straps clipped on my tartan pants. But here in adult life, my persistence and refusal to be ignored had forced them to lift the lid on their own incompetence. I had made them acknowledge their mistakes, publicly apologise and reopen an investigation they had never wanted reopening. I had embarrassed the county's force, exposing their ineptitude in the local and national press. I think she may have been right.

The two officers, Lauren and Parky, were very different. Less good cop bad cop and more shit cop, slightly less shit cop. One of the officers clearly remembered the training course on displaying empathy they attended at some point in the past. Though I have no doubt it was all an act, they were doing a fair job of seeming sincere. Fluctuating soft vocal tones, leaning into the conversation at the right points and maintaining just enough eye contact. I think I had been on a similar course when I was selling mobile phones, their tutors would be pleased.

The other was a pale balding middle-aged inspector whose straining shirt buttons suggested increasing amounts of time spent at a desk, and who in one of the worst rural traditions we are so used to in Cumbria, appeared to have risen stratospherically beyond the level of his incompetence. I imagine him on one of those motivational courses where the speaker encourages people to download a screensaver showing a kitten looking into a mirror with a lion looking back at them. The message from such simplistic exercises is that you are as good as you think you are. A nice thought but clearly untrue and in some cases positively harmful to both yourself and others if you are not as talented as you might think you are. Brain surgery anyone? However, he clearly believed his own hype and as he climbed slowly but steadily higher onto his soapbox, it became obvious he was going to harness his softly spoken inner roar.

The senior officer was part of what could loosely qualify in Cumbria as a policing dynasty. His siblings were on the local force and his parents had been long-serving senior officers. Hazard county can be incredibly and unhealthily nepotistic and parochial. In a peculiar twist of fate, or maybe a cleverly planned effort to avoid embarrassment, I will let you decide, this particular officer's dad served on the force at the same time as the commander who had been on the board of North Cumbria NHS during the first bungled investigation of 2001.

Though quietly spoken the lead officer was as subtle as a sledgehammer. His impatience with us and the case we had forced them to reopen, oozed from him. Such was his contempt he made no secret of saying he disagreed with his own head of professional standards about the quality of the original investigation in 2001. Despite their own official findings, he said he felt it had been of an acceptable standard. The implied message being that he had never seen the need to even reopen the case. He then seized on his deflating and defeated captive audience and took the opportunity to defend the indefensible ineptitude of his former colleagues as he continued to justify their original efforts.

Sarah and I couldn't believe what we were hearing. Here was the officer tasked with heading-up the latest investigation into the events leading to Alison's death, and he was making it clear he felt the first investigation had been fine. He didn't care what his senior colleagues in professional standards thought. Come hell or high water he was going to use this sensitive emotionally charged occasion to put us in our place, to let us know that as far as he was concerned our desire for justice had been a storm in a teacup.

After misguidedly telling us the investigation of 2001 had been treated seriously by his colleagues, he went on to say it was treated every bit as seriously then as they had taken it now in 2017. Knowing how bad the investigation in 2001 had been, this was not reassuring.

Not for the last time, I started wondering if the person across the desk from me had taken the wrong medication that morning. Was this detective really trying to defend the same botched publicly discredited investigation his own head of professional standards had already apologised for in writing just a few months earlier?

The same one in which they lost the evidence.

The investigation where they failed to interview any of the people on a carefully compiled list, we gave them, including the last person to see Alison alive.

The same investigation they failed to create a basic investigation plan for.

The investigation in which officers lied about conducting an interview with the suspect.

The same investigation they handed a file so inadequate to the CPS, it was rejected for prosecution.

An investigation so poor it did not even officially qualify by the polices own standards, to be classed as an investigation.

Yes, he was. Displaying all the sensitivity of a drunken rhino, he appeared to be relishing the opportunity to use this raw painful occasion on which we were being given news we never wanted to hear, to set us straight and defend the actions of his brothers in arms inside the police family. Perhaps the only reason he wanted to see us in person, the reason he would not answer my emails or phone calls and made us wait to meet him face-to-face was to enable him to say his piece. To get on his back-legs and tell us what he really thought. If he had stuck his foot in his mouth anymore, he would have disappeared up his own arse.

Rather than accommodate or even share our sense of frustration. Cumbria police used the meeting with Sarah and I to let us know they didn't even see the need for the reinvestigation we had fought so hard to get.

The mistake he made was thinking we trusted him. After all we had been through, we were unlikely to trust a police officer again. We recorded the meeting. Our mistake amongst the many we have made, was thinking Cumbria police would care what he had done. It is a statement about the entitled aloof sense of untouchability the force feels it has, that even though we taped and shared every word, he was supported by Cumbria police when he denied saying the very things, we recorded him saying.

They also had the arrogance to say to our faces the new investigation had taken so long because they were juggling it with current workloads. It seems Alison's case didn't qualify as part of current workload. I wonder what is, current workload, if it isn't dealing with crimes committed in the past. I've never heard of a police force dealing with crimes from the future. As far as they were concerned, the reinvestigation into sex crimes committed inside a public institution, crimes which had now been explicitly admitted for the first time in almost thirty years, had been nothing but a drain on their precious diaries. Something squeezed in between other more important matters like training courses on communication skills, or how to lie while maintaining eye contact and looking sincere.

Worryingly, a word I feel I have nearly exhausted, during the latest investigation it became abundantly clear to Cumbria police what happened to Alison was not an isolated case. It seems the hiding of what occurred when she was in the clutches of the NHS in Carlisle was planned and deliberate, involving several people. Were the police really saying that investigating an institution in which the sexual abuse and possible rape of patients was probably widespread, was not a priority? They now had a confession, they had other witnesses saying the culture of the hospital was broken, that sex between staff and patients was commonplace, and rule breaking was the accepted norm. What could be a more worthy priority for investigation, for police time and resources?

Over the years I have had many conversations with former patients and staff who after hearing of our experiences have confided and shared their stories. It is now beyond doubt what happened to Alison was not an isolated incident. The fact that I as a citizen have been able to unearth this suggests the second investigation Cumbria police undertook was only marginally if any better than the first lacklustre effort of 2001. The obvious question is why? Was someone or more than one person being protected? Maybe this is the right time in this book to call out what I and many others will be thinking. Knowing what we all now know about the way things were in publicly funded institutions of the seventies and eighties, would any of us be at all surprised if widespread sexual abuse was not the norm in an isolated dysfunctional mental health facility on the furthest edge of England's most rural county?

The Crown Prosecution Service had sent a letter to Cumbria police addressed to us which outlined their decision. Weirdly, the lead detective clung to this letter and insisted on reading it out loud as if conducting some strange ceremony for people with dyslexia. In it the CPS explained in their finest cut and paste public-sector-jargon, that they had decided not to prosecute the NHS Employee who had sex with Alison on hospital premises.

The reason they said, was that it was not in the public interest. Not being in the public interest was the second stage of the CPS's own two-stage test and it was the stage of the process I had been convinced we would sail through. In their letter the CPS pointed out the case had passed the first stage of the test, the evidential part, because the trainee nurse had confessed what he had done. Their letter then went on to say they did not feel the case met the public interest test and had therefore decided not to progress to prosecution. The rationale offered for this was a mixed bag of reasons, none of which when looked at closely made any sense.

The letter, signed by someone with the grand title of Senior Crown Prosecutor, stated that one of the reasons they did not think the case was in the public interest was that the events occurred a long time ago; so much for respecting victims of non-famous perpetrators of historical sex crimes! Their recognition of the time that had passed was in effect rewarding the perpetrator for keeping quiet. As if being good at holding secrets about the crimes you have committed should go in your favour rather than be viewed as duplicitous.

In using the passage of time to excuse his acts, the CPS failed to acknowledge their own role in cocking-up the first investigation.

They themselves were a large part of the reason for the lengthy passage of time that occurred. In 2002, fifteen years previously, they had asked Cumbria police for a more complete file, yet never followed-up their own request.

The letter from the Senior Crown Prosecutor, now being read to Sarah and I like a teacher would read an afternoon story to a group of infants, noted the perpetrator had admitted what he had done, wrongly inferring he came clean of his own volition. He did not. In 2001 the suspect had refused to be interviewed following advice from his union. It was obvious to all involved, he had only owned up now because concrete evidence of his wrongdoing was placed in front of all to see. He would doubtless still be refusing to speak to the police and ignoring knowledge of his crimes had I not located the medical records which revealed what had occurred. He confessed because he had to, not from any sense of civic duty or morality.

Ludicrously, in a decision I think has significant ramifications for the wider application of law, the letter went on to say that because he said he didn't know what he was doing was wrong, his culpability was reduced. Ignorance it would seem, is now a valid excuse for breaking the law, including crimes of a sexual nature. In short, the nurse in question told the police and CPS he shouldn't be held accountable for his actions because he didn't know he was doing anything wrong? He was thirty-five, not five. I am tempted to repeat the sentence you have just read for effect, instead I will ask you to just take a moment to reflect on it…

…and I still can't believe he thought using this playground line of defence would work. What is infinitely worse is that it clearly did. Not for the life of me can I understand the police and CPS seeing this as a legitimate reason to defend his actions.

In the aftermath of the CPS decision, it became evident that during the investigation, neither the CPS or police contacted the Royal College of Nursing. If they had, as we advised them to do, they would have discovered guidance on relationships with patients was issued to all practicing and training nurses some years before what happened to Alison. We had extensive contact with the Royal College of Nursing and suggested the CPS and police should get in touch with them; our suggestion was ignored.

Lastly, and most insultingly of all, the letter from the Senior Crown Prosecutor did not reference the most sinister and harmful aspects of the whole case. These being that the criminal acts committed led to a vulnerable mentally ill young woman having a crisis pregnancy and being subjected to a hastily arranged abortion, which the suspect himself and Alison's psychiatrist helped arrange. The CPS conveniently ignored the fact that information about these events was then withheld from records and concealed from other health professionals involved in Alison's treatment.

I now see that side-lining these egregious facts was wilful on the part of the CPS. Ignoring the most harmful transgressions that occurred was the only way they could legitimately justify not prosecuting the case. In our efforts to help them understand the life altering impact a crisis pregnancy and abortion had on Alison's state of mind, we had supplied the CPS with significant amounts of medically relevant information and sources of clinical and academic expertise. They ignored it all.

In deciding not to prosecute this case the CPS essentially ignored their own guidance. This states if a case passes the evidence test there must be very good reasons not to prosecute. To most rational people it would seem there was an abundance of extremely good reasons to prosecute and take the case to trial. The rationale, or lack of it, the CPS used to support their incredulous decision not to prosecute this tragic case, remains beyond logic.

Before leaving the meeting, the lead inspector asked what we planned to do next, a question I am sure he had been encouraged to ask by his head of public relations. I told him we would go away and think and then I asked if we had the right to request a review of the decision the CPS had made. He said we didn't. It turns out we did, though it took a month to get the CPS to understand their own guidance on which cases are eligible for review. I pity people who take the authorities at their word, people like the person I used to be.

The prize we could almost touch had been snatched cruelly from our hands. We had come so far and done so much only to be denied justice at the final hurdle. The scant two-page letter from the CPS finished with the sentence, I appreciate you will be disappointed with my decision but I would like to assure you that the report to the police was taken very seriously and I have given this case a great deal of careful consideration.

Disappointed! Fucking disappointed. No, disappointed is how you feel when you get a crap Christmas present or the Bluetooth on your phone stops working. It's not how you feel when the man you believe took advantage of your sister's mental illness and drove her to suicide evades justice. We were absolutely devastated, crushed.

The CPS and police seem happy to spend time and money pursuing celebrities based on spurious accusations about unproven alleged offences that date further back than the crimes committed against Alison. Yet here they were, in possession of a confession, not an allegation, of sex-crimes that occurred while she was in the care of the state, refusing to prosecute an individual on the obtuse grounds it was not in the public interest. Can there be anything more in the public interest than prosecuting such crimes when they are committed by publicly funded people in positions of trust upon patients in the care of mental health hospitals run by our National Health Service?

Most of us never even get off with a parking fine. Yet here was a man who admitted having sex with a mentally ill patient on hospital premises on multiple occasions, who acknowledged she had become pregnant with his child and who was party to arranging the crisis abortion. He had helped destroy her mental health and he was being allowed to walk away Scott-free from the consequences of what he had done. Not in the public interest, which public were they thinking of?

As we left the building, the Salvation Army food bank next to the police station was open and busy. A timely reminder of the better side of humanity. Volunteers adding value in the shadow of well-paid publicly funded employees who seem intent on doing anything but.

Sarah and I went in search of tea, or something stronger. We didn't speak much. I think we hugged each other and muttered a lot. We couldn't believe what we had just heard. I still can't. Afterwards I drove Sarah to the railway station, we agreed to speak on the phone once we had taken time to regain our composure and gather our thoughts.

We already knew we both wanted a chance to speak to the faceless wizards behind the curtain who seemed to be the architects of this incredible decision. We would get our chance to meet the CPS, and we would be ready for them.

Chapter 17 - We're off to see the Wizard

Some people without brains do an awful lot of talking, don't they?

Scarecrow; The Wizard of Oz.

In May 2018, almost a year after we had first been informed of their decision, Sarah and I finally got to meet two of the CPS prosecutors involved in our case. By this time, we had both lodged and lost our appeal against the original decision they had made not to prosecute the case.

The process of lodging our appeal had, as we had learned to expect by now, been infuriating and frustrating. Any notion we were dealing with an effective efficient group of professional people was rapidly dispelled as we found ourselves guiding various CPS employees around the finer points of their own processes. Our plea to reconsider their original decision, as well-constructed and dripping in logic as it had been, was rejected. The clear rationale we offered, completely ignored. Having exhausted all the review stages available to us, further requests to the CPS to revisit and apply their own guidance were dismissed out of hand.

In one terse email, sent bizarrely by someone nameless from the Special Crime and Counter Terrorism Division, presumably situated next to the Un-Special Sexual Predator Protection Department, I was told in no uncertain terms the matter was closed, that we had no business sending correspondence directly to Alison Saunders, then Chief Executive of the CPS, and all further contact would be filed without response. Binned, I imagine that means. Filed without response, disapplied, our publicly funded agencies have such polite ways of telling us to fuck off and stop bothering them. Alison Saunders recently became a Dame. I and countless others would argue she has held a leading role in pantomime for many years.

We had requested a meeting with the CPS to help us try and understand what seemed on the face of it, an utterly unfathomable decision. Importantly we also wanted to meet the faceless bureaucrats we felt were preventing us obtain justice. We needed to look these strange illogical people from planet CPS in the eye. After a protracted period of correspondence with emails toing and froing, we were at last granted an audience. We arranged to meet at their premises in Carlisle. I have known the border city well for many years and had never noticed the building before, hidden behind a non-descript understated exterior overlooking the cathedral. Religion and justice huddling closely together, what could be more reassuring. Once inside the building seemed a strange mix of the old and new, a Tardis like quality revealed a large open plan office full of expensive ergonomic executive chairs and modern desks with no-one at them. It felt soulless and was eerily empty.

The meeting was memorable for many reasons, the first being their inability to work their own recording equipment. The two CPS ladies present were each dressed in that classically corporate non-descript way which says, I don't bring myself to work, I bring the person I think others expect to see. Each had the title of Senior Prosecutor; Christ only knows what the juniors are like. Between them they were unable to fathom out how to start the large recording device perched on the edge of the desk. In a scene to compete with any comedy sketch, they played with the machine for what seemed like an eternity, muttering to each other, occasionally looking up to reassure us they had tested it that very morning and it had been fine. Pull the other one I thought. I don't think they wanted the meeting recorded. They were simply observing one of the many unwritten rules contained in the public sector handbook of best poor practice. This particular one being, that if there is no record of what is said it makes your incompetence harder to prove. Leave no trace was a strapline of the public sector long before the environmentalists got hold of it.

Its lucky I took my Dictaphone. I watched them mess about for as long as I could bear and then pulled it from my pocket before placing it on the desk. You don't mind if I make a recording of this meeting, do you? They seemed disappointed.

We felt we deserved answers from this meeting. To state our serious intent, a week before we met, we sent a four-page letter outlining our concerns. It contained twenty-four agenda items in the form of questions we wanted to discuss. We were not going to let these wizards of waffle bullshit and obfuscate in their attempts to tick a box marked, yes, we have met with the family and addressed their concerns.

As the meeting progressed and we sought to go through the agenda, one of the prosecutors seemed to become increasingly exasperated and impatient with our deliberate, calm, reasoned and structured approach. Neither Sarah nor I were prone to ranting, maybe we should be, and so one by one we worked our way methodically through the list of questions on our agenda.

Perhaps running late for lunch with a friend or missing an important message on her WhatsApp group, she clearly had enough of our awkward thorny time-consuming and probing questions. In a thinly veiled effort to move this obviously tedious meeting along, the prosecutor leapt in to address what she felt was the heart of the matter.

We wouldn't even be here meeting today if the acts had occurred somewhere other than on hospital premises, she stated. She went on. The only crime the suspect committed was having sex with Alison in the wrong place. No shit I thought. But before my mind could explode completely, she continued, in the process making it abundantly clear she felt the entire case was essentially a trivial matter, pretty-much a waste of time. We were treated to the enlightening observation that sex itself was not a crime. In her view the accused's actions were merely legitimate loving acts undertaken in the wrong place.

This was a real wow moment. As the prosecutors' mouth continued digging her deeper into the hole she had opened, for the first time on this long journey Sarah and I sensed the absolute lack of understanding the CPS had about this entire case. Alison had taken her own life, but the CPS had never even considered her action could be a consequence of what had been done to her when she was in the care of the state. They had not entertained the idea that the criminal acts committed were an abuse of the duty of care she was owed. Nor had they given a second thought to how what happened was dealt with and then hidden. As far as they were concerned, this case had only ever been about a bloke who happened to have sex with someone in the wrong place because he didn't know any better. We were stunned at this clumsily stated and deeply flawed reasoning. What was done to Alison was more, so very much more than they were willing to grasp or allowing themselves to consider.

And even if having sex on hospital premises was the only thing he did, other than the small matter of exploiting a vulnerable mentally ill patient and getting her pregnant, helping arrange an abortion, withholding information and contributing to the implosion of Alison's mental health, the lady from the CPS was right; his only crime was having sex with a patient on hospital premises. A patient in the care of the NHS Trust he was working for and to whom he had a duty of care. Was that not a significant enough crime in itself?

I wondered when in the mind of this senior prosecutor, had nurses having sex with mental health patients on hospital premises become an okay, I understand, don't worry these things happen, kind of excusable activity? How long had this prosecutor lived in England I wondered. Was she even a CPS employee, perhaps she was in the wrong meeting, was she missing from an outing and should we try to contact her guardians? Don't worry, we've found her, she's just having one of her episodes where she pretends to know all about the law and spouts platitudes unworthy of an imbecile. Yes, it's fine, we'll keep her safe until you get here.

Our attempts to highlight the wording of the law in relation to the care of the mentally ill, quoting sections of those Acts of Law, were ignored, not referenced once by the people we had been led to believe were experts in the law and existed to uphold it.

As diplomatically as I could, I attempted to explain the flaw in the prosecutors thinking by pointing out the simple laws of space and time. Where and when are the very parameters defining what is acceptable behaviour from what is not. What is criminal activity from what is not. If I jump into my car and drive at motorway speeds through a pedestrianized area and kill somebody, shall I say in my defence the only thing I did wrong was driving at the right speed in the wrong place, shrug my shoulders and ask what all the fuss is about? Space and time, where and when we do things, define what is and isn't lawful behaviour. Shall we excuse Saville because his only crime was having sex with people who were underage at the wrong point in time?

The calm exterior I had brought to the meeting was slipping. Other than trawling the lists of unsuccessful applicants for Big Brother, I found myself wondering where these organisations possibly find such stupid yet wildly over-confident people. Let's not forget, you and I are paying these idiots salaries. We are constantly forking out huge sums of money to cover the wages of such public servants, who as well as being unable to work their own tape-recording equipment and understand their own processes, are incapable of understanding the basic premise of their jobs. It is bad enough these highly paid panjandrums did not understand their own guidelines, but to be unable to grasp that the law is a tool to differentiate and categorise events which occur at different points in space and time, is beyond infuriating.

Then, to be at the mercy of such people, who think we are even stupider than they are, is rage inducing. Sitting opposite this latest set of corporate lobotomised automatons, trying desperately to tolerate their ineptitude, I could see why people protest at injustice by jumping out of windows, setting themselves on fire or harming themselves in public spaces. It cannot be much more painful than listening to them spout their nonsense, while knowing you are paying them to do it. I live with the knowledge we were denied justice by the sheer incompetence of such people.

His only crime was having sex in the wrong place. I ask you.

Her colleague, slowly recognising the obvious flaw in her partners assertion stepped in to try and save the day with a different but even less sensitive, equally inane and ill thought out approach. In what was becoming an increasingly desperate bid to defend the indefensible decision they had made, she told us the suspect himself had been suffering with depression at the time in question and suggested we should see this as a mitigating factor on his part. The meeting was now well and truly entering the realm of the surreal. Not only was it crassly insensitive to use his mental health as an excuse for his actions, Alison had after all been the mental health patient and they had not taken her state of mind into account, it was misleading. Records we have subsequently accessed which the CPS were already in possession of, show the perpetrator was not depressed at the time in question but allegedly suffered the following year. Perhaps no longer having sex with younger women on the hospital premises was getting him down.

I asked the prosecutors, if being depressed is an excuse for committing sex-crimes, then why hadn't they taken Alison's mental health and obvious vulnerability into account? Being as mentally ill as Alison was, meant she was not able to be a willing knowledgeable participant in the unprotected intercourse he seemed happy to encourage her to have. Citing his depression as a reason to excuse what he had done seemed contradictory. The CPS were attempting to use his condition to let him off yet ignoring Alison's serious mental illness as the very reason she should have been protected. The hypocrisy they were applying to bolster their reasoning was sickening. Then without a hint of irony, the CPS went on to talk of his good work in the community as a volunteer DJ in hospital radio.

Again, we pressed the prosecutors as to why in all their waffling correspondence they had never referenced the impact a crisis pregnancy and abortion would have on Alison. A review of the literature about the psychological effects of abortion on young women reveals a wealth of information. With the help and cooperation of people from the UK and abroad we had unearthed and then shared significant amounts of relevant research material with the CPS. This made it clear the impact of a crisis pregnancy through pre-marital sex would have caused great anxiety in a mentally ill young woman with deeply held religious beliefs. We then talked about research which clearly links crisis pregnancy and abortion to increased risk of self-harm and suicide in patients, especially young women with existing mental health conditions. Once more we emphasised that the negative consequences are amplified if the woman in question is deeply religious, they remained unmoved.

It has always been our assertion that the illegal sex was simply one part, albeit a significant and very wrong part, of a wider series of failings that occurred. We felt once it had become clear Alison was pregnant, her consultant, the hospital and the wider NHS, had a duty to protect and look after her. We earnestly and patiently offered to reshare the evidence base of research and publications we had amassed with the CPS. We begrudgingly acknowledged they had now made their final decision in relation to Alison but explained that the information and access to expertise we had amassed could help them make more informed choices in the future. They declined, complacently, arrogantly, and as it would later emerge, incorrectly, reassuring us they had access to all the expertise on these complex matters they needed.

Next, we sought to understand why they insisted on continuing to refer to what happened between Alison and the trainee nurse as a relationship. Their use of the R word highlights a profound ignorance about mental illness and the unequal power dynamics that would have been present. It is both annoying and incredibly inappropriate for them to refer to what was clearly a breach of trust, not a meeting of two equals able to make informed choices, as a relationship. Their response was to reference the diaries of the nurse which talked of it as a loving consensual relationship. This is an incredibly twisted interpretation of what were no more than a series of crimes. Applying this logic ignores the illegal nature of the acts. If the same logic were applied to accusations of rape within marriage, no prosecutions would occur, as long as one half of the couple could say it was a loving consensual relationship.

Alison had been sectioned to a mental health hospital because it was recognised in law her ability to make choices and act in her own interests was compromised. She was severely mentally ill. Yet reading the CPS notes you would think the story of Alison's encounter with an older male nurse was a romance novel, not the seedy tale of illicit, illegal, immoral and irresponsible criminal acts committed by a man who abused a position of trust to repeatedly satisfy his physical desires. A man who had been warned about the inappropriate nature of his behaviour and had chosen to ignore the warnings he was given.

I asked if the diaries of a man who had taken advantage of a mentally ill young woman should be viewed as anything other than a necessary illusion and possibly a pre-planned deception, a means he used to rewrite history and justify what he did in his own mind. They didn't think that was the case, once again citing the mutually consensual nature of the Mills & Boon romance they clearly thought the whole sordid business had been.

Finally, we asked the CPS why they had not referred to the medical records from Alison's psychiatrist at the Garlands. These appeared to show he had been deliberately kept out the loop about her pregnancy and abortion. We did not anticipate the answer we were given. This was the first time we became aware Alison's Consultant Psychiatrist had apparently known what was going on all along. The CSP informed us that his had been one of two required signatures authorising the pregnancy termination.

The revelation the CPS shared with us that day turned Alison's psychiatrist from merely an ineffective health professional to a co-conspirator in covering-up what occurred. He had created medical notes and sent correspondence to other health professionals which made no reference to the crisis pregnancy or abortion, which we assumed meant he hadn't known about them. The reality now seemed very different. Rather than being ignorant of events as we had thought for years, the records Alison's psychiatrist created and shared, appear to have been inaccurate at best, perhaps even purposefully misleading. The CPS prosecutors told us Cumbria police tried to speak with him during the latest investigation. He apparently refused an interview saying he could not remember anything. Had he arranged so many other abortions he was able to forget one?

Our meeting with the CPS was drawing to a close. It was clear we were getting nowhere. We had one question left. In light of the explicit confession the police had now obtained, would we be entitled to use this evidence to take a private prosecution forward. The CPS replied that they retained the right to block private prosecutions and would apply this to Alison's case if we attempted to pursue it. They were intent on closing the door to the justice we deserved by any means. The question remains, why?

The meeting ended. We had met the wizards behind the loudhailer and like Dorothy we had found them wanting. I felt as low as I had felt high when I first learned an arrest had been made in February 2016. But the opposite of punching the air screaming yes, fucking yes at the heavens, is not screaming no, fucking no, it is just numbness, a tired void emptied of energy. At moments like these I don't feel so bad about bunking off school, there were no classes in how to deal with this sort of shit.

As we left, the senior prosecutor who had been so contemptuous of our quest was ringing someone to arrange where to meet for lunch. As one of the two latest additions to my mental dark alley list, I couldn't help hoping she would choke on her ciabatta or better still be clipped by a speeding motorist as she walked through town. I would fundraise for the driver's defence lawyer. My client did nothing wrong your honour, their only act was driving at the right speed in the wrong place. If they had been on the M6, they would have been well within the legal limit. And as for the spurious allegation this incident caused life altering imbalances in the mind of the victim, we see no reason to take those matters into account. Suck that up, let's see how much you like your own twisted logic.

Am I allowed to be confused and disappointed by so many of the female species apparent willingness to mimic the stubborn stupidity of their male counterparts as they carve out careers and climb greasy poles? I believe we all stand to gain from living in a world in which women bring the best of who they are to the table. But the sisterhood that offered the promise of change to an increasingly compassionless world too often seems to manifest itself as little more than a fresh set of arseholes in disguise. Don't we have enough of these already?

When we had been handed over to the CPS following our meeting with the Pontius Pilates of Cumbria police the previous year, we were told the CPS would make themselves available to listen and explain any unanswered questions we might have. They had been sold to us by the police as fonts of legal knowledge who were firmly on the side of the wronged. A cross between a benevolent legally knowledgeable Google and a sensitive counselling service for the families of victims. We were assured all would become clear once we established contact with them. Nothing could have been further from the truth. We found out very quickly the CPS were most definitely not there for us. I'm not sure I have worked out yet who they are there for? We left our meeting with even more questions and concerns.

What counts as abuse? In my mind, in my family's mind, in almost everyone's mind I have shared this story with, what happened to Alison when she was in the care of the NHS in Carlisle was abuse. Abuse on many levels and by more than one person. Abuse of trust, abuse of responsibility and abuse of power for personal sexual gratification.

The fact it may have been committed by an inexperienced unaware individual who had no idea of the boundaries he was crossing, or the unequal power dynamics present between patient and health professional, is incidental, indicative only of wider failings in relation to training and supervision. However, what was then done with planned coordinated and undeniable clarity, was the handling of the crisis pregnancy, the arranging of the abortion, and the withholding of information from others.

We have never suggested Alison should have been wrapped in cotton wool and insulated from the natural desires present in every young person, but it's important to remember people suffering mental health problems often need protecting from themselves and their own choices. Alison was at a point in her life where she was unable to make informed decisions about such important issues as who to trust her body to and who to be intimate with. One of the reasons we have hospitals for the mentally ill is that they need places of safety, protected managed spaces where they are shielded from the cruel chemically influenced tricks their minds may be playing on them and the people who would take advantage of them. A physician noted many years ago that there are no health conditions that are improved by seeing a Doctors genitals.

When Alison was admitted to hospital in a seriously unstable state of mind, the last thing she needed was to be the subject of sexual attention from a randy amoral nurse. She was vulnerable, isolated and confused. She needed professional compassionate help, not a complex confounding imbalanced connection with an individual whose prime focus appears to have been grooming and using her for sex. The horrendous way Alison was treated and her needs for help ignored, amount to nothing less than ill-treatment and wilful neglect. Both of which are recognised as crimes carrying significant prison sentences.

Yet here we were again. We had been fobbed off with more poor police work, undertaken by reluctant obstinate detectives. Now, not only were we being asked by the CPS to view the abuse of our sister as insignificant, but in what seemed to be the justice systems final slap to our faces, sympathise with the perpetrator because he was depressed and hadn't known he was doing anything wrong.

In all that has happened these last years, one of the most difficult things to deal with is the unshakeable sense I have that Cumbria police and the CPS have behaved more like the perpetrators defence team than guardians of justice. What was done to Alison is recognised in law as a criminal act, yet in all our dealings it feels as though the justice system has been looking for every reason not to prosecute. In their efforts to defend the indefensible, they have scraped the barrel through to the ground below and entered the realms of the truly fantastical and utterly unbelievable.

What started out as a quest to obtain justice for Alison had turned into a protracted energy-sapping mind-boggling battle with a close-knit group of inept, defensive and insensitive publicly funded organisations who appear to be unaccountable to anyone.

At every point where we provided empirical evidence to illustrate the damage done, we have been countered with anecdote and carefully chosen selective views. There is no greater example of this than the CPSs refusal to acknowledge the damage a crisis pregnancy and abortion had on Alison. During the investigation and in all the correspondence we have, they have never once referred to these events. As if by ignoring them they could avoid taking their impact into account.

The relevant respected scientific research shared with the CPS suggests young women with pre-existing mental health conditions are up to six times more likely to take their own life following an abortion. We have attempted to introduce them to experts in this field who can show them the effect a crisis pregnancy and abortion would have on someone with deeply held radical religious beliefs. They have ignored it all. More disturbingly they continued to insist they had their own sources of expertise to provide the insight and guidance required on such matters.

It has subsequently emerged the CPS knowingly misled us in vitally important areas of this case. In our efforts to ensure success we repeatedly sought assurances from them on two matters. Firstly, we wanted to know the impact of the crimes would be taken into account, not just the act of the crimes themselves. This felt entirely logical and is in line with their own guidance. The CPS assured us they would take the impact of the crimes into account.

Secondly, we wanted to know the CPS possessed the necessary expertise to understand what the impact of the crimes in these specific circumstances would have been. It felt appropriate that if we were asking them to take the impact of the crimes into account, we needed to know they understood what these impacts were.

During our meeting with the CPS and in our correspondence, we specifically asked them to confirm they had sought information relating to the impact of crisis pregnancies and abortions on young, mentally ill, and highly vulnerable women with strong religious beliefs. They assured us they had. They said they had colleagues who specialised in such matters and told us the required expertise was at their disposal.

We now know that not only did they explicitly ignore the impact of the illegal sex-acts that were committed, the CPS did not possess or seek any relevant knowledge or expertise in relation to the impact these criminal acts undoubtedly had.

In an email to an MP from the CPS Parliamentary and Complaints Unit, they acknowledge in private what they have never said in public. This being that they did not consider the impact of the crisis pregnancy and subsequent abortion arising from the illicit sex acts, in their decision-making process. Even though the impact of a crime is something they are obliged to consider when assessing cases for prosecution. They effectively admitted ignoring the most significant aspects of the crimes that were committed, side-stepping their own guidance in efforts to sweep what happened under the carpet.

To add salt to our still open wounds, despite all their assurances of having access to up-to-date knowledge and expertise about the specific impact on victims of the matters in question, a freedom of information request we submitted revealed they did not possess or seek any such sources. The FOI request we made took over a year for them to deal with. It was only answered, following yet another enforcement notice issued by the Information Commissioners Office on our behalf. The CPS were not only prepared to mislead us, they then used every trick in the book to hide their own duplicity. Maybe it's no wonder they empathised with a perpetrator who was adept at withholding information.

This is alarming. Not only does it mean the CPS misled us when they said they had access to the expertise they needed to assess the impact of sex crimes on the mentally ill and vulnerable. It means important decisions about prosecuting sex crimes will continue to be made on the whims and varying levels of understanding of individual prosecutors. Which as we have witnessed first-hand, leave a lot to be desired. How can the CPS possibly assess such sensitive cases in a consistent equitable manner without access to the research and knowledge which would enable them to understand the impact of the crimes that have occurred? The answer is they cannot, and they are not.

I would not have believed the levels of ineptitude and deceit I've encountered unless I had experienced them. Justice is one of the cornerstones of our society, of democracy. The absence of justice erodes democracy. You cannot have functioning democracies without justice, the two are inseparable. When justice is withheld from taxpaying citizens without good reason, it's like denying water to people dying of thirst who paid for bottles of it in advance. Its denial to us in such an obtuse fashion has left an unquenchable angry fire in our hearts and our heads.

Chapter 18 - Insult to injury

There can be no peace without justice.

Martin Luther King

When something goes wrong in the NHS, in public sector health and care services, the long-term impact of the damage to patients and their families is enormous, in many cases irreparable. But any initial harm done is often merely the start of a lengthy list of hurt, pain and unnecessary scarring inflicted on patients, where they are still alive, their families, friends and carers.

Those affected who seek answers to help them deal with whatever has occurred are quickly and clumsily turned from heartbroken grief-stricken victims into unwilling and unwitting adversaries. Tired and ill-equipped for the fight ahead they don't even yet know is coming. If you had told me ten years ago, of the challenges I would face in my future dealings with public sector services, I would have called you daft at best, possibly paranoid and maybe thought you a borderline conspiracy theorist. People in responsible publicly funded posts wouldn't knowingly behave that way, would they?

Families of the victims of wrongdoing and harm, where they are aware a wrong has occurred, become victims themselves. They are deliberately ostracised and distanced from the system and the very people within it who can provide them with the answers they need. Answers they deserve.

A pop-up ocean of bureaucracy appears consisting of wave after wave of unfeeling archaic processes. We want conversations, we get forms to fill in. We want quick replies to emails requesting simple details. Instead we get signposted to an online complaints process, pitting us against the organisation and people we want to communicate with and funnelling us into confrontational situations we didn't wish to enter.

We want to be able to pick up the phone and ask a question about the letter we have just received written in a strange public sector quasi-corporate language we are unfamiliar with. We are drowned in gobbledegook and generalisations phrased so they can be said to mean just about whatever the sender wants them to mean.

We are thrown into a high-stakes game of snakes and ladders in which the dice is loaded to ensure we are sent back down the snakes to the beginning of the board at every possible turn.

When we have the audacity to ask if we can meet to speak face to face with a real person, someone we think may have insights that will shed light on matters, we are intercepted. Tersely contacted by their superiors and told to stop emailing or calling them and direct all future queries to a manager. On the rare occasion when we reach someone on the phone, perhaps by disguising our number or ringing from a different one, when we manage to speak briefly to the person who sent us the letter to ask if they can clarify its content and tell us what the next steps are, we are told they have fulfilled their part of the process and what we are now asking for is the responsibility of someone else in another department. And no, they won't contact them on our behalf, we must do it ourselves, and no, they don't have the number.

We want to deal with one person, a real human-being we can talk to whose job it is to guide us up the ladders and help us avoid the snakes. Instead we acquire an endlessly growing list of names with vague titles as we are sent from pillar to post swifter than a package in a terrorist game of pass the parcel.

We would like a copy of a document or a report we think may help us understand what has happened. This may be something we had already been promised access to, but now we are told it will not be made available and instructed to submit an official Freedom of Information (FOI) request if we want to try and obtain it.

So, as respectful citizens we do as instructed and jump through the bureaucratic hoops now placed in front of us as if we were show-dogs at Crufts. But our legitimate request for what seemed a simple piece of information gets rejected and we can't understand why. We try to explain in a polite email that we just wanted a conversation, we never really wanted to go down the route of submitting an FOI request, we were shunted into it. We are told we can appeal against the initial decision not to respond to our FOI, and so we spend more precious time filling in appeal forms. Then our appeal is rejected, and we are told we have now exhausted the internal processes of the body in question. Of course, we can appeal against the rejection of our appeal if we get in touch with another organisation; perhaps the Information Commissioners Office (ICO) or the Independent Office for Police

Conduct (IOPC), because of course we have nothing better to do with our time.

At this point we are becoming severely pissed-off and frustrated, yet we also realise we are too far in to turn back and we are still naively clinging onto the eroding shoreline of our belief in the justice system. So, we contact the ICO or the IOPC and there is of course a further form to complete and we spend more of our time completing it. The time and attention we are using are the most precious finite resource we have, but we have no choice. We have no personal assistant, no dedicated admin department; nobody will step-in and do what needs to be done on our behalf.

Then, if we are lucky, really lucky, the Information Commissioners Office agrees to support our request and sends a letter to the organisation that first refused to provide what we asked for telling them to comply with our original request. But the public sector service we wanted answers from then appeals against the ICO decision, and sensing they are cornered or perhaps just holding out for the death of their pesky persistent inquirer, they stall for more time and send a desperate response full of meaningless increasingly nonsensical reasons. Data-protection this, data-protection that, it was a full moon, it is the Chinese year of non-transparency, anything to hamper the acquisition of the information that was asked for.

And so the dance continues, the Information Commissioners Office is then obliged to send us a letter outlining the response they have received, asking if we want them to continue with the quest for the information sought, of course we say we do. Then, eventually, months after they have finally been told they must comply with the original decision of the ICO to support our request, the public body in question sends us what we wanted. What started as a phone call or email asking for a simple non-complex bit of information, has taken a year to get our hands on. Why didn't the bastards just save all this time, money and effort by giving us what they knew we were entitled to when we first asked for it.

In short, right at the moment when people need answers and help, often the darkest lowest point in their lives, the organisations we fund to provide services to us shed their thin veneer of compassion, bare their sharp legal teeth and eagerly and deliberately expend their energy and our money in erecting every perceivable barrier to make things as difficult as possible. The mission and values statements hanging on the walls of the offices these people work in must make grim reading.

And the precious time we are using is the time we used to spend with partners or loved ones, at leisure, relaxing, undertaking professional development or earning money. Behind the scenes you find yourself adjusting other areas of your life to accommodate this new and unwelcome pressure on your time, your mind and your relationships.

You ask the University for a break in the course you are studying because it is becoming clear there are not enough hours in the day to work, study, seek the justice a dead sister deserves whilst maintaining anything loosely resembling sanity. You then ask your employer to let you work a four-day week because the pressure of chasing organisations and individuals who can only be physically contacted between Monday and Friday means your employer is not getting the best of you. The drop in your pay is a pain, especially when you need money for legal fees, but the time is needed.

As we do all this, as hundreds if not thousands of people like my sister Sarah and I, sit at small desks in the corner of lofts with ageing printers and limited supplies of second class stamps, battling it out with the well-resourced fully-equipped information governance and professional standards departments of our public services, time ticks on. Responses become delayed and the days quickly turn into weeks, the weeks turn into months and before we know it a year has passed, and then another year and so it goes on.

They are the experts, they have all the tools, tricks and time, and they know it. This is no fair fight. It is not even David and Goliath; it is way more unequal. The harder we try the higher and stronger the relentless waves of bureaucracy keep coming, the tide and strength of current become almost impossibly difficult to swim against. Each wave seems designed to push people further away from understanding what happened, from information, from knowledge, insights and ultimately truth. And while we tolerate the systems endless appetite for bureaucracy, biting our lips at its inherent ineptitude, brazen lies and misdirection. If we so much as send an overly eager email which may be construed as snotty in the slightest, they delight in reminding us of the precariousness of our position and their munificence in acknowledging us. Their staff will not tolerate our forthright emails. We must tolerate everything.

Being at the mercy of such fuckwittery and double standards is debilitating and dehumanising. It's no surprise people become frustrated, isolated, angry, feeling invisible and unheard. I have felt incredibly frustrated, isolated, angry, invisible and unheard.

People's mental health and their relationships suffer. Savings where they exist are spent on legal fees, travel, postage and any other amount of activities arising from seeking the truth. Jobs are lost and lives can fall apart, and all because public sector bodies, the police, NHS Trusts, Care Quality Commission, CPS, take your pick, are more concerned with maintaining their shop windows than accepting the challenge of dealing with their own mess and learning from their mistakes.

These are messes they know exist but which they are simply not prepared to acknowledge. To acknowledge a problem would mean dealing with it and dealing with it properly may mean someone loses a cosy well-paid job and a pension, and they don't do such things to each other in the polite closely-knit senior management circles of the public sector.

The society I thought I was part of, the one I contribute to as a volunteer and a taxpayer, the society I believed in, will now only welcome me at its table if I promise to stop rocking the boat and sit down and shut up. Fuck that. That's not my idea of the freedom people fought and died for. Is it your idea of freedom or democracy?

Trying to seek justice for Alison has used more of my time than I have time to calculate and more than you would believe. It has placed more pressure on my marriage than most relationships would bear, and it has cost a significant amount of money. It has distanced me from family and friends and cost me my career in the NHS. Most worryingly though probably not surprisingly is the impact it has had on my mental health and my outlook on life.

Unlike Pauls sudden moment of revelation on the road to Damascus, the scales have been slow to fall from my eyes. The change in my outlook crept up on me gradually. With each inevitable disappointment in the integrity of our institutions and those within them, I have been slowly robbed of the rosy optimistic attitude I once had. The belief I was brought up with that good prevails, that all I need is truth, has been replaced with what some would call cynicism, which I call informed knowledge. The bitter product of being constantly let down. Persistence and courage is not to rise in the morning with a positive affirmation, it is to get up and keep going even though you know how shit things can be.

The farce in all this is that people like my sister Sarah and I and the countless others seeking truth, accountability and justice must fight so hard for something which is our right. We do not live in a banana republic, a third world country where justice and favour are bought and sold like fruit in the marketplace. This is supposed to be a great first world nation whose democracy and justice systems are the envy of the world. It is utterly inexcusable and a blight on us all that the victims, the many, many victims, of public sector wrongdoing are treated so appallingly.

Some of the young people recruited to ISIS who were stripped of their UK citizenship have been granted legal aid in their efforts to regain it. I also read more recently that the wife of the London Bridge bomber has been offered legal aid to support her at an inquest into the atrocity. My sister Sarah and I needed to launch a crowdfunding campaign relying on the goodwill of well-wishers to pay for the seeking of a fresh inquest into Alison's death. I feel aggrieved my family has never received any kind of support from the state in our efforts to get justice for a sister who was abused and died in its care. We are just one of many families who will doubtless feel this way.

My closest childhood friend killed himself in January 2011. He was forty-three. I grew up with him, dismembering Action Man, climbing the machines on the building site, headers and volleys, fighting with the fifth formers at Grammar School before finally progressing to interest in the fairer sex. Johnny was another of the few boys from single parent families on the council estate where we lived. Birds of a feather, I guess. We spent many hours and days together playing in the woods at the end of the estate. We climbed trees and the walls of the old farm hall building. We lit fires, which we would roll through to replay scenes from war movies, and we threw grenades at enemy tanks; crab apples at passing cars. I still have a small chip in a front tooth to remind me we didn't climb every tree and wall unscathed.

Johnny was the naturally gifted one. Incredibly bright, good looking with a broad smile and talented, he was able to turn his hand to anything. He would take his pushbike to bits as I stood in the background, chuntering he would never be able to put it back together again. He did, with seeming ease. And continued to be able to do so when he progressed from his Raleigh three-speed to the souped-up Harley Davidson's he came to love. Sickeningly, with a half-decent singing voice he was as much a hit with the girls as he was academically able. He introduced me to the guitar, something I have retained a passion for trying to play if not mastering, to punk music, pornographic magazines, cigarettes, a rite of passage for many teenage boys in the eighties, and Leeds United; I didn't say it was all good. Johnny grew up to become a well-travelled and respected worldly-wise man with a responsible job.

Early in January 2011 following a serious mental health episode for which he was initially admitted for treatment, Johnny took his own life. He had a meeting as an outpatient with a junior Doctor that morning and was sent back home from the mental health hospital in an already depressed state with medication known to increase the risk of suicide. The lead clinician treating Johnny was on leave and the senior consultant on-call was not contacted before he was discharged. No risk assessment was done. At the inquest into his death the Trust told the coroner lessons had been learned, but that's just what they all say after every occasion where poor practice gets exposed. Surprisingly, they never seem to stand up and say, we fucked up your honour. My cat got more highly regulated attentive treatment from our local vet than Johnny got from NHS mental health services.

I was later told by someone who worked in the service in question, that the hospital he attended for his outpatient visit, and with hindsight should have been immediately readmitted to following the meeting with the junior Doctor that morning, did not have enough staff on duty to support the patients. They said festive party season had taken its toll and absence rates amongst staff who were supposed to be on duty were even higher than normal. Having seen how NHS staff are managed it's no surprise absence rates are higher than the national average, even on a good day. And let's not kid ourselves, some of this will be down to people's over-indulgence; they are only human. The unacknowledged realities of real life are the messy space we occupy which never features in reports or strategies. I myself have never needed to drink so much red wine and smoked as many cigars as when I worked for the NHS. Without a steady supply of these necessities I would have crashed and burned even faster in the dysfunctional, duplicitous and destructive culture I found myself working in. I was not the only one self-medicating.

Johnny should never have been sent home in the state he was in, certainly not with the medication he was given. He hung himself, it was his mother who found him dead. She has, understandably, never been the same since.

What is less understandable is how poorly she was then treated by the people who had been charged with the care of her son. Staff who had previously been responsible for Johnny's care became unavailable to speak with her. The Chief Executive of the NHS Trust who's care her son died in sent a letter of condolence in which he repeated an entire paragraph, he had obviously not checked the letter himself. There are clearly more important things for such important people to worry about than patients who die in the care of the hospitals they are running.

Johnny's mother knew something had gone seriously wrong and in the absence of honest open dialogue, she sought legal support. The costs of the case quickly mounted to a sum that would buy a small house. The Trust, in classically defensive NHS public sector style, applied all its legal guile and resources to keep her in limbo for almost five years, before finally offering compensation on the court steps. Is there a more perverse way to spend public funds than on legal fees to conceal the truth, to defend the indefensible from the very taxpayers footing the bill?

I find it difficult to think of a less compassionate way to deal with the grieving mother of a son who died due to your negligence than to put them through the wringer only to tacitly acknowledge liability at the very last possible moment. Surely, if there was ever a time for an NHS Trust to show some compassion, to hold its hands up and acknowledge they got it wrong, to say we fucked up, this was it.

A cavalcade of Harley Davidson's ridden by friends from across the UK and Europe attended Johnny's funeral at the crematorium. He was much loved and greatly respected. We said our final goodbyes to the sound of Neil Young's Rockin in the Free World.

Not long after Johnny had taken his life, I found myself at an NHS staff meeting amongst a room full of mental health practitioners and managers. The agenda was issued the same morning, the main topic was support for staff following the suicide of a patient. I nearly choked on my coffee. I fully support the idea of looking after the emotional needs of employees who have been close, not too close, to patients who take their own life. I can see how good clinical staff identify with their patients as people. I recall the mental health consultant who had been treating Alison in Doncaster expressing a sense of personal failure and responsibility in the letter he sent to the original coroner's inquest.

But the focus of the discussion I now found myself in was way too inward looking for me to be comfortable with.

The support families, friends and carers might need after the suicide of their loved ones, was never mentioned. I couldn't understand how these seemingly clever intellectually able people were not joining the dots. I was waiting for one of them to jump up in a Eureka moment and say, if we think we need help and support following the suicide of a patient, then perhaps the families of the dead patient themselves might need it as well; nobody did.

I had visited Johnny's mum during this time, and hearing first-hand how cruelly, defensively and indifferently the NHS were dealing with her, was heart-breaking. I was utterly gobsmacked that a room full of mental health professionals could be so self-absorbed in the process of ensuring their own needs were met, they ignored the needs of the families of suicides that occurred on their watch. I raised the point as diplomatically as I could.

I was told not to worry as numerous charities and voluntary services existed to provide support to the families, it was not a priority for the Trust. Without any hint of irony these people were saying charities would pick up the pieces after the NHS had dropped the ball. Was this what the Trust meant when it said it was becoming patient centred and working more closely with voluntary services?

Dealing with the death of a loved one is difficult enough without thinking the state was not only complicit in what happened but is hellbent on protecting itself from dealing with the consequences of its actions. Double whammy doesn't get close.

My family and I have now been misled by so many people from so many different public sector organisations there are times we don't know whether we are coming or going. When people ask me for an update on the situation, something they now do less frequently, I don't know where to begin. Should I tell them about the thirtieth Freedom of Information request I have just sent to the CPS, or the content of the three thousandth email in my inbox folder? What sets off as legitimate grieving for a loved one lost is so often and needlessly turned into anger at the way people are dealt with.

People dealing with such intense and often unexpected grief should not have to navigate the internal machinations and politics of bumbling duplicitous public sector bodies. In the case of what happened to Alison, the anger and sense of betrayal we feel about what happened to her in Garlands and her subsequent death by suicide has now become secondary to the anger and betrayal we feel at the way we have been dealt with.

We were kept in the dark in 1988 and we have been failed at every point since. The memories and stories my family could be sharing about Alison should be directed at remembering how brightly she burned in the short time she was with us. Instead our emotional energy has been taken captive by facts that were hidden from us. Our energy is redirected from the perpetrators of wrongdoing to the organisations and individuals who allowed crimes to be committed without redress. Carrying the burden of this lack of justice we feel entitled to is an almost unbearable weight, draining me, robbing my family of our right to grieve and remember Alison without sadness or anger, even rage.

I never wanted to spend my time and effort chasing publicly funded organisations and their employees to do the right thing, I can't think of a more frustrating less rewarding way for anyone to spend their time. I want to spend my time with the people I love, people who matter to me, I want to go out more on my old mountain bike, learn to play blues guitar, I want to watch a Michael Moore documentary on Amazon Prime, I want to build that website I bought the domain name for years ago. I continually ask myself, why must I spend my precious time pleading with people who are supposedly employed as public servants, corralling, cajoling them to do their jobs properly, diligently, transparently, honestly, the jobs we pay them for. Am I asking too much!?

It isn't like this to begin with. At first the process of working with public sector bodies starts with willing compliance to their bureaucratic requests. You work with the system and jump through the hoops put in front of you because you still hold the illusion it will deal with you reasonably, fairly. You haven't yet realised there are things, so many things, you don't even know you don't know. You have no idea of the scale of Machiavellian intent and the levels of administrative firepower being lined-up in readiness to halt any attempted advance toward the truth.

If you are like me, you will be doubly unprepared because you will naively feel the universe should now be inclined to be kind to you in the wake of whatever bad thing has happened. The delusional rationale doing the loop in your head is saying, we have been through enough haven't we, karma will restore balance, we will get to the truth. Funniest of all, you may still be under the impression the organisations and people you are dealing with will be keen to help you because as responsible public sector bodies and guardians of the public purse, they would want to learn from their mistakes, wouldn't they?

Scandals within hospitals, lying policemen, nepotism and incompetency in the justice system are things that happen to other people, not reasonable half-intelligent people like you. And at first the organisations you are dealing with will tell you they will be helpful. I can still see the sincere and sombre face of the former chief executive of the NHS Mental Health Trust in Carlisle as he earnestly assured me, they were doing everything within their power to locate Alison's medical records. The same records we now suspect were singled out for destruction to ensure the uncomfortable truths they contained would never see the light of day.

The way public sector services often deal with families after people have been wronged, harmed, sometimes killed, is beyond disgraceful. There seems to be no consideration of their emotional and practical needs or acknowledgement of the role the organisations themselves had in creating them.

Your most unhappy customers are your greatest source of learning, is a slightly cheesy but very useful quote attributed to Bill Gates. I and my colleagues often used it when advising businesses. Gates was simply underlining the benefit of listening to customers. This listening learning attitude creates improvement, and organisation's in the private sector have had to adopt it to survive and thrive in competitive markets. It is the other end of the spectrum from the fingers in ears, nah, nah, nah, run around the playground shouting I can't hear you school of thinking permeating many of our public sector services and most of our NHS.

Public sector bodies should have dedicated customer service departments led by directors with integrity, lived experience, influence and private sector know how. They don't, because they see their real customer not as the people who use their services, but the ministers, civil servants, regulators and government departments who provide the funding they depend on. Strictly speaking you and I provide it, but we'll skip that technicality for now.

This means there is little if any incentive to listen to people who use and experience the services, we fund them to provide. Perversely, they have a stronger interest in hiding problems from the departments that channel funds to them and from regulators like the Care Quality Commission, who are supposed to oversee them. Managing reputation, keeping the lid on problems, these are the things that keep funders happy and ministers off your back, so these become the priority. It is easier to manage the expectations of regulators and civil servants than deal with the complex messy problems patients and service users might have; however severe the impact on individuals may have been.

If these organisations devoted half the time, attention and significant amounts of taxpayers money they currently spend building administrative barriers and defending their reputations, into listening to patients, victims, and families, and improving their services, they would have better services which would fail people less often. But of course, that would be logical. Whatever was I thinking...

Chapter 19 - Healthborough

The women watched the men, watched to see whether the break had come at last. The women stood silently and watched. And where a number of men gathered together, the fear went from their faces, and anger took its place. And the women sighed with relief, for they knew it was all right - the break had not come; and the break would never come as long as fear could turn to wrath.

The Grapes of Wrath; John Steinbeck

I made a point of starting to write this chapter on the 15th April 2019, thirty years to the day since the Hillsborough tragedy. In March I had been watching BBC Breakfast news. David Duckenfield, the hapless copper in charge of policing the game at Hillsborough Stadium that fateful day in 1989, walked away from court in the small city of Preston. The jury were unable to reach a verdict. He was being prosecuted for gross negligence and the manslaughter of ninety-five Liverpool fans.

This awful avoidable era defining event, now etched like a scar on the face of recent British history, was made more tragic because of the subsequent cover up and misdirection by people in trusted positions of influence and authority. Including both senior and rank and file officers of South Yorkshire police. The tragedy and its shameful aftermath has rightly featured in the news and in our minds for many years. Though some may argue, and I would be one of them, it has not featured heavily enough.

Hillsborough has come to epitomise not only a David and Goliath struggle of citizens versus corrupt state, but truth versus lies, good versus evil. There is no older story. To stop for a moment and think that the search for truth, accountability and justice should be such a difficult goal to obtain in the UK in the twenty first century is both a sobering thought and a heart-breaking realisation. Lady justice has seemed increasingly fallible and deeply flawed.

But I wonder if the wrongdoing of Hillsborough has helped cement the role of dishonesty in our public services, making obfuscation and denial accepted ways of doing things. If only extreme tragedies are worthy of attention, how much else goes on that none of us are aware of? Though disgraceful, where it occurs the appalling behaviour of authority figures somehow no longer surprises us. It's as if we should almost expect and not be shocked by blatant abuses of power in public office. The deny, delay, defend, denigrate and deceive tactics employed in the public relations and communication departments of our public services, the same services we pay for, have become accepted, expected behaviours. It's almost a shock when someone in a position of trust is held accountable for their behaviour.

Public sector services and those representing them continue to reach out to us with one hand constantly demanding cash, telling us we can't live without them. Yet with the other they treat the taxpayers who fund them like dirt. Their ability to consume our money whilst viewing us with utter derision is confusing. Like being beaten up and spat on by a gambler you have just given your last fiver to.

The easy thing to think and easier thing for others to repeat is that they appear to have lost all touch with the people they are supposed to serve; us, we, the people who pay for their very existence. But I'm not sure that's the case anymore. I can't help thinking the problem is not that people occupying positions of trust and influence are out of touch, though they undoubtedly are, I just think some of them don't give a flying fuck what people think anymore. They are becoming increasingly untouchable, and they know it.

Following the conclusion of fresh inquests conducted in 2016 into the deaths at Hillsborough, the government asked Bishop James Jones of Liverpool to produce a report to capture the perspectives of those who had been directly affected. To some it may seem strange he was deemed the right person to lead such a task. Calling the Bishop seems only one step removed from calling Ghostbusters. I think the choice of a Bishop reveals the gap in trust in our society.

Even more recently, following revelations the lives of more than four hundred and fifty people were cut short at Gosport War Memorial Hospital, Bishop Jones was asked to lead an inquiry into what happened. Doesn't it strike you as strange that the well-paid heads of the organisations which already exist to regulate the NHS were not deemed appropriate for this task? Where were the Care Quality Commission, NHS Improvement or NHS England?

Why are we reliant on the clergy to do such things? Why can't the public figures already in post be trusted with these tasks? Why have we no faith in the existing bodies already funded to the tune of many, many millions, to monitor and oversee the quality of public services and the integrity of those who run them?

The establishment knows these figures, grey suited and overly well-rehearsed to the point of obvious insincerity, are simply not trusted. The experience of Mid-Staffs, Southern Health, Liverpool, Gosport and now Shrewsbury, has shown patients, their families, friends, and carers, that all these people seem interested in is making problems go away, not seeking to identify and deal with their causes. Though it sticks in my atheist throat to say it, it seems there is presently no one better than the men and women of a god, to fill this unspoken vacuum of trust. Who ya gonna call?

The report Bishop Jones oversaw was entitled The Patronising Disposition of Unaccountable Power, and though to me it seems well written and throws some punches, it lacks the brutal honesty about human nature the Hillsborough tragedy deserves. The term cover-up is used only once, and the document contains no mention of the words, conspiracy, dishonesty, liar or liars. Why not?

Sure, I get it, a Bishop can't be seen to call officers of South Yorkshire police a bunch of lying arseholes in a report being paid for by the government, more accurately the taxpaying public. But we all know it's the darker side of human nature which led to police officers colluding. Collectively agreeing to lie and falsify information to maintain status and continued acceptance in the gang to protect pay packets and pensions.

Hillsborough and its aftermath is not about the patronising disposition of unaccountable power. It is about the absence of morality, the result of the choices to lie and be dishonest that people make when they are allowed to hide the tragic consequences of their individual behaviours, behind the drawbridges of faceless unaccountable organisations.

If Bishop Jones own handbook of choice is to be believed, these same people were created in the image of God and fully able to choose their own path. It has become too easy to excuse the behaviour of individuals by removing their personal agency and labelling the system or the wider organisation as the cause of the problem. We shouldn't forget the excuse for cruelty and injustice of all types across the ages has been, I had no choice, or I was told to do it. Systems and organisations are nothing but the people within them. Its people who make decisions, not shifting entities with transient labels and logos. Does the Bible say the wages of sin are death, or does it say, don't worry what you do, it's all down to the culture of the environment you exist in.

I corresponded and spoke with Bishop Jones in 2018. He seemed a genuine sincere man. Unlike much of the apparatus of our state he replies to his emails. Perhaps heaven has issued customer service response guidelines for all employees; reply to your emails within one working day and pick up the phone within five rings. If only the public sector were as responsive. We had a good conversation and I greatly appreciated the time he made for me even though he was incredibly busy. It was around the time of the publication of the report into deaths at Gosport hospital he had overseen in June the same year.

If you feel in need of sleep-inducing reading, the Gosport report hits the spot. It is another lengthy tome, 387 pages, to add to the long and growing list of publicly funded reports into the clusterfucks occurring in our public sector institutions. A further attempt to unpick why the indefensible and unreasonable are allowed to happen in the services we fund to help us.

Again, a search of the Gosport document reveals no mention of the words amoral, colluded, concealed, duplicitous, liar, liars, self-interested or underhanded. It does contain a single reference to the words self-preservation, which I imagine is a polite way of saying someone or more than one person made choices to conceal or mislead. Self-preservation within the confines of a dysfunctional institution sounds so much better than, they withheld key information or lied through their teeth to protect their pension; something probably nearer reality. The word misled is used only once, and this is in relation to a conversation a patient had with a member of the local constabulary. No surprise there. In my experience if you've never been lied to by a policeman then you've probably not spoken to one at length.

There is also a new phrase in the report I had not come across before, clinical collusion. I think it means collusion amongst medically qualified staff, calling it clinical collusion is just a more palatable way of saying, people who were clinicians agreed to lie and mislead. It feels a little like trying to rebrand a group of lying bastards as Homosapien deception purveyors.

So, when are we going to learn I wonder? When will we realise the polite genteel language used in these reports achieves little if any real change? These lengthy volumes, even when overseen by the well-intentioned, appear to do nothing other than condone inexcusable behaviour and placate victims to ensure their anger is directed outward from the closely managed tent.

Like others, the Gosport report unwittingly legitimised the murderous, that's my crude interpretation of life-shortening behaviour, that lay behind the face of the NHS Trust under scrutiny. If people, clinical or not, in responsible influential positions in the public sector services we fund, want to take our money, they need to understand they must also be accountable for their actions. They should not be encouraged, able or allowed to hide behind words and phrases which excuse their choices because someone says the culture was broken, or the organisation was preoccupied with achieving arbitrary targets, or clinicians were subjected to excessive work pressures. These things may all be factual, but they feel more like excuses than reasons. People should be able to acknowledge their mistakes and we should all benefit from the learning that emerges.

No burglars or benefit cheats get away with theft or fraud using the defence of feeling pressure to keep up with the neighbours or telling the judge the culture of their neighbourhood is broken. We don't excuse knife crime on the basis everyone else was doing it. The narrative trotted out to justify the inexcusable actions of people in the public sector seems like middle class reasoning for bad behaviours we would never allow people from other walks of life to fall back on.

I had got in touch with Bishop Jones because I had read the Hillsborough report he oversaw, and I wanted to ask if he had any ideas about how to tackle the challenges we were facing, in our quest to obtain justice for Alison. We discussed similarities with the numerous incidents and cover-ups in the NHS and what happened at Hillsborough. The Bishop acknowledged he was inundated with similar requests for help. I got the distinct impression he felt like a bottle of water in a desert. I suspect there are many others like me, reaching out to him for help in their search for answers. Reaching out to God's ambassador in the face of failure from our all too earthly public sector institutions. I reminded myself a little of the desperate atheist come to the end of the road, praying for a miracle, earnestly pleading to heaven that if God will just do this one thing for me then I will repent and live a good life for the rest of my days. I made no such promises. God wouldn't have believed me anyway.

I shared my concern with the Bishop that more people die each week from poor treatment at the hands of the NHS than died in total at Hillsborough. I directed him to a report written by an organisation called Patient Safety Learning, at the time led by James Titcombe. James's son Joshua tragically and infamously died due to poor care at Furness General Hospital in Barrow-in-Furness. Nurses failed to spot a serious infection and Joshua died nine days after being born. The subsequent conspiratorial behaviour of those involved in Joshua's preventable death was appalling.

The report by Patient Safety Learning suggests one hundred and fifty people die avoidable deaths each week due to issues in NHS Hospitals across the UK. This number doesn't include the many other incidents related to treatment in mental health hospitals or community settings that lead to harm or death. The report touches on what we think we know rather than the things we don't know we don't know. In other words, the estimate of one hundred and fifty avoidable deaths in the NHS each week is probably on the low side, the very low side. And yes, lots and lots, millions and millions of people have a smooth and hassle-free encounter each week with our NHS, as they should. Hillsborough is memorable because even though millions of fans attend football matches in the UK each season, we don't expect ninety-six people to die each week.

I didn't share and compare these numbers with Bishop Jones to suggest tragedies in healthcare are more worthy of attention and support than Hillsborough, they are equally unacceptable. I did it to highlight the same shadow of public sector behaviour that straddles all these tragedies and demonstrate the massive scale of this largely invisible problem. A problem concealed because most issues occur as single incidents and do not warrant national inquiries or reports. I also wanted to highlight the scale and intensity of the hidden struggles every isolated family and disparate individual is coping with in their attempts to seek truth, accountability and justice from the NHS, for loved ones harmed and lost.

I explained as sensitively and diplomatically as I could that for people like us there is little press attention. There is no memorable chant or song called Justice for the Seven Thousand Five Hundred. Or an instantly memorable collage of the faces of the deceased, there would be too many to put in one image.

I have only the deepest heartfelt sympathy for the victims of Hillsborough and huge empathy and admiration for their families. But as strange as it sounds, I can't help envying the sense of togetherness and shared outrage the Hillsborough families have been able to harness to support their case for justice. I don't envy what they have been through and are still going through, who in their right mind would. No, I envy them for the collective way they have seemed able to support each other. I have never met them, and I only know some of their faces and the faces of the loved ones they lost from the media. I imagine them sometimes, meeting each other, talking about their loved ones, crying, howling at the moon together, thumping the walls and screaming at the brutal injustice of their situation, perhaps even laughing together as they share stories of the insanity they have endured and the loved ones they have lost.

And I imagine they do not judge each other, that nobody looks awkwardly at the floor or makes a crude attempt to change the subject to something lighter, more positive and uplifting. I also imagine they have gained great strength by being amongst a group of people who understand, who really understand. Fellow sufferers, victims, human beings who actually get it, who feel the same pain and share the same thoughts. Who else other than those who have experienced such things could ever really empathise?

What I wouldn't give sometimes to be amid such a group of people is only less than what I would give not to need to be. But the tragedy of my family is small, too small for a national campaign, not worthy of attention in its own right. I and my older sister Sarah only have each other and our partners and friends to unload upon, and there is only so much we can expect them to put up with. I would give my back teeth to sit with a group of people who understand what I and my family are going through, really going through. To offer support, to vent, listen and share our frustrations. To hold each other up when the going gets tough. The anger and sense of isolation I sometimes feel can be almost unbearable.

I also pointed out to Bishop Jones that if you criticise the NHS, you risk being labelled an enemy of the people. Unlike the police or the CPS, public sector institutions many have developed an informed and healthy disregard for, the NHS is the UKs most cherished asset, some would say best loved brand. Corona virus has cemented its place in the nations heart.

The NHS is one of the most inconsistently managed brands in the world. A loosely handled franchise consisting of hundreds of separate NHS Trusts, many supporting bodies and thousands of individual GP practices, all with their own ways of doing things. National it may be, joined-up and consistent it is not. Once you say you have had a bad experience with the NHS people assume you mean, The NHS, when in reality there is no such thing as, The NHS.

There is the nice blue and white logo we all know and love, but it is nothing more than a simplistic banner sitting astride a plethora of organisations offering different services of varying quality. The response from the majority when they hear any criticism of the NHS, is to drape themselves in patriotism and talk about the hard-working nurses who do a fantastic job. Despite repeated well-documented failings, the kneejerk reaction to any observations made about our NHS, is to perceive them as unwarranted criticism. It is not easy to have a meaningful debate in the UK about our NHS when most people in the country don't know what it is or how it is made up. This stifles debate and suits those who benefit.

It is said a job is done by people combining three things; knowledge of what to do, knowledge of how to do it and the willingness or motivation, to want to do it. What this widely accepted truism means is that people who need and want to engage with public services to understand incidents that may have occurred, are immediately disadvantaged. Often, the only thing they have going for them is willingness and motivation. With regards to knowledge of what to do and how to do it, they occupy the unenviable space of not knowing what they don't know, sometimes not even knowing where to start. My sister Sarah and I have spent a lot of time in this space. It seems there are many others fumbling around in it with us. A quick look at the number of appeals for justice and answers on social media reveals the tip of a very large iceberg.

The things Sarah and I possess are some tenacity, a small degree of intelligence, a little knowledge, a tiny bit of expendable if shrinking income and whatever time we are prepared and able to give. Time being the thing we have needed most to enable us to pursue all the threads and avenues that have emerged along the course of this ongoing quest. Starting this journey was like unwittingly opening the door to an impossible maze. There are so many different bodies and organisations to deal with and they each have their own processes to go through. Being committed means giving yourself to this process. It means being both patient and responsive. Understanding that there is lots of waiting punctuated by bursts of activity. Sometimes responses, complaints and appeals must be submitted in short arbitrary timescales, regardless of our health, availability or capacity to deal with them.

I feel a great sadness for all the people who know an injustice has occurred and simply don't have the time, inclination, resources, health or mental strength to pursue it. More worryingly are the many, many people who won't even know, as we didn't for ten years, that there was ever a problem to be addressed.

There must be thousands of individuals and families across the UK who have received disingenuous misleading letters from the police, the CPS, NHS, care services and local authorities, telling them everything that can be done was done, that they understand their disappointment, but there is no further action to be taken.

Most of us are brought up to believe what these organisations tell us. We do not think to question their competence or integrity. They wouldn't have knowingly done anything wrong would they? They wouldn't hide wrongdoing to protect their own careers, would they? They wouldn't lose the evidence sent to them, would they? Of course, they would have interviewed the list of people we gave them, wouldn't they? They would never put their reputation above the need for justice; that could never happen, could it? Important well-educated people like that don't need to tell lies, do they? You get the gist.

The last thing I pointed out to Bishop Jones was the actual quantity of work we have done in the last few years. Work which many others are also doing in their own isolated bubbles of despair and rage, and for which there is absolutely no guaranteed return. In truth, there are times when I think all we have gained by unearthing the lies and deceptions played on us, has been an unquenchable anger and a deep scarring sense of injustice. But I knew this was not going to be easy and to not even try was never an option. Since our initial attempt in 2015 to reopen the investigation into the events leading to Alison's death, the number of emails and letters we have sent and received runs into thousands and grows each week.

As of December 2019, I have over three and a half thousand related emails in my inbox. We have engaged with well over a hundred different organisations including public sector bodies, the press and sources of expertise and research in the relevant areas. These bodies include the Police, CPS, Police and Crime Commissioners, locally and nationally, the Victims Commissioner, multiple NHS Trusts and NHS commissioning bodies in pursuit of information and records, Academic researchers, The Nursing and Midwifery Council, the Royal College of Nurses, the Royal College of Psychiatrists, the Care Quality Commission, independent experts in the field of sexual abuse and the power dynamics between health professionals and patients, numerous regulatory bodies, NHS Improvement, NHS England, local MPs, government ministers, coroners offices, mental health charities, religious oversight bodies, safeguarding experts, the ICO, the IOPC, the list goes on and on. The number of separate individual contacts within these bodies runs into many, many hundreds. We have dealt with around fifty separate points of contact in Cumbria police and the CPS alone as they have passed us around the houses from department to department.

We have submitted dozens and dozens of freedom of information requests, and subject access requests to obtain information. Nearly all of these had to be appealed and some then escalated to the Information Commissioners Office. We have even been refused documents on the grounds they contained personal information when the personal information referred to, was our own. There have been countless phone calls, many Skypes, multiple meetings and the travel and time that goes with them.

I spend time on social media and endless hours seeking information and resources to help our cause. We set-up a website, which Alison's nefarious seducer asked the police to get taken down. He was concerned it revealed his identity. His fellow elders from Hebron Evangelical Church in Carlisle did not answer the solitary email I sent asking them if they knew what he had done. Instead they called the police saying it raised issues that caused them upset and promptly reported me for harassment. And the truth shall set you free.

Like everyone else I have used the internet to find my tribe. Going online these last few years has been a humbling and alarming experience. Seeing the number of people seeking truth, accountability and justice for loved ones who've been harmed in the care of the state is eye-opening. Many of these people have been a great source of strength and encouragement to me. I might have given up if I had not seen that I wasn't alone. I am unfortunately and most definitely, not alone.

The financial cost of what we have done, legal expense, travel, postage, time off work, runs into thousands of pounds and the hours given would be more than I needed if I had wanted to study for another degree. Multiply what we have done by thousands and you will start to get a slight sense of the scale of activity being undertaken to secure truth from public sector services in the UK at any one point in time. In July 2019, the NHS itself acknowledged that it's collusive culture of blame and cover-up is contributing to the deaths of eleven thousand patients a year. It may be more.

Aside from money and time, I shared the emotional cost of taking on this task with Bishop Jones. The bouts of depression I have experienced as a direct result of what I have been through are beyond anything I could have imagined or prepared myself for. At times, my head has been an incredibly unpleasant place to be. My marriage and relationships have been strained as time and emotional energy have been directed elsewhere.

I told him I was no doubt the decision I made in 2015 to push Cumbria police to reopen the investigation into events leading to Alison's death, cost me my career. At the time the investigation was reopened I was still an employee of the same NHS Trust, albeit with a different name, on whose watch the offences against Alison occurred. Efforts to make me uncomfortable at work were escalated and poor treatment towards me became less subtle and more obvious. Work became an unwelcoming hostile place and some of the meetings I was asked to attend were moved so they could be held at the same hospital site where the trainee nurse had sex with Alison all those years ago. The sudden choice of location for these was insensitive at best, deliberately upsetting at worst. People who previously chatted regularly with me now distanced themselves as life at work became increasingly unbearable. And though the Trust ultimately acknowledged its behaviours toward me had been regrettable, words don't pay bills and it was ultimately me that lost my job, income and whatever future I had in the NHS.

My treatment was just another visible exercise in humiliation and a showboating demonstration of authority to anyone else with differing views. The message was clear; rocking our comfortable isolated rural public sector boat, however dysfunctional it may be, will not be tolerated.

Bishop Jones listened patiently and attentively, but ultimately, I sensed that even this man of God would not be able to fully understand what he himself had never experienced.

I wanted this chapter, indeed this book, to be about more than the injustice we have suffered. Witnessing the courage and persistence of people like Julie Bailey, Melanie Leahy and Sara Ryan to name but a few, is humbling, heart-breaking and inspiring. I think of all the other people, some of whom I have spoken with or engaged on social media, the families, friends, and carers of patients who have been harmed and worse. If somehow all our individual struggles for truth, accountability and justice could be captured and collected, if we weren't dispersed, disparate, and if all the effort's we make in isolation were made visible in one place, what would it look like?

How many hours, days, weeks, months, and years have we collectively amassed pursuing justice? How much money have we spent? How many emails and letters have we sent? How many Freedom of Information and Subject Access Requests have we completed? How many phone calls have we made? How many appeals against decisions have we lodged? How many meetings have we attended? How many fob-offs, high-handed dismissals and disappointments have we been subjected to? How many lies have we been told? How many tears have we shed?

What is the collective weight of the hurt and anger we have felt and are yet to experience?

Chapter 20 - Flat Earth news rules now

In England, the Press is more centralized, and the public more easily deceived than elsewhere.

Homage to Catalonia; George Orwell

It is over ten years ago Nick Davies first published Flat Earth News, an excellent highly readable expose on the declining state of the media. The book shines a penetrating and disturbing torch into the world of journalism and the art of public relations. It introduced readers to a new and wonderfully descriptive word; churnalism.

Churnalism was the predictable outcome of the growth of what were referred to as News Factories in which journalists were given unrealistic targets for the number of stories they needed to cover, with little time for getting out the office. The book cited the case of journalists who typically spent less than three hours of each working week away from their desks building contacts, networking and fact checking. These being the essential building blocks of effective journalism.

The rapid demise of meaningful journalism was further reinforced by the need to speedily and unquestioningly cut, paste and recycle whatever information news desks received to enable them to meet their targets for content. Adequate time to check sources and accuracy no longer existed. Under increasing pressure to streamline and reduce costs in the face of new web-based competition, the traditional media didn't so much slimdown as hollow itself out. In the process losing the capacity and capability to fulfil its basic requirement of providing informed impartial and original news.

We live in what many are calling a post-truth era. I think they mean post-honesty. An age in which we seem drawn to people who lie politely over those who swear honestly. Fake news and finely polished bullshit are now the norm. We exist in a social media fuelled furnace of kneejerk soundbites, hate, half-truths, narcissism, nonsense, propaganda and of course the ultimate distraction from the things that matter, face-aging apps and kittens on YouTube.

Good quality investigative journalists who set out to get under the skin of issues that matter have become an endangered species. And their demise has not gone unnoticed by those who benefit from their absence. Trump, Johnson and their kind are obvious visible examples of people who have seen this new fragmented media landscape as open virgin territory across which any chosen narrative can blaze a trail. These people know we know they are misleading us, but they also realise it doesn't matter. No one seems able to hold anyone to account anymore, and we quickly forget todays lies as new ones emerge tomorrow. Herd Immunity, NHS Brexit Bus ringing any bells?

Say what you want to justify what you want to do and to hell with the people who must pick up the pieces. Our attention is the scene of a battlefield, whether we know it or not, and the first casualty of war is always the truth. In this fight for our headspace there is no room for the thoughtful and the considerate. Logic and reason are less able to be seen or heard in the constant digital cacophony and twenty-four news surrounding us.

But the role of a well-resourced functioning press, able to speak truth unto power is an important part of democracy. Whoever owns the media controls the collective mind of the people. In the decade since Flat Earth News was published, hundreds more local and regional newspapers have closed and what news media is left, whether press, TV or radio, has been paired to the bone to survive. This is not good news for anyone wanting to live in a society built on trust where transparency is the norm. Though the internet provides opportunities for individuals to be heard and social media revelations have their place, there is no substitute for a well-resourced press willing and able to stand toe-to-toe with vested interests, to hold our public institutions to account.

As the rise of social media and millions of new channels through which to consume the content of our choice has mushroomed, the traditional press has been squeezed out of view and out of business. The present truth is that whilst England's public may be more easily deceivable, it's no longer because the press is more centralized. The unregulated echo chambers broadcasting their messages to billions every day through cyberspace have created a fragmented press landscape. For many papers and press channels the need to maintain advertising revenues to secure their very survival has become the primary focus, overtaking the need to provide news coverage with any integrity.

The present truth is that whilst England's public may be more easily deceivable it's no longer because the press is more centralized. It's because the press is more fragmented, in some cases almost non-existent. For many local papers and press channels the need to maintain advertising revenues to secure their very survival has become their primary focus, overtaking the need to provide news coverage with integrity.

In Cumbria, the county I have lived in for nearly fifty years, there is only one independent newspaper publisher of note left. The Cumberland & Westmorland Herald first published in 1860 and based in Penrith is now the last local flag flying in a media warzone littered with casualties. In February 2020, the Herald entered administration. It was saved by a local businessman. Its long-term future remains uncertain.

In 2018, its long-established, last and largest local rival, the Cumberland News Group, sold itself to a company called Newsquest Media. Now one of the largest publishers of regional and local newspapers in the UK. Newsquest is owned an American mass media enterprise with a reputation for cutting jobs and centralising as many functions as possible to achieve the rapid payback needed on its acquisitions. Googling the titles of papers in Cumbria one is guided to generic templated pages and standardised blurb. Bland in the extreme. Homogenised and seemingly designed to remove all sense of localised individuality.

Following the takeover, in the first action of its kind, Newsquest's own employees, members of the National Union of Journalists lodged a complaint with the Independent Press Standards Organisation. They accused their employer of lacking commitment to quality journalism, including fair and balanced reporting. When journalists are prepared to call their own papers out in public, something is clearly wrong.

Many people in the county now follow a newsfeed called Cumbria Crack, which while occasionally informative, appears to have no journalistic capacity to assess, analyse or critically appraise the content it promotes. It seems its sole intent, like many other similar sites is simply to be the first to spread a story. I imagine the financial model relies on a growing number of followers to help sell digital advertising space. Calling itself an independent online newspaper the website appears to contain a host of automated news feeds that pull content from various sources. Entertaining it may be, but it's a poor substitute for the presence of properly resourced journalism. The last time I looked the site had almost one hundred thousand followers on Twitter.

Questioning nothing and promoting everything, to me it seems the antithesis of an independent informed source of news.

So obvious are the blatantly poor levels of local news coverage we are experiencing in the UK, in efforts to redress the imbalance the BBC recently agreed to fund the salaries of a small amount of locally based journalists. Strangely, these journalists were then employed in the very companies like Newsquest that sacked them to improve their bottom line. This is a new and worrying stage in the history of UK news-coverage. The idea that part of my licence fee is used to prop up the unsustainable business models of American mass media companies as well as the overpaid executives of the BBC does not sit well. Why the BBC doesn't just use licence payer's cash to employ more local journalists is a complete mystery.

Because the ability of the press to locate and investigate the important issues affecting us has been decimated. We now exist in a climate more conducive to flawed decision making, cover-ups, corruption, nepotism, poor and even dangerous practices in our public sector services, than at any other stage in our recent history. We are in a spin doctors dream.

In times of increasing austerity when demands on people's finances are more than they have been in living memory, the temptation to cut corners, to hide mistakes in order to maintain employment, and commit crime for personal gain become significantly greater. A country in which there is less and less capacity to scrutinise the unscrupulous, combined with a population subjected to extreme financial pressure is not a good combination. If you are the senior manager of a public sector service earning significantly more than your ability would earn you elsewhere, with a good size mortgage, university fees to pay, a status symbol car to maintain and a large safe pension pot to look forward to, will you be the one to blow the whistle on financial irregularities, poor practice, sexual abuse or unexplained deaths occurring on your watch?

For Cumbria's public sector, the absence of a well-resourced press and the risk of personal alienation in a rural community is a perfect greenhouse for the choking, sometimes lethal weeds of indifference and impropriety.

When it comes to dealing with the press, my family and I, through no fault of our own and with no wish to be in the situation we find ourselves, in fact an almost constant longing to be anywhere other than where we are, have found ourselves in a strange surreal space we are entirely unfamiliar with. Some sections of the press, and by sections, I mean individuals, have been incredibly helpful. Guiding us in our efforts to navigate the unchartered waters we've now been in for some years. Despite all the effort we have committed, we were, and in many ways still are, novices in the complex game of cat and mouse public sector organisations seem so adept at playing. Aside from lacking the truth, a minor detail in these matters, they appear to hold all the cards. A castle sized cupboard of tools and techniques and seemingly limitless financial and legal resources at their disposal.

Some of the journalists we have dealt with have shared their personal insights about the unwritten rules of the game we are in, demonstrating great empathy and making time to keep in touch whenever possible. They have given advice and offered immensely useful suggestions about what to do and how to handle and respond to the bodies we are trying to hold accountable. We will always be extremely grateful for this.

However, the lack of interest locally and nationally from all press channels, online, radio, print and TV, has opened our eyes. Even those journalists and sections of the press who have been supportive would be the first to admit that if we hadn't done all the spadework, they would not have covered Alison's story. It is not that they did not think the story was newsworthy, interesting and to many, as I'm sure it is to you, deeply shocking. They simply did not have the capacity or time to investigate it properly. For newsworthy stories of any complexity to make it onto the radar of busy reporters already tasked with carrying their own recording kit and editing their own work, they must be gift-wrapped, oven ready. The only group of people with less capacity to investigate the untoward and the illegal would seem to be the police.

The loss of press capacity in the UK means many local papers and radio stations, including the BBCs regional networks, are unable to provide anything other than basic levels of news coverage to increasingly time poor, distracted and apparently uncurious audiences. It's nice that Hugh Jackman visited the local pub for a meal on his way through the Eden Valley. Live here and love it deeply as I do, this is still a place most people pass through on their way somewhere else, a temporary stopping point on their travels or in their careers. And the ultimate transit station for the ageing population who come here in increasing numbers to retire. Yet even in this rural media desert, Hugh's smiling confused face as he is surrounded and selfied with a selection of star-struck locals, should not qualify as front-page news.

Much of our local press is now so stretched for content to fill the pages of its increasingly thin editions, it has become entirely dependent on the asinine news releases that stream like cheap confetti from the bullshit departments, I mean public relations teams of our public sector services. These articles and press releases often go unchecked by editors and are reprinted or broadcast exactly as they are submitted; unscrutinised and unquestioned. This means that where it suits them, the spin doctors in our public services exploit an incapacitated press to spread rose-tinted messages of success. Sometimes in deliberate efforts to divert public attention from something less savoury. The new set of values from the local NHS, not the tens of millions paid in compensation to patients and their families.

This constant unchallenged stream of unicorn fluff is now the sandwich filling for much of our local media. Perversely, their growing reliance on large swathes of content from the very organisations they should be holding to account, means local press channels are not only unable to challenge, they appear increasingly unwilling.

I recall telling Alison's story to a journalist from a commercial radio station in 2016. They agreed to cover the story on the condition they would only report the less contentious aspects, they said they didn't want to risk upsetting their relationship with Cumbria police.

The station is owned by a global media group and I was looking at the corporate values behind them as they spoke. We create unique, high quality content that delights our audiences. We think big and bold, pushing boundaries and embracing change. Their approach came to typify the caution much of the local press, with exceptions, would display towards highlighting Alison's story. Only the Guardian had the appetite and courage to report it nationally. I never got the chance to give the interviews or write the news releases I really wanted to. The press would rather broadcast soundbites to a public more animated by online spats between footballer's wives than social injustice. We really are a strange fucked-up society aren't we.

In recent years, the press of every persuasion in Cumbria, along with the local healthcare regulators, have been more absorbed in tales about the difficulties of car-parking at the local hospitals than the unnecessary deaths occurring on wards and in communities. The uncovering of the most significant healthcare tragedies of the 21st Century in the UK, in Cumbria and elsewhere, has unfortunately had little to do with the press.

Our local papers and TV channels are effectively glued-together with unedited public sector propaganda and fatuous feel good stories. A situation which it seems will only get worse. We use our neighbour's old newspapers to line the cat litter tray or keep warm the hedgehogs we overwinter.

Debbie and I once saw the illusionist Derren Brown performing live. During the act, a gorilla, strictly speaking a man dressed as one, ran on stage. The appearance was not fleeting, the impersonator made their entry, taking time to make themselves visible. The illusionist then paused his performance and asked if anyone had spotted a gorilla in the last few minutes. Everyone shook their heads, no one in the audience had seen a gorilla. It was only when he replayed video footage of the incident as it had unfolded only minutes earlier, we realised what had occurred. The entertainer did such an exemplary job of throwing the entire audience's attention in another direction that a man dressed as a six-foot ape was able to strut the stage unnoticed in front thousands of people.

It is a classic brilliantly executed example of misdirection and a wonderful metaphor for the role of public relations in the public sector. Look this way, look this way, keep looking this way, there's nothing else to focus on, nothing else to worry about, there really is nothing to see over there, just keep looking this way, this way, this way.

The undeniable demise of our public sector has been accompanied and enabled by the rise of the role of public relations. The importance these practitioners of the dark art of spin have to their paymasters is undeniable. If you are going to hold onto your overpaid publicly funded job, please your political overlords and feed them the messages and soundbites they crave, whilst living within shrinking inadequate budgets, keeping the pesky regulators off your back and looking good in the eyes of the public you are paid to serve, then you must become better and better at reporting on the less and less you are doing. Brilliant at documenting the nothing you are achieving. Public relations is the tool of choice that will enable you to show you are holding all these plates in the air, or at least create the illusion you are.

A well-resourced communication department and public relations practitioner is a must have for the street-savvy chief executive of any self-respecting public sector body. When it comes to celebrating success without being honest about the all too often avoidable mistakes they make, the NHS has read and memorised the illusionists guide to life. It is this contrast between what public sector bodies want to be seen as, versus the reality of how they behave behind closed doors that causes much of the mistrust and anger between them and the families of service-users they have failed.

They talk of compassion and values in their press releases when they are anything but in their day-to-day dealings. They talk of being listening organisations yet seem happiest running round with their fingers in their ears ignoring the people that fund them. And they tell us they are patient centred as they scrap budgets for patient information. Our press is filled with a narrative of disingenuous concern fed to them by public bodies, who behind the scenes, continue to display the swaggering organisational body-language of entitled indifference and insouciance. Taxpayer funded corporate sociopaths who listen and answer to no-one. Talk is cheap in the public sector, and all too often a distraction from reality.

The language of public relations professionals is the very essence of insincerity, of feigning authenticity in pursuit of self-interest. Public relations thrives in the absence of positive personal and organisational character traits. Practitioners of the vile art fully understand demand for their services is highest where principled leadership is absent, underhand, amoral and detached. The bigger the back, the bigger the need for a front.

The development and widespread use of the term public relations is itself an exercise in rose-tinted positivism and rebranding. Public relations was acknowledged by its founder Edward Bernays as simply a more politically acceptable way of describing propaganda. Bernays was a relative of Sigmund Freud and is often referred to as the father of PR. The word propaganda acquired negative connotations after its widespread use by Hitler's Nazi party.

The online Cambridge Dictionary defines propaganda as, information, ideas, opinions or images, often only giving one part of an argument, that are broadcast, published, or in some other way spread with the intention of influencing people's opinions. Google currently defines it more straightforwardly as, information, especially of a biased or misleading nature, used to promote a political cause or point of view. Considering such sinister albeit entirely accurate associations, it's easy to see why Bernays and co decided the word propaganda itself, urgently needed a remake. I guess Edward couldn't be accused of not practising what he preached? Did I say preached? Sorry I meant suggested following a period of extensive consultation with stakeholders. I would love to know what the inscription on his headstone is. I have some ideas…

In the very midst of crisis, the scandal-stricken hospital at Mid-Staffs was describing itself in documents as having a can-do attitude. At the same time, it was getting rid of registered nurses to meet financial targets. Using misdirection to fool an auditorium in the name of entertainment is a skilled and clever feat. Using misdirection to fool patients, staff and regulators into thinking everything is hunky dory when what's being concealed is not a man dressed as a gorilla, but neglected patients dying unnecessarily, is a callous, deliberate, and disgustingly duplicitous act. One in which the use of taxpayer's money to support it seems doubly inappropriate.

Many of the public relations and communication departments of NHS Trusts are now staffed by former journalists, plucked from amongst the rubble of what is left of local media. These game-keeper's turned poacher who have experience of what news outlets look for in a story and with existing contacts inside the press are welcomed enthusiastically by publicly funded services desperate to manage their reputations.

When I joined the Cumbria Partnership NHS Foundation Trust in January 2012 it had a well-staffed and well-resourced communication and public relations department. The combined budget for the team salaries and their associated activity was around four hundred thousand pounds a year. At the time they were one of about two hundred and fifty NHS Trusts. I spoke with a good deal of other Trusts during my time in the NHS, many of whom had much larger communication and public relations departments.

Simple arithmetic suggests if the average annual budget for communications and public relations of each NHS Trust is half a million pounds, then collectively they spend about one hundred and twenty-five million pounds on these activities each year, over a billion each decade. This figure does not include the public relations and communication budgets of all the other NHS bodies and associated agencies in the healthcare system. When I left the NHS five years later, there were fewer nurses but more people in the communication department than when I had joined, and still no budget for patient information leaflets. The well-resourced public relations departments of our public sector are running unchallenged rings round the shrinking skeleton of our media.

Though the reasons may have changed, the observation Orwell made in 1938 about the public being more easily deceived seems more accurate than ever. Our collective awareness is now deep in the territory of not knowing what we don't know and more and more at the mercy of misdirection and spin.

Covid-19 will provide an unparalleled opportunity for the unscrupulous to bury bad news and cloak ineptitude. In the wake of recent events our public services will be under great pressure to manage a wide range of increasingly unrealistic expectations, for which they will turn to their public relations departments. As a result, they will require more scrutiny than ever. I wonder if it would be too much to ask the BBC, the nation's publicly funded broadcasting service, to create a public sector monitoring team in each region of the UK. The primary responsibility of which would be to scrutinise and hold local public sector services to account, police, councils, social services and healthcare. Without fear or favour.

And now, here's a sheep that thinks it's a dog...

Chapter 21 – Lions led by donkeys

If you can keep your head while those around you are losing theirs and blaming it on you...then there's probably something they're not telling you.

Kipling and Anon

Kipling's most famous poem If, is often touted as our nations favourite. I myself have often looked to the poem for comfort. Its message of stubborn focused stickability, leadership, stoic endurance and ability to be all things to all people, like most poetical messages can be interpreted to suit the mood, motivations, biases and character of the reader. It offers the bland the keys to life, solace for the isolated, encouragement for the entrepreneur and gives the self-appointed hero an excuse to ignore everyone around them, to plough on without thought or regard for the opinion or wellbeing of others. It is the last of these the public sector and our NHS appears to have latched onto.

It is now just over a hundred years since a German general is said to have observed during the First World War, that the English troops fought like lions but were led by donkeys. He was observing in the most poignant of settings, that leadership matters. It impacts; for better or worse, and in this case was costing lives. Thankfully you and I will never know what it feels like to jump over the top of a trench into a hail of bullets, but anyone who has ever worked for a boss who behaved like a total ass can identify with the sentiment. It's an interesting fact most people who leave a job, leave their manager, not their employer.

When I worked in the NHS, the preeminent challenge facing health and care services was the recruiting and retaining of staff, especially nurses. I had many discussions about the challenges of trying to attract people to work in the NHS Trust I was employed in. During one of these I recall my director pronouncing in a lofty knowing tone as he tolerated my presence in his office, "working as a nurse for the NHS was just a job like any other", he said, as he gazed out his office window, hands held together behind his back as if addressing a crowd of invisible onlookers. Then like a comedian misjudging his audience he mistook my stunned curious silence for encouragement and went on to explain in a rising increasingly oratorial voice, that to him, in his job as a director, this was more than just a job; so much more. To him, his voice climbing steadily to the finale, it was about the very future of the organisation. Patients take note, you didn't feature.

I pondered what was going on in his head as he pictured the fictitious listeners applauding from the carpark below. What an unparalleled feat of mental acrobatics to have performed I thought. To turn caring for patients from vocation to commodity, whilst simultaneously raising his own acts of pen pushing, bean counting and spreadsheet navigation to the status of noble selfless deeds, ranks as one of the greatest pieces of self-delusion I have witnessed.

My former bosses at Carlsberg seemed more able to recognise the value of their staff in the service of spreading sugary alcoholic liquid to the masses than NHS leaders and managers seem capable of doing for people employed in the greatest vocation of our times. If there truly is no wealth but life, then those tasked with leading our NHS should strive to make serving its continuance one of the most fulfilling roles a person can undertake. How did we get to a place where before the outbreak of Covid-19, NHS Trusts had to offer signing-up bonuses and financial incentives to get people to work in healthcare? The thousands now coming back to practice their craft in the fight against the Corona virus were attracted by duty, altruism and the chance to make a difference. It has taken a global pandemic for people to understand the true value of our doctors, nurses and care staff. They have been undervalued and mismanaged by their employers for too long.

Of course, when my director dispensed his wisdom to me, he had no idea my mum, my gran and my aunt had all been nurses. They remembered their time in the NHS with great fondness and no small amount of pride. They recalled a time before the introduction of multiple layers of management, the arbitrary targets dispensed from ivory towers that diverted effort from caring to counting and the centralised relentless short-sighted outsourcing of everything possible; food, cleaning services, maintenance and hospital buildings themselves.

They had real skin in the game. Often serving communities they lived in and knew, sometimes forming lasting friendly professional relationships with many of their patients. They saw the hapless bureaucrats, managers and directors, self-proclaimed leaders without followers who possessed little knowledge of the world outside their office were a problem, not the solution. If they'd been in the room when he expressed his ill-informed opinions, he wouldn't have got out alive. Sure, not every nurse is Florence Nightingale, I understand that better than most. But whose character would you rather trust on the balance of probabilities; a man who has spent three decades kissing arses or someone who knows what it's like to wipe one?

Despite what happened to Alison, it's still my belief most people attracted to nursing see it as a vocation, they want to serve. The majority of nurses I have met as a patient and during my time in the NHS are hard-working and dedicated. But of course, they are just mortals, not angels. They are prone to the same temptations and habits, good and bad that befall employees in any setting. In most instances where they have behaved badly, sometimes incredibly harmfully, even fatally, it is generally the result of feeble characters working in bullied teams or collusive cultures that won't let them admit their mistakes. And of trying to achieve targets which detract their effort and attention from caring for patients.

The nurses I used to work with laughed at the idea they needed sets of values, patronisingly dished out to them at expensive launches every few years by directors who appeared to have jettisoned their own moral compasses some time ago. These same nurses told me they were under pressure covering vacant posts that managers were refusing to advertise so the Trust could save the money to maintain its reserves. Values; really?

In April 2019, the Nursing Times carried an alarming story about the number of nurses taking their own life by suicide. Over three hundred nurses in England and Wales took their lives between 2011 and 2017. In a profession which exposes them to the extremes of the human condition, they are trapped in an invidious and increasingly unmanageable situation. Exposed to the full spectrum of emotions and subjected to the unnecessary seemingly endless pressures of keeping tick-box happy managers at bay. The number of lives being lost may be much less than the troops of the First World War, but it would seem nurses, and for that matter many of the frontline health and social care staff we depend on, even more so now, are the modern-day lions being led by a large and very well paid cohort of inept donkeys.

I have never fathomed out if the ill-judged words my director spewed about nurses that day were designed to motivate, appal, or simply make me feel special in the presence of greatness. I think what he really meant about being focused on the future of the organisation, was maintaining his own very well-paid role within it. Figures from the Office of National Statistics reveal corporate managers and directors have the lowest rates of suicide. I guess to many NHS directors who flit seamlessly from one healthcare system or Hospital Trust to another, there is no real attachment to areas or communities, it really is just a job. To most nurses, I think it will always be much more.

A couple of years before the outbreak of Covid-19, I was online following a speech given by Simon Stevens, head honcho of NHS England. He was addressing a gathering of highly paid senior minions. A day on which these people are all in one room meaning the NHS probably performed better than usual, so perhaps not a total waste of our money. As if on demand, like trained monkeys the assembled great and good applauded Simon, when he announced with obvious pride that the UK spends less money per head on healthcare than Germany.

I sighed, deeply. Did he really say that out loud as if it was something to be proud of, I thought? Have I just watched the chief executive of the nation's most treasured asset, crassly announce that the country who led the industrial revolution spends less on the health and care of its citizens than its neighbours? Is this man proud to hold our NHS aloft as a leading competitor in a self-destructive race to the bottom of the, which government can get away with healthcare for its citizens on the cheap league?

Who will he compare us to next year? Mexico, Estonia, Lithuania; in ten years, Zambia, Sierra Leone, or possibly Armenia? Pundits place your bets now. I watched in amazement as the besuited primates not only greeted this depressing revelation like compliant chimps, but then, just as caged apes in a zoo hurl their own waste at the unsuspecting curious who are unfortunate enough to be within range, they started tweeting this deeply saddening fact into cyberspace, presumably to be shared even wider by the next layer of minions as unquestioningly sycophantic as them.

Why weren't they booing, chanting for his resignation while making gestures in the air? Had the audience consisted of frontline staff, over-worked nurses, unpaid carers, cash-strapped charity volunteers, poorly paid homecare visitors or patients on hospital waiting lists, they would be throwing their chairs at Simon like punks at a Bay City Rollers gig. Before placing him unceremoniously atop piles of expensive unread values and mission statements and auctioning the opportunity to light the glossy pyre to an eager baying crowd. But no, the upper echelons of our NHS applauded as they nodded their unthinking admiration.

Of course, Simon, recently knighted for services to healthcare, doubtless endorsed by funeral directors and coffin manufacturers, neglected to tell his adoring audience that Germany has around a third more Doctors and many more hospital beds per head than the UK. A statistic meaning it will naturally spend more per person on healthcare and one I imagine the Germans take great pride in. Nor did he mention Austria, Belgium, Canada, France, Iceland, Ireland, Norway and Sweden, who along with dozens of other countries, spend more per head on healthcare than the UK. Citizens of these countries live longer.

He also, rather importantly and many would argue very ungraciously, forgot to remind his overpaid audience that the hospitals and services they are paid large amounts of public money to manage, are more and more reliant on a growing army of unpaid volunteers. That we have reached the stage where a cadre of self-serving public sector profligates are dependent on the selfless to give their time and effort for nothing, should make us all think.

Recent estimates prior to the pandemic, suggest the UK has between three and five million unpaid carers and some of the highest levels of volunteering in Europe. The country and its healthcare system runs, in no small degree, on the goodwill of unpaid labour. Your NHS needs you, says the Daily Mail as it promotes a campaign to recruit unpaid volunteers into the NHS. The last time I looked its owner Viscount Rothermere was a non-domicile who pays no UK income tax. The heroic fundraising efforts of Captain, now Colonel Tom Moore, are filling a revenue gap many have knowingly created. But even the fruits of a legends labour are wasted if the barrel leaks, and at current levels what he has raised will plug a hole in the negligence claims bucket of one NHS Trust for about three few years.

When did reliance on charity to enable a government to spend less on the health of its own people become something to be proud of, in anyone other than the darkest hearted, Ayn Rand loving, die in the street like a dog or pay for your own healthcare brigades mind?

When did our national dependence on lotteries, bucket rattling for donations and endless campaigns to fund overstretched voluntary services become a good thing? Spending less than other civilized countries on the health of your own citizens would never be something to shout about, other than inside the safe cosy sycophantic and thoughtless echo chambers NHS management circles have become. What is the opposite of brightest and best?

I wondered if anyone in the room with Simon, perhaps an intelligent quick-thinking journalist from one of the specialist health publications or possibly the national press would have the courage to challenge. To raise their voice above the crowd and ask; Simon, should we be proud of spending less on healthcare and being increasingly reliant on social care, charities, volunteering and private sector services to fill the gaps our under-funded, under-resourced, mismanaged under-led NHS is leaving? Of course, nobody did. The conventional wisdoms always triumph in rooms filled with those eager to please and everything to lose.

Desperate to show support for their leader the acolytes continued filling Twitter with the ignoble content of his speech. Yay, let's hear it for our NHS, clearly dying on its arse and more reliant on charity than other countries, woo, woo, #but-just-keep-saying-the-right-thing-to-secure-your-significant-salary. Simon says put your hands in the air and your posts on social media. I picture the conference goers after a few publicly funded drinks in the hotel bar that evening. Oh god, I thought Simon was brilliant when he stuck it up those overly caring compassionate and sickeningly efficient Germans today, don't you think?

I was ashamed, saddened but not surprised by the lack of courage, thought and challenge. As a former NHS employee, I have seen the unbearable pressures under-funding and mismanagement place on staff and witnessed the harm, sometimes fatal, done to patients. As Chair and Trustee of a local charity I know how stretched resources have become. And as a patient myself I have first-hand experience of the impact. In the last few years alone, due to the lack of capacity in the system, I and many of my friends and family have spent money on private health services including mental health counselling, surgery and physiotherapy.

Once again, the Germans can observe the ineptitude of their ass-like English counterparts. I could almost guess the content of the German Health Minister's next speech, and it would not have been how proud they are of spending less on the health of their population than the Brits.

German patients get such speedy access to hospital services, data on waiting times is not even collected at the national level. Proof if it were needed that chasing meaningless targets is nothing but a harmful distraction, a wasteful misdirection of scarce resources that should be deployed in adding value to patients. Germany also publicly funds much of the activity that we in the UK rely on charitable donations to provide, including a fleet of fully equipped air ambulances. The German healthcare systems capacity and swift response in dealing with the initial outbreak of the Covid-19 pandemic, was acknowledged globally as exemplary.

Unfortunately for the UK, while other countries health systems have been investing and innovating to meet the needs of their patients, the preoccupation of NHS managers has been the manipulating of data and gaming of numbers to meet meaningless flavour of the month targets. Reinterpreting NHS data has become an industry. An array of specialist well-paid consultants work with NHS Trusts to help them "manage" their performance data. We not only spend less money and attention on the healthcare of our citizens than other countries, we waste huge amounts of it focusing on the wrong things. Simon forgot to mention the minimal waiting times German patients enjoy to his audience.

Of course, many of those attending his presentation were old hands. Long serving directors and senior managers. When someone tells me, as such people seem inclined, that they have many years of experience in senior positions in the NHS, I worry. It often means they have one years-experience repeated many times and no experience of anything else. It also indicates they have learned to successfully navigate and survive and thrive in collusive dysfunctional cultures and rigid organisational structures.

And the longer they have been in post and the higher they have climbed means they have more to lose than most if they challenge the hierarchy. The results of long service in NHS management are not the benefits generally associated with experience; they are the harmful side effects of unquestioning compliance. Challenge has been largely eradicated from the most senior circles, the very place we need it to exist and intercede on our behalf. Spineless, self-serving, obsequious, applauding nodding acquiescence prevails.

The NHS Nye Bevan envisioned was surely not created to be like this? These traits are simply by-products of an increasing focus on the wrong things and rewarding those amoral enough to exploit and perpetuate the systems frailties for their own ends.

The appalling treatment of whistle-blowers, truth tellers to you and me, is all the evidence needed the hierarchy does not respond well to unflattering observations. What does it say about the people at the top of our nation's health service that they would rather let patients suffer harm and families experience the pain of injustice than acknowledge and deal with poor practice? What happened to their humanity?

Nearly twenty years after mental health services in Cumbria were justifiably harangued in parliament, and the local NHS told to pull its socks up by the regulator, many of the important and vitally needed recommendations made, had still not been implemented. Grand plans were created, sincerely worded assurances the matters raised had been taken seriously were issued, but little if anything was done. To me it seems the collusive self-preserving harm accommodating culture that infected the NHS when Alison was a patient in 1988, and that was clearly present when NHS executives sought to conceal evidence of the crimes committed against her in 2001, is still thriving today.

Our NHS does not appear to have been led in any meaningful sense of the word for quite some time. The ideological interference of politicians, the proliferation of career managers and directors, the increasingly obvious absence of humanity at senior administrative levels, and the accompanying lack of a strong spinal cord in the limp lacklustre body of what passes for leadership, has brought it to its knees.

The lack of courage and willingness to challenge the pursuit of meaningless targets has destroyed workforce morale and created perverse management behaviours with horrific and fatal consequences. Patients continue to be needlessly harmed, lives unnecessarily lost, and justice denied to the victims and families of a self-serving bureaucracy that seems pathologically incapable of acknowledging or learning from its mistakes, unable to empathise with those it fails and unwilling to challenge and hold accountable.

If we continue, on the path we are on, necessity will drive more and more of those who can afford it to purchase healthcare from private providers as the last vestiges of confidence we had in our once iconic NHS disappear. If there is a silver lining to be salvaged from the dark cloud of Covid-19, it is an opportunity for the current crisis to highlight a need for systemic changes to the capacity, capability, structures, management and leadership of our NHS.

Chapter 22 – Reasonable expectations

When mores are sufficient, laws are unnecessary; when mores are insufficient, laws are unenforceable.

Emile Durkheim

Austerity and its purveyors of course have much to answer for. However, many of the woes plaguing our public services have more to do with the absence of morality than money. Evidence of the significant, growing, increasingly obvious and damaging deficit of courage, humanity and humility in the senior circles of our public services is all around us.

A quick recap of just some of the inhumane NHS hospital crimes and cover-ups which have emerged with depressing predictability since the 1960's; Ashworth, Alder Hey, Blackpool, Bristol, Ely, Gosport, Liverpool, Mid-Staffs, Morecambe Bay, Southern Health, the infected blood transfusion fiasco and now the Shrewsbury Maternity scandal, to name but a few, would suggest we are in the midst of a genuine and deep-rooted crisis of leadership.

And these are the things we know about. In candid moments NHS directors and executives, will tell you themselves these scandals are just the tip of a very large iceberg. By their own admission, there but by the grace of God go they. Social Care has another large, growing and well-publicised iceberg of its own; Vielstone, Whorlton Hall, Winterbourne.

As for the police, what we know is a drop of water, what we don't know remains an ocean.

Durkheim was a French sociologist I first came across as I looked through Alison's textbooks in the months after her death. I think she would have made a brilliant incisive social scientist. Distilled to its essence, what Durkheim's phrase means is that laws and rules on their own don't work. What holds society together, what makes people behave in certain ways, what makes some things okay and other things not, is the collective sense we have about what is and isn't acceptable. We are bound together, our actions and behaviour influenced and guided more by each other's beliefs and expectations than laws or rules. People who repeatedly break the law do it regardless of the law. They know the law, yet it doesn't stop them flouting it. What stops most people is the belief what they are considering doing will be viewed as morally repugnant or unacceptable by their peers.

The real crime within public sector circles is seldom the act, it is being found out. Possessing and displaying humanity, humility and morality has become a disadvantage, a weakness and hindrance to career progression, not qualities to be cherished or encouraged. As managers continue to replicate the behaviours of leaders, the system will continue to produce more of the same so long as everyone within it sees such behaviours as a blueprint for success. Nice guys and gals really do finish last.

Senior executives in NHS Trusts, police forces, councils, and other public bodies, never in my experience step forward and say, we lied, I lied. Deceptive behaviours and the subsequent doublespeak used to disguise them, are of course dressed up as something else, something noble. The greater good, the need to maintain reputation, the need to rebuild public trust, the need to be seen as trustworthy, not to be confused with actually being honest or trustworthy. But at their heart all these excuses are, is duplicity masquerading as noble intent. I imagine the public relations department in Cumbria police used this reasoning to justify the lies they told to my family in their efforts to conceal past failings. Just as I am sure executives at the NHS did in 2001. The Universal Declaration of Human Rights asks us to treat one another in a spirit of brotherhood, equal in dignity and rights. Aren't we as citizens of a civilized democracy entitled to be treated with dignity and respect? And at the human level, didn't we then and don't we now, simply deserve the truth?

Where there is no threat to national security, shouldn't access to information and truth be the default position? Why are public services so predisposed to secrecy, hellbent on never admitting or owning their mistakes? We all know they make them. We all know they are human, fallible. All they succeed in achieving when they continue to deceive and obfuscate so obviously, is the destruction of trust. I wish their public relations teams would stop trying to distract us, dancing like demented cheerleaders chanting merrily that the team is performing brilliantly when we can all clearly see the stadium is on fire behind them.

Poor cultures cost lives in healthcare. When these cultures cost the lives of people precious to you, it changes your view of the world. You acquire, albeit slowly in my case, knowledge and insight about organisational and human behaviours those without experience might call cynicism. You find yourself with a level of knowledge and skin in the game others who study and teach can only imagine but will never truly understand.

The tipping point for my descent into depression when I worked in the NHS, was seeing first-hand how it slipped so effortlessly into self-defence mode when anything untoward happened. My disappointment at discovering the immense chasm between what I optimistically thought I was becoming part of and the reality of what I had become part of, was utterly soul-destroying. I never dreamt the default mode of the NHS would be to manage its own reputation ahead of thought or concern for the deceased and those left hurting in the wake of avoidable tragedies. It's like causing death by dangerous driving, then sloping away from the crash site after sticking a post-it-note on the wreckage saying; shit happens, nothing to see here.

I tried explaining to an NHS director the growing sense of internal conflict I felt between my values and the Trusts actions, how my past experiences made it impossible to turn a blind eye to the harmful management behaviours I was witnessing. I contrasted the polished positive messages the Trust was busy communicating to the press with the reality of the views of GPs and the poor care patients were receiving. I shared the profound discomfort I felt at being part of what appeared to be an exercise in self-delusion and misdirection. Instead of acknowledging the validity of my views based on real-world experience, he questioned my mental resilience.

He interpreted any emotional awareness and empathy with the needs of patients and their families I was displaying, as a lack of commitment to the Trust. My desire to understand the needs and wants of others was taken as a sure sign I was going native, not an honest attempt to learn and find out where we might improve. In his world to be resilient was to stick to a script regardless of the facts, to park your humanity and morals in defence of the indefensible. The Trusts reputation and the status of directors came before any sense of responsibility, being open and transparent, or acknowledging it could do better. Scrutiny was resented. Being truly accountable to the people and communities served was to be resisted fiercely.

Regulation of our healthcare services is not working. More legislation and increased bureaucracy will not change the culture or cure the harmful behaviours in our NHS or any of our public services. When management cultures are so dysfunctional, simply creating further boxes to tick and asking for more reports from organisations predisposed to duplicity, is a fool's errand. The bumbling failed introduction of the fit and proper persons test for NHS directors offers ironic proof of this. To succeed in demonstrating compliance with an act aimed at promoting honesty by behaving duplicitously, is a new level of irony.

Regulation exists and multiplies in the absence of trust. Without the presence of trust, real trust, hard-earned and evidenced in the honest daily acts of individuals at all levels, the introduction of more and more measures becomes a never-ending game of cat and mouse. A constant circle of evasion and misdirection. Healthcare regulation in the UK has turned into a confrontational arms race of conniving duplicity in which the regulated displace their focus from doing to deceiving. The people who suffer are patients and staff. Precisely those the regulations are supposed to protect.

The summary version of the full report into the scandal at Mid-Staffs where patients died of neglect is a hundred and twenty-five pages long. Yet this report like others I have referred to, contains no mention of the words, amoral, amorality, deceive, lied, liar, liars, misled, moral, morals, or morality. But it is blindingly obvious it was the presence and absence of these behaviours and traits that enabled what happened. Not regulations, or sets of new values, or plans or standards for directors. The importance of the most basic personal ingredients of good character continue to be ignored by regulators who feel every issue can be addressed with a target or a checklist. The complete report into Mid-Staffs published in February 2013, comprised three volumes consisting of well over a thousand pages. It contained two hundred and ninety different recommendations. Even in the full report there are few references to the absence of morality and the word amoral does not feature.

Without morality at the level of the individual, and trust that is earned and evidenced by honest actions rather than empty promises and strategies, it won't matter how many recommendations regulators make, they will all count for nothing. Ministers are tossing our money to the wind if they think they can legislate for morality whilst continuing to recognise and reward the dishonest behaviours that chasing meaningless targets encourages.

It seems to me the pride I had in working for the NHS, the responsibility and accountability I felt at being paid for from the public purse, were the exception. I thought public-service at any level was a privilege bestowed on anyone fortunate enough to undertake it.

What has happened. Why do people occupying significantly well-paid positions of trust, funded by you and I feel justified in behaving dishonestly, evasively, amorally? Is it an old-fashioned view of the world that public servants should have integrity?

All I have to draw on is experience. But is my experience of how I and my family been dealt with, shaped by unrealistic or unreasonable expectations? Have my expectations of the individuals and organisations behind this unfinished tragedy simply been too high?

Was it unreasonable for us to expect Alison to be safe in the care of the NHS, protected from the sexual desires of nefarious employees? Were our morals overly rigid to expect the people, fellow-workers and managers in the NHS, who knew their colleague was having sex with a mentally ill young patient on hospital premises, to step in and do something?

Were we stupid to think once Alison's Consultant Psychiatrist knew what was going on, he would intervene and ensure she got the help needed to deal with the mental challenges an illicit crisis pregnancy would raise? Was it naïve to expect him to tell the police that a student nurse on his watch had broken the law and got a patient pregnant? Have we been misguided in our expectation that the professionals we trusted with Alison's recovery would share vital relevant medical information about what had happened to her in their care?

Were we then gullible to think senior executives from the NHS would treat our concerns seriously and share information openly with us, with the police? Were we simply foolish to expect that once the committing of a serious crime had been uncovered, the authorities would do everything in their power to ensure justice was done?

Were we overly trusting in assuming the police would act diligently, competently and not lose the evidence we gave them? And was it just plain old delusional for us to think the NHS, Cumbria police and the CPS would act together in the interests of a victim's family? That they might collectively seek to understand, to empathise with our need for justice.

With the benefit of hindsight, I fear we may have been all these things. Our expectations of honesty, integrity, decency, now feel like a quaint notion, a flawed paradigm and disabling anachronism in a post-honesty era. It is said the crooks know all the tricks so honest men should learn them in self-defence. If that's the case, then each day still feels like a school day.

I love to watch my detective hero's, Bosch, Endeavour, Rebus, Vera. My newest idol is Dr Max Goodwin, the bureaucracy busting solution focused Medical Director of the New Amsterdam Hospital in New York. His compassionate can-do attitude and willingness to go the extra mile is a welcome antithesis to my experience of directors in the NHS. Such make-believe characters are the escapism keeping my belief alive in what conscientious public service might look like. I know they and their fictional attributes, the fallibilities, traits and quirks which make us love them are not real. Their attention to detail, the personal emotional investment in each case they become involved in, are a fantasy. It may be unfair that I use them as the benchmark against which I compare my own experiences of dealing with box-ticking bureaucrats. But I want to believe there are people who might go the extra mile.

Can you imagine Brenda Blethyn's earthy detective character Vera Stanhope, saying in her finest Geordie accent, ere, this case aboot that wee lassie and them historical sex crimes is a nee brainer like, but its ganna invalve a fair amount ah work. It'll bugger up ma detection rates an ah cannit be arsed we it, as she screws up the notes she has just taken from a distraught witness, throwing them casually over her shoulder into the nearest bin. Vera would never do such a thing. As for Cumbria police...

When they are good, they are very, very good, but when they are bad, they are horrid. How is it our public services can behave so brilliantly one minute yet so malevolently the next? Like Jekyll and Hyde, they morph from an air of caring attentiveness to sociopathic and abusive in the space of a nanosecond. Why are they so difficult to deal with? So quick to display indifference and thoughtlessness, desperate to feign perfection and hide their mistakes from the people they are paid to serve?

When did employment in public service funded by taxpaying citizens, turn from a privilege to a right? When do people change from who they were into scheming storybook villains who feel it is better to lie to the families of victims than talk honestly to them? I wonder if these are the sons and daughters of the hat wearing churchgoers from St Andrews. Were they always destined to become these people?

Some business writers will tell you public services are poor because we expect little from them. They simply give us what we anticipate getting. We don't expect to be delighted by them, to get great service from them, so they don't provide it. Have we now reached a point where we have only ourselves to blame if we want anything more than incompetence and duplicity from the public services we pay for? That would be an incredibly sad place to be.

At this point it's worth remembering the gap between our experiences and what we might reasonably expect often exists because of the mistaken assumption many of us hold, that we are the customer, the focus of all effort. Most citizens who use publicly funded services remain under the impression that they are the important part of the process, the epicentre of each public sector organisations attention and efforts. We are not, you are not, I am not.

Can this ever be changed? Should we matter more to the organisations we fund to serve us? What should our expectations of them be? How do we want to be treated by them? What are the behaviours we should expect from them? What sort of people do we want to lead them, to manage them, to work in them? How should they be helped and held to account when they don't meet our expectations?

Trust is the only currency that should truly count in public services. Not only should we be able to rely on them to do what they say on their respective tins, acting honestly and with integrity as they do it, we should have a say on what is written on each tin. Public services are after all, ours, whether we like them or not. They belong to us. Are paid for by us. And whether they like it or not, they should be there to serve us.

Being trusted is the fruit of being honest. Trustworthiness is not a product to be manufactured by knitting sincere sounding words together, by mimicking its characteristics. Such constant obviously disingenuous acts, charades of false contrition when things go awry have brought us all to the point of screaming or yawning when we hear someone standing on the court steps or outside a hospital, speaking as if from a script, saying lessons have been learned. Fuck save us all from another hollowed-out publicly funded excuse for a human looking earnestly into a camera saying, lessons have been learned.

We have simply stopped believing what many in public services say; and while we are losing faith in them, an army of the hapless and well-paid, the chairs, chief executives, directors, and senior managers sits on its hands looking impotently on, hopelessly saying they are unable to make change, that their hands are tied, they are only doing what the system forces them to do. These well-paid bystanders, pompous, indifferent parasites, will never acknowledge their role as leading actors in the post-honesty post-trust crisis we are undoubtedly in. They and their kind are not stuck in traffic, they are the traffic. They have always been the traffic and the change we need is unlikely to come from such people.

It is said for every complex issue there is a simple answer, which is generally wrong. We know legislation is failing, and growing lists of recommendations not only achieve little, they divert resources from where they are needed and create measurement fatigue. There are certainly no obvious simple formulas for addressing the poor behaviours crippling our public services. No straightforward answers to these huge ethical challenges exist.

This book is not anti-public sector or anti-NHS, it is very pro-public sector, pro-NHS. We get angry about the things we care about. I have been to numerous third-world countries where people would give their right arm to pay fair taxes in exchange for decent public services; sanitation, education, health, policing, the list goes on. I am a passionate believer in a publicly funded National Health Service. Health and care services collectively funded by all, to serve those who need them when they need them, regardless of their ability to pay. This is the very essence of a civilized society. The principles behind the NHS do not represent the best of what it means to be British, they embody the best of what it can mean to be human.

The BBC recently called the state of Social Care in Britain a national disgrace. And there is no serious informed or respected commentator of note who would argue the NHS wasn't in the direst of trouble even before the Corona outbreak. The UK is the world's fourth largest economy. There is no reason we should not expect our healthcare and public services to be amongst the very best in the world. We will never achieve this ambition if we continue to ignore the hiding of incompetence, the amoral management practices and short-sighted self-interested actions of public leaders, those who accommodate them and those who lack the courage to challenge them.

The circus of regulating, monitoring and whistleblowing has become an absurdity. Can honesty, ethics and morality be taught and learned, or just be shown to be being taught. I don't know. I don't have the answers; they are much bigger than me. I know real change is difficult, but I also know we cannot collectively continue to stick our heads in the sand. The absence of a moral compass is costing lives. Room must be made for candid conversations about honesty, integrity and morality in public services, and how we reached this point.

We are not losing our trust in public services for their lack of resources. We are losing trust in them because they stopped being honest. The challenges facing them are not purely financial. The absence of honesty and integrity is the greater crisis facing us.

Our knowledge has made us cynical.
Our cleverness, hard and unkind.
We think too much, and feel too little.
More than machinery, we need humanity.
More than cleverness, we need kindness and gentleness.
Without these qualities life will be violent, and all will be lost.

The Great Dictator; Chaplin

Chapter 23 – From despair to where?

I'm at the stage, where everything I thought meant something, seems so unappealing.

Brilliant Mind; Furniture

Martin Luther King said the arc of the moral universe was long, but that ultimately it bent towards justice. I used to believe it. I still want to believe it.

After all, justice ultimately prevails, doesn't it? The good guys and gals win in the end, don't they? Perhaps the hope of justice endures because it's only those who survive and succeed who get to tell their story. The journey I have found myself on is a journey that found me. It isn't one I sought, nor is it one I could avoid. Foolishly, it is one I thought I could control.

When I set out seeking justice for Alison for the second time, I had no idea the genies I would unleash. What I approached and tried to manage like a project, calmly, logically, objectively, somewhere along the line turned into a quest. I clung to the illusion that the institutions who failed us were not inherently broken. I thought they would not only acknowledge their failings but want to address them, to make things right.

Then I found out the universe doesn't work the way I thought it did, and my world, my sense of who I am, my place in society and my emotional wellbeing, came crashing down around me. I didn't know how much a person could need hope until I found myself without it.

Writing this book has been necessary, cathartic and at times incredibly painful. I have taken a journey through time, viewing history through the eyes of a young boy, now deciphering, judging with an adult's mind. Looking back over the years without blinkers and with time to reflect has been immensely emotional. The loft I have spent so many hours writing in has taken on new life, flooded with thoughts and memories. Each alive with renewed energy, poignancy, joy, sadness, anger, pain, rage. Memories I did not even know I had acquired to enable me to forget, have come back with crisp clarity. I have admitted things to myself, faced truths I have been hiding from and that have been hidden from me for many years.

I met my cognitive behavioural therapist this morning. As I drove to the lovingly restored scent filled rustic barn outside

Penrith where she is based, I found myself listening to Women's Hour on Radio Four. Jane Garvey and guests were talking about Love Island. Love Island, fucking Love Island. The world is going to shittery on a rocket-fuelled twatting handcart, my mind is taking me to hell almost as quickly, the pillars of our justice system are crumbling in front my very eyes, my family has been royally screwed over, an increasingly impotent press seem uninterested in anything that really matters, and all the pseudo-intellectuals on Radio Four want to talk about is Love Island. What the fuck; I want to puke.

The intelligent sounding ladies are desperately trying to convince me there is more to Love Island than a parade of publicity hungry scantily clad shallow vacuous dullards set against a backdrop of sickening clawing music. They talk about how the show highlights important issues affecting young people. They talk about something called the Girl Code, then the Bro Code. They try to tell me the show provides a conversational totem round which young people can gather and share their views on the challenges facing them. Totem my arse. What utter bullshit, horseshit and any other shit you can think of. Who the fuck do they think they are kidding? The anger that seems to constantly simmer under my surface these days breaks out as I realise my licence fee is paying for all the shite they are talking. I turn the radio off. I am really in need of therapy now.

I am becoming more comfortable with anger. I realise I have earned the right to be angry, really, really, angry. I'm still asking myself, when will it be time to relent, to stop seeking justice. When? Will I ever get back the sense of wellbeing I used to treasure? I don't have the answers yet. I used to be a nicer person. For nice read slightly gullible, or perhaps a little too trusting, maybe even naïve. I have felt distinctly underfoot for some time. Writing this book has helped me lift my head and straighten my spine.

This morning I am here to see the counsellor who is helping me deal with issues I faced after being knocked off my pushbike by a driver who had been drinking. It may sound strange after everything else I have had to deal with, but this incident was the straw which nearly broke this camel's back, mentally and physically. My mind suffered more than my body and I am grateful my legal cover is footing the bill for therapy. I stopped screaming at Jane Garvey a mile ago. I pull up outside the barn and find myself repeating the words, stupid silly bitch, stupid silly bitch, as I recall the driver who knocked me off my bike and remember why I am here.

As we neared the end of our allotted time my therapist asked what I wanted to get out of my sessions. I said I want to feel able to participate in life even though I know people can't be trusted and I feel life is basically a bag of shit. I explained I had lost the happy comforting illusions I once held about the world and my place in it that used to get me out of bed with a spring in my step. I used to tell myself and those around me the best was always yet to come, and I believed it. I trusted people, I had hope. It seems like that has gone now and I need to find another way forward. My therapist has been great, but I'm not sure she knows what to make of me.

I have veered back and forward from hope to despair, and I know the journey is not yet over. My beliefs have been shaken from their foundations. I am struggling to come to terms with how ill-informed and ill-equipped I have found myself to be. It's as if I have been in my own version of the Truman Show, blissfully ignorant of the world around me, believing others were playing by the same rules and subject to the same moral boundaries I was.

It was so affirming to hear my therapist say I was entitled to my anger. That it is natural, expected and completely logical. I needed to hear those words. Though it is getting easier to live with I know I will need help if I am going to make it. In the meantime, I can enjoy laughing from my lofty perch of experience at what I realise now were the ill-informed ramblings of the positivity gurus and bullshit merchants I paid attention to when life was less challenging. The motivational books, Ted talks, throwaway phrases, social media posts, presentations, papers and posters quoting the teachings of Buddha or the Dalai Lama. Posturing about how to live and deal with anger from isolated ivory towers built on emotional distance and non-involvement. Don't hold onto your anger, they exhort, it will only harm you. Holding onto anger is bad for your health. You must learn to transform your anger into patience.

Fuck off. Have they been denied justice for a sister abused in a mental health hospital, failed and lied to by the police, misled by the justice system? Anger and hatred of injustice are underrated. Too many people mistake tolerance, unawareness and ignorance of injustice for positivity. As the saying goes, if you're not angry, you haven't been taking notice.

I realise hope is the thing we all need. It's the force that keeps us hanging on in there when everything around us is crumbling. My world stopped working the way I thought it did and the institutions I was brought up to believe in failed. As I have watched the foundations of my beliefs disappearing, I have been left thinking I no longer fit into a world I don't comprehend. I question if I ever have. I think I am starting to understand it more now; I just like it less. I feel the ground around me, the things I thought I could count on, the principles of a fair and just society in which I could live and contribute, these have turned to sand and given way. Perhaps they always were sand, perhaps my faith in them to this point was utterly misplaced, my comforting illusion.

Alison's needless death and the circumstances that led to it still make me incredibly angry. What makes me infinitely angrier is the way we have been dealt with. Lied to, and misled. It's no longer the initial crimes committed against Alison which hurt the most. People will do bad things; they always have, they always will. My anger is now directed toward a system, a group of organisations and individuals that allowed it to happen and then failed to deal with it after it happened, and their subsequent unwillingness to be honest, to acknowledge and be open about their failings.

To not only be the recipient of incompetence, but to be the subject of concerted efforts to lie and misdirect; that hurts. Our public sector services, the ones we fund to help us, they add to the challenge of moving on, they make it almost impossible. Dealing with them becomes the challenge, right at the point when it should be part of the solution.

Our public sector institutions have mastered the art of defence. The drawbridges of denial, the energy sapping process filled moats of doom and the walls made of the solid stones of stoicism with narrow slits through which no empathy can flow. They are seasoned pros in handling small fry like me. On the rare occasion the little people find a chink in the fortress wall, the bureaucratic occupants of the castle take note and vow to get better at defending that section next time. They have the benefit of a thousand encounters under their belts, I have only persistence and righteous indignation.

And the myth of closure persists. Talk of recovery focused mental health interventions to get me back to the person I used to be are misleading. Events have shaped me, changed me for ever. For better or worse I am a different person. It has taken me a long time to realise I can't deal with things, put them to bed and move on. It doesn't work like that. It's not that I don't want to, but even if it was within my power, contentment doesn't seem a fitting gift to give myself just yet.

Depression brought me to my knees and to tears at the foot of the stairs as I found the things that gave me pleasure meant less and less. I used to be a lover of music, a bringer of joy, a teller of jokes and like Alison, a mocker of pomp. Doing my best to bring frippery to a world I thought often took itself way too seriously. I wasn't always Eeyore. Now, I daren't let myself get happy, overly content or look forward to anything too much. I watch for the emergence of spontaneous happiness like a hawk scanning a meadow. I know deep darkness follows light. I expect hurt and disappointment. I am frequently visited by what others tell me is an irrational fear of losing everyone and everything precious to me. Something I have not felt since I was a drifting homeless teenager.

Depression is a complete and utter bastard. Dark, shark-eyed, relentless, unfeeling, energy sapping, sleep depriving, esteem eating, memory stealing, joy denying, libido crushing Viagra consuming depression, is ever circling. I tread water as we watch each other. Flight feels futile, impossible. I worry that with a deft flick of its powerful chemical tail it could get the drop on me, catching me out, fucking with my head and tearing at the fabric of my being as it pulls me down, again. The thought of depression's return is its ever-present evil twin. Medication, science, has become my life raft.

The only things that have kept me from taking my life in recent years are the hurt I would inflict on the people I left behind, and anger. The intensity of anger and rage I feel can at times be ferocious, almost unbearable. Yet the energy it gives is often the only thing sustaining me. When I was young and ignorant, I used to think of suicide as the sole preserve of the mentally ill, the rotten fruit of an infected tree. But sitting in the still smouldering wreckage of my emotions, I think I now understand it as a logical choice in a selfish dysfunctional world. In bullish moments, I tell myself that even if I feel like doing it, even though I know the mind can lead anyone to take the ultimate step, I will be damned if I let the bastards grind me down to the point of suicide. Fuck them.

I have a good life in the traditional sense of the word, and I know it, but depression doesn't come and go based on material circumstance. Its power is that it exists in-spite of the facts. The idea it depends solely on the presence or absence of hardships, perceived or real, is misguided. I now know that. What have you got to be depressed about, is an ill-informed question. Depression is an illness like any other. Nobody says, what have you got to have cancer about. I know I would have been swept out to sea were it not for the anchors in my life. The strongest of these being my wife and best friend Debbie. Love and concern for the people that matter to me, the beauty of the place I live in and deep reserves of rage and injustice being the others. I think anger and love are sides of the same coin.

The decline in my mental health was fuelled not only by the sense I didn't understand the society I live in, but that I just don't matter to it. I feel as if the unwritten contract I had with it, the one which says if you work hard, pay your taxes, contribute to your community and keep your nose clean then the state will be there when you need it. This implicit contract if it ever existed has been well and truly shattered, smashed into a million pieces that can never be put back together again.

I don't want you to think I felt I should matter in a significant or extraordinary way. When I say I have realised I don't matter, I mean I now understand that as a citizen I see how essentially meaningless I am to the institutions underpinning the society I live in. I mean something to the people who love me, these same people mean the world to me. What I want to convey is the incredible sense of betrayal I feel when I realise the institutions I thought existed to help, institutions that kept telling me when I didn't need them that they would be there for me when I did, iconic institutions held aloft as embodiments of the principles civilized society is built on, structured around, they simply don't care about me and they don't seem to care about justice. Worse, if I attempt to engage them or try to question them, they will actively work against me. I just didn't see that coming.

It feels like an important connection bonding me to everyone around me has been removed. Their contract with society and their illusion remains untested and intact. My experiences have made me feel insignificant, unimportant, unwelcome even. When it comes down to it, we should feel we matter to the societies and communities we live in. I think we need some sense our lives matter, that we are part of something bigger than ourselves.

Where next? The state that caused the death of Alison and nearly destroyed me, offers no support. Where do people like me go to find help? The NHS, the police, the CPS have offered nothing but words, duplicitous utterances given without sincerity. It is incredible when I look back and see how shabbily my family have been treated. I feel sick and naive.

I hope with all my bruised tormented heart, what happened to us never happens to you or those you love, this is also a problem: it means I know you will never really understand, what it has felt like to be in the middle of this. I used to think people were lazy when they wrote that words are not adequate in condolence cards, now I get it. There are more and more instances I feel the words at my command are just not up to the task. I don't think I need you to fully understand, just to have heard my voice, to have granted the precious gift of your attention if only for a short time, is enough. Thank you.

Epilogue

Only the rich can get justice, only the poor cannot escape it.

Henry Demarest Lloyd

I thought the objectives we set at the start of the second investigation; truth, accountability and justice, were simple, achievable. How wrong I was. It is now early 2020. The passage of time and no small amount of persistence continue to reveal an astonishing, disturbing and tragic sequence of events and failings, before and after Alison took her life.

In 2016 charges against Cliff Richard were dropped in the absence of evidence. The cost to the taxpayer of police and CPS time is estimated at over a million pounds. In July 2019 Carl Beech was sentenced to eighteen years in prison for creating false allegations of murder and child sexual abuse. The Metropolitan police spent over two and a half million pounds investigating the unfounded allegations this clearly troubled man had made. They obtained search warrant's based on spurious claims, people were questioned, detained and some put on bail for almost two years. And all this was done without a shred of credible evidence.

There is no doubt we have done more investigating, researching and probing than the NHS, Cumbria police or the CPS in our efforts to reveal the events leading to Alison's death. As well as the admission of guilt from the trainee nurse, Cumbria police are in possession of notes and an audio recording suggesting sex between staff and patients at Garlands Hospital was widespread, and the rape of patients by nurses occurred. This information was offered to me as I turned over stones the police were unwilling to look under. Though I have no faith in Cumbria police, as I have unearthed evidence of wrongdoing, I have shared it with them. At the time of writing they are yet to act on any of the information given to them.

In November 2019, the CPS were forced to admit that arbitrary internal targets they imposed on their employees had deterred their own prosecutors from pursuing complex cases. A subsequent report by Her Majesty's Crown Prosecution Inspectorate concluded that victims of complex sex-crime related cases were being let down by a combination of an understaffed CPS and under-resourced police force. The CPS promptly announced to the press it was seeking a further five hundred prosecutors to address the gap. Round numbers work so well for soundbite driven public relations exercises. In simple terms, the organisation we fund to provide justice in the UK, the same organisation which has been telling us all it was working effectively on our behalf, is now admitting it has been under capacity, under-performing and failing the victims of sexual crimes for years.

In a recent twist of events, following a freedom of information request made early in 2020, it appears the CPS have not only misled my family and I in their efforts to conceal ineptitude, they are now attempting to mislead the Attorney General's Office. Unknown to us, in 2019 the CPS provided a briefing to the Attorney General in relation to their handling of Alison's case. In this briefing they have told the Attorney General they took all relevant factors into account and adhered strictly to their own guidelines. We know this to be untrue. The CPS and Attorney General's Office are refusing to share copies of this briefing.

A vulnerable disturbed young woman was groomed, manipulated, and her condition exploited to enable an older male nurse to engage in unprotected sex on hospital premises. To me these acts, committed on a mentally ill patient are predatory, akin to rape. Having got Alison pregnant, he and his colleagues arranged an abortion to make the problem go away. All reference to these events was omitted from correspondence her psychiatrist then sent to NHS services in South Yorkshire only months later.

As if that weren't enough, near the anniversary of what would have been the third birthday of her baby, the same vulnerable patient who had been shamelessly used to gratify the earthly appetites of an unsupervised NHS employee, stepped in front a train to take her own life. She died while she was an inpatient in the care of the state. These events are empirical; captured in records and documents and acknowledged or admitted by those involved.

But to prosecute, potentially, perhaps inevitably uncovering other serious sexual crimes occurring in Garlands at the time, is not deemed in the public interest? Alison's mind was sacrificed on the altar of sexual self-interest between the soiled sheets of a seedy student nurse's bed. And nobody has been held accountable. I am still troubled acknowledging this fact to myself. I feel as if I am missing something obvious everyone else but me knows. I find myself wondering if I am in some sort of parallel universe, a dream from which I will awake.

I have a juvenile criminal record for the theft of cigarettes which will follow me to the grave. Yet a nurse who had sex with a mentally ill patient, a psychiatrist who withheld information, managers and mentors who turned a blind eye, directors who withheld evidence, police officers and civil servants who lied, they have no such stains on their character.

There is little doubt what happened to Alison contributed massively to her suicide. If a celebrity of any kind were involved, the CPS would be falling over themselves in the rush to prosecute. We have watched as the CPS and police throw millions of pounds of our money at high profile cases in the absence of evidence. But neither Alison, her family or the perpetrator are famous, so we must put up with the second-rate service that is the preserve of ordinary people like us. Perhaps like you? Where is the equality in our justice system, we as citizens and taxpayers deserve? It is my sincere wish you never have to find out.

In the summer of 2019 in a final effort to get near the truth, we launched a crowd-funding campaign to support the legal costs of obtaining a fresh inquest into Alison's death. Having been told the CPS would block our attempt at launching a private prosecution, a fresh coroner's inquest is now the only option that may enable the facts to at last emerge. Thanks to the generosity of friends and strangers alike, the money needed to start this process was raised. I wonder what the Pastor of mum's church will say should the Coroner return a new verdict of suicide. Will Alison be allowed to remain in heaven on a technicality?

Relying on goodwill to deal with the failings of the state was a strange sobering experience. However, the messages we received, the amounts we were offered, the money in envelopes put through the front door, rekindled some faith in humanity. I have been amazed and incredibly humbled. My neighbour, a World War Two veteran of Normandy, Arnhem and Belsen, invited me in as I passed his window. Pressing a ten-pound note into my hand he and his wife wished me all the best in our quest for justice. I didn't know what to say. I had to hold back tears. I know I owe him more than I could ever give. Taking money from a reluctant hero to pay for the failings of a state he was willing to die to defend, feels wrong.

We who believe in justice cannot rest until it comes

The content, information and influences drawn on within this book come from a wide range of sources, the largest of these being personal experience. I am resisting the temptation to try and gain academic credibility by listing everything I have read and everyone I have spoken with. As well as being impractical and incomplete, it would simply give the world another exhaustive lengthy index section that few if any will ever refer to. This book kicks against much existing theory and practice and grasps the unruly nettles of human behaviour the establishment is often unwilling to acknowledge and many academics and experts ill-equipped to comment on. It feels appropriate to break with tradition.

For anyone who may experience a flaring up of their OCD upon reading this, please be assured that a wealth of reading, research and correspondence relating to the themes touched on has been undertaken and numerous experts by experience have contributed.

The people who I think shaped my outlook and approach to writing this book the most are the systems thinkers, Bellinger, Deming, Seddon, individuals who seek to contribute to and build our collective understanding that nothing exists or happens in isolation. Everything is connected.

The many other topics touched on in this book have been explored in depth through reading, conversation and correspondence with a broad audience of knowledgeable people, including those with strong opposing views who were willing to contribute their insights on issues such as the breaking of professional boundaries, crisis pregnancies, post-abortion trauma and the impact of radical religious beliefs on the mentally ill and vulnerable.

I have read more sleep-inducing reports and papers than anyone should as I have unwittingly compiled a growing dossier of disaster; Mid-Staffs, Gosport, and Hillsborough to name a few. I have perused an ever-growing collection of books, old and new from numerous notable authors in many disciplines. Business and management gurus such as Covey, Kotler, Peters, Porter, Rosenzweig; observers of organizational culture, Heffernan, Seedhouse, Neal, Phillips; political commentators like Chomsky, Jones, Klein, McGarvey, Monbiot; public sector specialists, De Bruijn, Ormerod; writers of religious critiques, Dawkins, Ellerbe, Harris, Hitchens; and of course, large smatterings of the good book itself. This list does not include the countless academic papers and documents from healthcare think tanks like the Kings

Fund and Nuffield Trust, the various government strategies and a seemingly limitless number of NHS England plans and publications, triumphs of hope over experience, that now hog an inordinate amount of space on my computer hard drive.

If you would like to ask questions about the sources and information I have used, please feel free to drop me an email using the contact details or social media links on the following page.

About the author:

Tom lives with his wife Debbie, two cats, several fish and various other visiting animals in Penrith.

If you would like to become part of shaping a movement for Honesty & Integrity in Public Sector Services or if you would just like to find out more please visit **www.hipss.org.uk**

For more information or to see many of the documents referred to that outline the specific details in relation to what happened to Alison, such as medical notes and copies of correspondence, you can visit **www.AlisonsStory.co.uk**

Email the author at **tom@hipss.org.uk**

Connect on Twitter **@TominCumbria**

Hook up on LinkedIn **www.linkedin.com/in/tomcumbria/**